Abstracts
from
The Edenton Gazette
and
North Carolina General Advertiser
Edenton, North Carolina
(Chowan County)
- 1806-1809-

Volume #1

Compiled by:
Raymond Parker Fouts

Southern Historical Press, Inc.
Greenville, South Carolina

This volume was reproduced
from a personal copy located in
the Publishers private library

Please direct all correspondence and book orders to:
SOUTHERN HISTORICAL PRESS, Inc.
PO Box 1267
Greenville, SC   29602-1267

Copyright 1990 by: Raymond Parker Fouts
Copyright Transferred 2023 to:
            Southern Historical Press, Inc.
ISBN #978-1-63914-177-7
Printed in the United States of America

In Memoriam

Martha Ballard Hawkins

Genealogist

1924-1990

PREFACE

These abstracts were compiled from microfilm of the original newspapers, obtained from the North Carolina State Archives, Raleigh, North Carolina. [Reel #EdEGw-1, Edenton, Edenton Gazette, Feb. 26, 1806-Dec. 1, 1818.] The locations and dates of the originals are noted at the beginning of each year. The years 1806 and 1807 are incomplete. There is a large number of marriage and death notices found in this paper.

This was a weekly newspaper, consisting of four pages. The first two pages were usually devoted to international and national news. This information was obtained from newspapers published in the large American ports and from letters received by residents. The state news was obtained from other North Carolina papers.

Items that follow a city dateline are from that city, unless otherwise noted. All issues have been included, though nothing may have been abstracted from them. Advertisements have been recorded only from the first issue in which they appear in legible form. Several advertisements that originally appeared in issues no longer extant have been preserved by having been continued in later issues.

Each item has been assigned a number, within parentheses. The name and location indices refer to these numbers. All spellings of every surname are indexed. Postmasters are listed only on the initial appearance in that office. Sheriffs are listed in all instances. All references to those persons are indexed under their individual names. Native Americans are indexed under "Indians" and Blacks under "Mulattoes" and "Negroes", the terms found in this newspaper.

Underlined letters emphasize verbatim spelling. "____" denotes missing or illegible letters or words.

TABLE OF CONTENTS

ABSTRACTS FROM THE EDENTON GAZETTE

AND

NORTH CAROLINA GENERAL ADVERTISER

EDENTON, NORTH CAROLINA

1806-1809

VOLUME I

(1)   [Note: The following paragraph appears at the beginning of this film.   The author is unidentified.]

"THE EDENTON GAZETTE AND NORTH CAROLINA GENERAL ADVERTISER

1806-1831

In the Raleigh Register of July 22, 1805, is a statement that a newspaper has again made its appearance at Edenton, under the title of The Edenton Gazette.   It was printed by BEASLEY and BACKUS. How long it was continued with these publishers is not known, as no issues are located. But it was re-established January 1, 1806, printed by James WILLS and Joseph BEASLEY with the title of The Edenton Gazette and North Carolina Advertiser. In 1807, BEASLEY started a paper in Elizabeth City and WILLS became sole publisher. With the issue of February 17, 1809, the title was shortened to The Edenton Gazette, but in October, 1813, it was changed to The Edenton Gazette and North Carolina General Advertiser."

1806 - Filmed from originals in the American Antiquarian Society-February 26; October 29; November 26. All other issues are missing.

The Edenton Gazette, and North-Carolina Advertiser.
Edenton, Printed by James WILLS and Joseph BEASLEY.

[Vol. I. Wednesday Evening, February 26, 1806. Number 9.]

(2) Edenton, February 26. .. On the 8th inst. in lat. 25, 50, N. long. 67, 50, W. Capt. NORCOM spoke the brig Industry.. On the 13th inst. spoke Capt. C. BIS-SELL, on the outer edge of the Gulf, from Occacock, bound to Jamaica, all well.

(3) William LANE, Saddler and Harness Maker, Edenton, Respectfully informs his friends and the public, that he has taken into partnership with him Mr. Thomas WILLS, of Norfolk; the business will be carried on in future under the firm of LANE & WILLS. They beg leave to inform the public, that they intend keeping a general assortment of Mens and Womens Saddles of the best quality..Bridles..Chair Harness... February 26th, 1806.

1

(4)   25 Dollars Reward. Run away on the 14th inst. a Negro Man by the name of
JACOB, about 5 feet 5 or 6 inches high, and about 28 or 29 years old, though of a
much younger appearance; short & thick, well made, dark complexion, commonly wears
his hair tied and cued, his feet point in-or much parrot-toed. .. He has a wife
at the house where George BARNS, jun. dec, formerly lived and a mother belonging
to W. LITTLEJOHN, Esq. near Edenton, where he is most likely to be lurking about;
he has been branded on the cheeks I. S. but the letters cannot be distinctly seen,
though some appearance of the burn-also, one of his heel-strings has been cut,
which is now visible. He has had a strong desire for some time to go to sea, and
may attempt to get on board some vessel.. I will give the above reward to any
person that will deliver him to me, or confine him in goal, so that I get him. ...
Jas. SUTTON. February 22d, 1806.

(5) Run away from the subscriber, on the 24th inst. a Negro Man named JIM, about
23 years of age, nearly 6 feet high, and very stout made, dark complexion, speaks
very quick and plain; he sometimes plays on the fiddle. .. He formerly belonged
to Mr. John MOORE of Perquimans county and I do suppose he may be lurking about
there now, or in Edenton. I rather suppose he has a free pass. I will give Ten
Dollars Reward to any person that will confi_e said negro in any goal so that I
get him again, or Fifteen Dollars if brought to me in Bertie county. ... Stephen
M'DOWELL. Bertie county, (near Colerain) February 25th, 1806.

(6)   Prize Medals, Offered by the Humane Society of Philadelphia. The Society
have observed, with gratitude, and admiration, the labours of the many learned and
ingenious benefactors of mankind, who have advanced to an high degree of improvement, the means to be employed in restoring to life those who have been apparently
deprived thereof. But they have at the same time to regret, that notwithstanding
much good hath been done, yet these means very often fail of success. In order to
excite public attention towards the further improvement of so important a part of
medical science, the society is induced to offer: For the best dissertation on
the means of restoring to life, persons apparently dead from drowning, and more
effectual than any yet in use, a Gold Medal, value Fifty Dollars. For the Second
best, a Silver Medal, value Twenty Five dollars. The dissertations to be sent to
the Secretary of the Society (post paid) by the first day of January, 1808. .. By
order of the Managers of the Humane Society, Jos. CRUKSHANK, President. Isaac
SNOWDEN, jun. Sec'ry. Philadelphia, Dec. 11, 1805.

(7) Washington, Jan. 26. Extract of a letter from a gentleman dated Wythe, Vir.
Dec. 27, 1805. "I cannot omit amusing you, with some items of a late discovery in
this country. About two miles east of Geo. WAMPLERs, an attempt was made to sink
a pit, to search for salt water. A few feet below the surface, have been found
several bones of the Mammoth of an unusual size. One tooth is said to weigh 17
lb. and proved to be of a creature that fed on herbage. With these bones are in-
termixed a number of those of an animal of the largest species of the carnivorous
kind; also a number of bones of young or smaller Mammoths; and one might conject-
ure from appearances, that these carcases have not been more than one hundred
years deposited in the earth. .. Our acquaintance, the Rev. Mr. SLONGER, is busy
in good weather in having a full search made, for the whole skeleton..."

(8) Extract of another letter from the same gentleman, dated Wythe, Jan. 4th,
1806. Sir, I wrote you in haste about two weeks ago. This day I went to the spot
where the Mammoth bones are found, and with my own eyes satisfied my own curiosi-
ty. The teeth, or rather the grinders are larger than those I have seen that were
found at CAMPBELL's Saline on Holston, or even those at the Big bone Lick in Kentucky.. But the singular appearance of this new Lick, and the variety of large

26 February 1806

(8) (Cont.) bones already dug up, proves, that a part of them belongs to large animals of a carnivorous species. A large tusk or horn has been found, inserted in the head or rather upper jaw, about two feet long and eight inches in circumference. There have been seven under jaw bones already found of this latter animal, as Mr. Michael KINSAR informs on whose lands this curious deposit is found by the shape of the horn, and its place so near the nose, the smaller animals may have been a species of the Rinoceros...

(9) For Sale, One Fourth Part of the Land, Juniper Swamp, Canals, Mills, &c. known by the name of the New-Lebanon estate, on the Great Canal, leading to Norfolk. This is one of the most beneficial Shingle Swamps known in this part of the country. .. For terms enquire of Wm. BLAIR, Esq. at Edenton, Wells COOPER, Esq. Gates County, near the Great Swamp, on the Suffolk road, who is one of the Proprietors; or of Mr. Geo. FORBY, at the New Lebanon Mills, All of whom are impowered to contract for a Sale. February 1st, 1806.

(10) The Subscriber, Lately removed from Nixonton to this place, intends practising Physic, Surgery, and Midwifery in their most extensive latitudes; and offers his services to the public in either of those branches. Having been engaged during seven years in practice in the West-Indies, under the direction of the most respectable Physicians, and having attended the hospitals and lectures of the most eminent of the profession in Europe for three years, with the advantages of an extensive practice in this state, he flatters himself he will be entitled to a share of public patronage. Widwifery, and the diseases of lying-in women, have been a particular branch of his studies, having had the advantage of being a pupil of the illustrious HAMILTON, of Edinburg, whose public lectures and lying-in hospital he attended 3 years.--His future place of residence will be in Mr. Alexander MILLEN's new house, on Water Street, and his shop at the corner formerly occupied by the late Dr. DICKINSON, where he has a fresh and general assortment of Drugs and Medicines, which he will sell very low. ... Andrew KNOX. Edenton, Feb. 7, 1806.

(11) Notice. All persons indebted to the Subscriber, by Note or Account, are earnestly requested to make payment, on or before the first day of March next, that he may be enabled to answer the demands of his creditors. Those who fail to comply with the above notice, may expect to settle with an officer. Peter P. LAWRENCE. Edenton, Jan. 16, 1806.

(12) Notice. All persons indebted to the Subscriber, either by Note or Account, are earnestly requested to make immediate payment, so that he may be enabled to settle with those to whom he is indebted. .. And for the future, all articles, or work done, the money must be paid before they are taken from the shop, as he intends keeping no open accounts. He returns his thanks to..his customers who have been punctual in their payments. Jos. MANNING, taylor. Edenton, Jan. 22, 1806.

(13) Martin NOXON, Gold and Silver Smith, Edenton Keeps constantly for Sale, a handsome assortment of Articles..consisting of..Gold ear and finger Rings, set and plain do. Lockets and breast Pins, silver Table and Tea Spoons, Sugar Tongs, Salt Spoons, Thimbles, Scissar Chains, Sleeve-Buttons, &c. &c. &c. .. Watches repaired as usual. ... Edenton, Jan. 15, 1806.

(14) Thomas BISSELL, Informs..that he has begun to Manufacture, and has on hand, a constant supply of Cut Nails, and Flooring Brads, which he offers for Sale, at the following reduced prices, by retail. 8d. 10d. 12d. & 20d. Nails, 15 Cts. lb. Also, for Sale, a few barrels of New Pork. Edenton, 20th December, 1805.

29 October 1806

(15) From the Farmer's Gazette. The Confession of Nathan TAIT, Who was convicted of forgery, at Hancock Superior Court, February Term, 1801, and sentenced to be hung, but was respited by the Governor until the meeting of the General Assembly, before which he made his escape; & who was executed on the 25th of August, 1806, in Sparta, on a gallows, which was erected for the same purpose five years before.

Georgia, Hancock County,) I Nathan TAIT, being convictd at February term, 1801, of forgery, but having broke jail and been since arrested, in South Carolina, and being demanded of his excellency Paul HAMILTON, Governor of said state, by the Governor of Georgia, and having been obtained and brought forward to August term, 1806, in the county aforesaid, I there received the sentence of death, which is to be executed on the 25th day of August, 1806.--Being truly impressed with the weight of my crimes, and wishing to discharge my conscience towards God and my fellow creatures, in my last moments, I have voluntarily made and signed the following confession, viz:

The first horse I ever stole was Mr. Samuel BUFFINGTON's of Warren county, in the state aforesaid, I kept him at my brother Robert TAIT's a considerable time--I was then taken a second time by Lewis GRAVES and confined in Sparta jail; in which time of confinement my brother Wm. TAIT took him to South Carolina, by my desire, and swapt him away, as I afterwards understood.

The second I took was a horse the property of Mr. C. LOFTON, of Jefferson county, Georgia;.. I rode him to South Carolina and there exchanged him with a Mr. George MARTIN of Martin town. Mr. LOFTON has since got his horse.

The third was a large bay horse belonging to Major MORGAN, on Broad river, S. Carolina. I rode him to the pine woods house, about 25 miles from Augusta, and let Mr. James TUTT have him in exchange; Mr. TUTT carried him to Charleston. Major MORGAN did not get him again.

The fourth was a bay mare belonging to Mr. Thomas SWEARINGAM of Edgefield district, South Carolina, I rode her to my brother Robert TAIT's; my brother Wm. TAIT returned her to Mr. SWEARINGAM.

The fifth was a sorrel horse called the Bull, belonging to Mr. MAXWELL, and a saddle and bridle. I rode him to Colerain, on the St. Mary's River; being pursued, the horse, saddle and bridle was taken from me at that place and delivered to Capt. LOWE.--I took this horse at Augusta.

The sixth was a horse belonging to Mr. Benjamin CHAPMAN, who was at that time overseer for my brother Robert TAIT. I carried him to the Creek Nation & left him in the hands of Jack CONARD. Mr. C. did not get him again.

The seventh was an Indian Stud horse, which I took at the confluence of the Oconee and Ocmulgee rivers; he was the property of Wm. HARDAGE. I went from there to near the Fishdam Ford, in South Carolina, and there turned him loose.

The eighth was a bay horse with a bald face, the property of Wm. CHAMPION of South Carolina, I also took a saddle from Mr. C. I rode him to this state, and turned him loose near FENN's Bridge.

The ninth was a bay mare the property of Peter AIKIN, which I took at the same time I did Mr. CHAMPION's horse. My companion, Charles BISHOP, rode her into this state. I let James BAITIE have her, in Burke county.

The tenth was a horse belonging to Mr. GRAISON of Rutherford county, North-Carolina. I let David GREENLAW, one of my confederates, have him. I think he carried him to Coosahatchie, South-Carolina.

The eleventh was a horse belonging to John MATHEWS, near FENN's Bridge. I rode him to my brother Robert TAIT's, and there he broke from me. His owner got him again.

The twelfth was a horse belonging to Mr. RENFRO, near the Shoals of Ogechee. I rode him about a mile and a half the other side of Campbellton, South Carolina,

(15) (Cont.) and turned him loose. His owner never found him.

The thirteenth was Mr. WHITE's split nosed bay horse. I rode him into Lincoln county, North-Carolina, and left him in the hands of Abraham COLLINS, where he still remains for all I know. I took this horse at Savannah.

The fourteenth was a horse belonging to Mr. M'LEOD, near Savannah. I rode him to my brother Rob. TAIT's-There he broke from me & jumped into Mr. JENKIN's field.

The fifteenth was a horse the property of E. BROTHERS, near the Shoals of O-gechee. I rode him to Abraham COLLIN's and left him to fatten.

The sixteenth was a mare belonging to Mr. SMITH. I rode her about 8 miles on this side of BAITIE's Ford on the Catawba River, North-Carolina, and there turned her loose.

The seventeenth was a large bay horse.. I rode him to Hancock county--There he broke away from me and is now in the hands of Larkin CHIVERS of Warren county.

The eighteenth, and last, was a horse belonging to Mr. ROBERTS just below Louisville. I rode him into Edgefield District, South-Carolina, where I was apprehended and confined in jail.

I took some goods from Benjamin JENKINS, who lives near the Shoals of Ogechee in Hancock county, the greatest part of which I afterwards delivered to him, and gave him some money (a few dollars) part of which I informed him was counterfeit. He then asked me if I could make counterfeit money; I answered him I could--If you will, says he, (JENKINS) and let it come into my hands or place it so that I can it, (sic) I will make you (Nathan TAIT) compensation therefor.

About the same time I had this conversation with Benjamin JENKINS I saw my brother Robert TAIT at his own plantation. He asked me if I could make counterfeit money, and if I did not make it; I told him I could and was about getting a parcel made, & had the means to make it--He said..that if I would get some & bring it to him that I should not be loser, as he was in great want of money; I told him I would get some made and let him have some, but he never got any from me.

The principal counterfeiters that I know are Abraham COLLINS of N. Carolina and Allen TWITTY, of the same state, on Green River; at the mouth of White Oak Creek. Thomas DAVIS engraved the plates for the 100 dollar bills and 50 dollar bills of the Savannah Bank; a plate for the 5 dollar bills of the Branch Bank of Baltimore; a plate for the 20 dollar bills of the Bank of the U. States; and a plate for the 10 dollar bills of the Branch Bank at Charleston. Martin COLLINS was a principal striker. A. COLLINS and Allen TWITTY struck at TWITTY's, on Green River, to the amount of 30,000 dollars to try an experiment with those plates made by Thomas DAVIS. Israel RIGGS, of North-Carolina, first tried to pass, for an experiment, the 100 dollar & 50 dollar bills, in this state, at Augusta, in which he was successful; as he passed four or five hundred dollars without being suspected.

James MOORY living on the Oconee river is a principal person in circulating those bills, before mentioned, in this state.

James BAITIE of Burke county; Jacob FARMER, living near TWIGGS' mills, Jefferson county; John VINZANT and his brother; John MARSHALL, a large man, pock marked, about five feet ten inches high; Robert CLARY, jun. Dudley KNOX, about six feet high, and has long black hair; Charles BIHOP?, of Jefferson county; Jacob BEA?DEY, of Burke county; & Richard Hathfield HOMAN, of Columbia, South-Carolina, are all circulators of those bills.

I Nathan TAIT, being of sound mind and memory, this 24th day of Aug. in the year of our Lord, 1806, do affirm, and I call upon God, at whose bar I must appear in a few hours, to witness the sincerity of my professions that the foregoing is the truth and nothing but the truth to the best of my knowledge. Nathan TAIT. Signed in the presence of T?iset? THOMAS. Jesse VEAZEY. John GAY. [The confession is signed at the foot of every page.]

(16) Philadelphia, 23d July, 1806. Peter MUHLENBERG, Esq. Collector of the port of Philadelphia. Sir, The importation from Great Britain and her dependencies of certain goods, wares and merchandize, being prohibited after the 15th day of November next, by an act of Congress passed on the 18th April last, and as the act does not particularly define sundry articles..we now address you with a view of obtaining the necessary information on the subject. .. (Signed) John LOHRA, Chairman. James WORTH, Sec'ry.

Answer. Collector's Office, Philadelphia, August 13, 1806. Sir, Your letter as chairman of a meeting of a number of Ironmongers, convened for the purpose of taking into consideration the effect which the act of congress prohibiting certain articles of British manufactures, may have on their importations..was duly transmitted to the comptroller of the treasury. We for various reasons which is unnecessary to enumerate, decline giving an opinion at present. ... John GRAFT, Dep. Collector.

(17) Edenton, October 29, 1806. An Imposition! I Came into this neighbourhood last Monday with a drove of Horses, and was enquiring for some good place to stay at for a few days to rest my horses, when I met with a Mr. John BOND, jun. who informed me he was well provided to accomodate me; and on Tuesday morning, not being well pleased with the usage, I was about to remove from the place, at which he seemed extremely uneasy, and begged me to continue with him, and said he would accommodate me with corn, fodder, pasturage, and board on lower terms than any other man in the neighbourhood; on which promise my horses staid at said BOND's till Friday morning:—Myself and a young man that was with me staid about two days. When I called for my bill on Friday morning, that being who calls himself BOND, stated it as follows:

Mr. Abner YORK,

To John BOND, jun.		Dr.	
	l.	s.	d.
To 5 1 2 bushels of corn at 10s per bushel,	2	15	0
To 130 wt. fodder at 12s6 per hundred,	0	16	6
To 4 days boarding,	3	4	6
To washing,	0	4	0
To pasturage,	0	18	0
	7	18	0

Now enormous as this bill undoubtedly is, I am able to prove I had but 3 1-2 bushels of corn, and called for but 2 dozen bundles of fodder, and as for the board for the two days, he fed me on plenty of salt fish and potatoes. I paid off the bill and took his receipt for the payment—I hope his relations will take no umbrage at me for advertising this circumstance, as I have not the smallest desire to injure their feelings; but as I find myself imposed on by the said BOND, I think it my duty to inform the public, that they may stand guarded against that imposter who calls himself John BOND, jun. There were several spectators present, who unanimously cried out shame. Among whom was Captain M'GUIRE. BOND flew in a passion & swore he would have his money, for he had charged low enough. Abner YORK, of Iredell county. Saturday, October 25, 1806.

(18) The subscriber has on hand a number of Classical & English School Books imported and kept by him for Sale for the particular use and in reliance on the Edenton Academy for their purchase; several of which have been laid in according to the directions of some of the Tutors... Henry WILLS. Edenton, Oct. 25th, 1806.

(19) Bernard DORNIN, Book Seller, No. 136, Pearl-Street, New-York, Respectfully informs the inhabitants of Edenton, and the country in general, that he has opened

(19) (Cont.) a Book Store in Edenton, next door to Mr. O'MALLEY's Tavern, which is now supplied with a handsome collection of Books, in Law and Miscellaneous Literature...October 22d, 1806.

(20) The following Verses were composed by Nathan TAIT, In Sparta Jail, on the 24th of August, the day before his execution. 1 Come gentlemen of ev'ry state, Listen a while and I'll relate, the tragedy that me befel, And the whole truth to you I'll tell. 2 In Virginia, there I was born, Now to my parents I'm a scorn; They handsomely educated me, And rais'd me up in piety. .. 4 When sixteen years of life was come, Then from my parents I did run; Into the state of Georgia came, And there awhile I did remain. .. 6 O MUSGROVE* he persuaded me, Persuaded me for to agree, Persuading me and thus did say Let's join and do some forgery. .. 14 O now my God of them take care, Both of my friends and wife so dear, Always be their strength and stay, and guide them still in virtue's way. .. 16 Farewell to Sun, Moon, Stars & Earth, and every thing that they bring forth, To all my friends I bid adieu, To my dear wife and children too. ... *His brother-in-law.

(21) The public are respectfully informed, that the Subscriber has procured a general assortment of all Classical and Reading Books, together with every article of Stationary used in the Academy. .. Ink ready made, will be furnished the Students at 12 1-2 cents per quarter. Simeon NYE. Edenton Academy, Oct. 21, '06.

(22) Advertisement. By virtue of a decree of the Honourable the Court of Equity for the District of Edenton, will be Sold, at public vendue, in the town of Winton, before the Court-House door, on Wednesday, the 26th day of November next, Two Lots or half Acre of Land, formerly the property of Mr. John BURN, deceased, situate, lying and being in the town of Murfreesborough, known in the plan of the said town by the number or figures 47 48; whereon is a good two story Dwelling-House, Ware House, Kitchen, Smoke House, Stable, and other out-houses, together with a large enclosed Garden.—The situation is airy, pleasant, and healthy, and a desirable stand either for a Tavern or Merchant. The sale will commence at 3 o'clock in the afternoon. ... A. MILLEN, C M E. E. D. Edenton, Oct. 21, 1806.

(23) For Sale, The Sloop Thomas & David, Burthen 52 tons, 3 years old, built in the city of New-York, of oak and red cedar; ... LITTLEJOHN & BOND. 21st October, 1806.

(24) Notice. All persons indebted to the estate of Henry E. SEARS, deceased, late of the county of Gates, are requested to make immediate payment, and those who have claims or demands against said estate are requested to bring them forward for payment, within the time limited by law, or they will be barred by act of Assembly for such cases made and provided; as the act will be plead in bar to them, if not brought within proper time. Wm. GOODMAN, Ex'r.

(25) For Sale. The subscriber is determined to remove to the country and improve his Lands, and offers for Sale the following valuable property, viz. In Elizabeth City, now thriving rapidly, Two Lots, or one Acre, on which I live, containing a Dwelling-House compleat, almost new, 30 by 27, with an additional new Chamber on the ground floor, 14 by 15, very airy; a compleat dairy and liquor room under one roof, with a snug Cellar, and a platform from the chamber to the dairy, which renders the passage dry in the wetest weather; a good Smoke-House and Kitchen; a snug well finished Store-House, with a shed room and fireplace; a new two story Ware-House, proof against rats, with a back shed, and every other Out-House and Garden compleat;—the whole seat decorated with trees and clover, and in every respect remarkable (sic) pleasant. Two other Lots opposite the Court House; on one

(25) (Cont.) stands a convenient Dwelling-House, with 2 good chimnies, now occupied as a store, and is an excellent stand for business; on the other lot is very convenient Stables and Chair House, all under the same roof, built of juniper, 45 by 15, stalls for six horses, and a loft sufficient to contain forage for a season, and room for two carriages below. Two Lots near the water, handsomely enclosed with juniper, one cultivated as a garden, the other well set in clover, adjoining each other, by far the pleasantest lots in town to build on, commanding a full view of Pasquotank River, from town to the entrance.. One Lot or piece of Ground back of said lots, occupied as a shipyard..with the privilege of a creek, and a handsome beach at the mouth, to draw a family Seine, where small fish are to be taken every day in the year. A Smith's Shop, with tools, if required, and negro House on the premises. One unimproved Lot on the south-east corner of the town. Sixty acres of Wood Land, adjoining the town..and on the public road, leading out of the main street.. One Lot, Ware-House and Wharf, formerly occupied by Charles & Francis GRICE. The Wharf is new, 104 feet in front, well framed of square timber, cyprus above water; a Ware House, 40 by 24, two story high, lately repaired, with every apparatus for cleaning & graving Vessels.. In Camden County, at RAYMOND's creek, on Pasquotank river shore, a piece of Land, at a very public landing, where much business has been done to advantage for a number of years, in the heart of a lumber and grain country, containing by estimation 14 Acres; on it is a good Dwelling House, with four rooms and a piazza, two good chimnies, out-houses, &c. a good Store and Ware-House separate, both two stories high. Some valuable Negroes.. All which will be sold reasonable by the whole or separate, to suit the purchaser, by application to Charles GRICE. Elizabeth-City, Sept. 16, '06.

(26) Tar and Turpentine. May be had by wholesale or retail, on application to John POPELSTON-A constant supply of these articles will be kept on John SKINNER's wharf. Jos. B. SKINNER. Edenton, May 19, 1806.

(27) For Sale, Between five and six thousand Acres of Land, in the County of Granville, on both sides of Island Creek, within five or six miles of Williamsborough. ... Edmund TAYLOR. August 27th, 1806.

(28) For Sale, A Valuable Tract of Land, belonging to the estate of George GRAY, dec. containing 1200 Acres, about 100 acres of which is cleared, & on which there is two Apple Orchards. This land lies on Cashie river, about one mile below the town of Windsor, and has sufficient timber to carry on Ship-Building to advantage- The payments will be made very easy, on receiving good security..apply to Wm. Lee GRAY, the acting Executor. Windsor, 1st Sept. 1806.

(29) For Sale, or Rent, The Strawberry Hill and Turnpike Lands.-Also, some likely young Negroes. John HAMILTON. Elizabeth-City, Sept. 16, 1806.

(30) For Sale, 14,000 Acres of Land, lying in the County of Washington, great part of which is equal in fertility to the lands of the Lake Company. There is a law for cutting a Canal from Plymouth to Pungo River, which, if effected, will run through the land. Terms made known by applying to Thomas JOHNSON. Washington County, Sept. 16, 1806.

(31) Notice. Found among the goods and chattels of George MACKLER, deceased, Watch-Maker, Four Watches, which it is supposed was left with him to repair. Persons owning the said Watches may have them by proving their property. If no application is made for them in..one month, they will be sold at public sale. John BULLOCK. August 5, 1806.

(32)   Matthias E. SAWYER, Has just received an extensive assortment of Drugs, Chemical, and Patent Medicines, Lancets, Phials, Corks, Perfumery, Court Plaister, Tooth Brushes, &c. &c. which he will sell to country Physicians, families or shipping, for cash... Edenton, Aug. 4, 1806.

(33)   Will be Sold, for ready money, On the 18th day of November next, at the town of Ederton, for the benefit of the Owners, Underwriters..the hull of the Sloop Pheasant, of Dighton, Massachusetts, wrecked in the late gale, and taken up in Pamtico sound; together with a quantity of W. O. pipe and hhd Staves and Heading, found on board said vessel-Also, a Boat and part of a hhd. Rum found a drift in said sound; of which all persons interested are requested to take notice.   Joseph BOZMAN. October 13th, 1806.

(34)   Joseph MANNING, Tailor, Returns his sincere thanks to those of his punctual customers & friends, for the generous encouragement he has received since he resided in this place.. All possible pains shall be taken to obtain the Newest Fashions, every spring and fall, and to keep the best workmen. ... July 28th, 1806.

[Vol. I. Wednesday, November 26, 1806. Number 48.]

(35)   From the Western World. The Kentucky Spanish Association, Gov. BLOUNT's Conspiracy and General MIRANDA's Expedition. [Continued.] We observed, that a few observations would be made in this number, on the letter of Dr. BROOKS, which was published in our last. The person whom BROOKS mention (sic) as having cursed Congress, & reflected upon the Magistrates as perjured, was one James SPEED, a notorious tool and trumpeter of Gen. WILKINSON, now living in Mercer..
   It is no ways astonishing that John BROWN "seemed much out of humour that he was so little attended to in the oracle way." and that he was extremely zealous to represent the Congress insincere. The loss of a Spanish Grandeeship was not a trifle..to a mind void of principle and inflated with ambition and love of power..
   Let it be remembered that when in the years 1794 and 1796, John BROWN and his friends were daily haranguing the people against the Excise Law, he & his bosom confident the late George NICHOLAS were contriving measures to carry it into effect.-The following letter which he wrote to Tench COXE, esq. commissioner of the Revenue, Philadelphia, is a sufficient proof of his political Jesuitry in this respect. "Frankfort, Kentucky, Sept. 30, 1796. Sir, I have the pleasure to transmit for your information, a letter received by me from Col. George NICHOLAS, stating the terms upon which, in his opinion, the Excise law may be carried into operation, in the State of Kentucky. I also forward inclosed the affidavit of Robert SAUNDERS, a distiller of considerable influence, which may serve to shew what the conduct and disposition of a great proportion of that class of men in this state, have been respecting that law for some time past. ... (Signed) J. BROWN."
   This political trick and finesse? which John BROWN invented to carry the excise law into effect, equals any species of duplicity of which we have heard. .. They were in reality planning a snare to entrap congress and the government of the union, whereby they might lose the confidence of the citizens of Kentucky, and therefore, rekindle the spirit of separation which had greatly subsided.   BROWN, WALLACE and SEBASTIAN were about the same period, incessantly convening meetings of the citizens..under the pretence of petitioning congress for the redress of some grievance or other..to procure an opportunity of pouring forth their vindictive spleen against the executive government. A celebrated meeting of this description was called together at Lexington on the 28th of March 1794..it was judged prudent that a person of opposite principles should be placed in the chair.   They fixed upon George MUTER for this purpose..

26 November 1806

(35) (Cont.) On Saturday the 24th inst. a numerous meeting of respectable citizens from different parts of the state assembled in Lexington; and after taking into consideration the degraded and deserted situation of this country, both as to its commerce & protection..the following resolutions were adopted. Resolved, 1. That the inhabitants west of Apalachian mountains, are entitled by nature and by stipulation, to the free and undisturbed Navigation of the river Missisippi. 2. That from the year 1783, until this time, the enjoyment of this right has been uniformly prevented by the Spaniards. 3. That the general government..have..adopted no effectual measures for its attainment. .. 10. That the inhabitants of the Western Country have a right to demand, that their frontiers be protected.. By the direction & in behalf of the meeting of the Citizens of the State of Kentucky. Attest, George MUTER, Chairman. John BRADFORD, Clerk.

We noticed in one of our late numbers, the name of Joseph BELLINGER, a celebrated tool of WILKINSON. The following extract of a letter lately received from a most respectable character in Upper Louisiana, will afford additional information respecting him. "I am strongly inclined to believe there are many persons in this territory, who, if they were not members of the Spanish association, are well acquainted with all the circumstances of this conspiracy. A Mr. Charles SMITH, of St. Genevieve (one of the firm of BULLITT and SMITH, at the falls of the Ohio), told me in the presence of several gentlemen, he was knowing to the payment of a certain sum of money to WILKINSON.. A certain Joseph BELLINGER, of Kentucky, and one among the many agents which WILKINSON formerly had in his employment..arrived here some short time previous to his departure down the river; and WILKINSON immediately gave him a commission, & started him in company with his son, Lieutenant James B WILKINSON, on an expedition up the Missouri.."

Of this BELLINGER..it was said about 8 or 9 years ago, by Governor GREENUP, to a Mr. Kincaid CALDWELL, whilst on a surverying expedition on the waters of Licking river, Kentucky, that if BELLIGER was called upon he could divulge an important secret concerning WILKINSON.. However, CALDWELL says, he did not require an explanation; for at that day it was well known, that the important secret was the transfer of Kentucky to the Spanish government..

The most suspicious circumstance regarding the secret embassies of BELLINGER occurred about 1790 or 1791.-We have repeatedly noticed that General WILKINSON was suspected of carrying on a treasonable correspondence with the several Indian nations to the north west of the Ohio.. The incident to which we at present allude, was the rupture of the treaty which Anthony GAMELIN was negociating with the tribes and villages of the Wabash river, and with the Indians of the Miami village. GAMELIN, who was a respectable inhabitant of Vincennes, was requested by the United States to conclude, if possible, a treaty with those Indians. The villages of the Wabash appeared earnestly inclined to pacific measures; but refused to give a decisive answer until they consulted with the..Miami village. A messenger was..dispatched..upon his arrival, found Joseph BELLINGER among them, who instantly upon learning the purport of his visit, set off for Kentucky. The chiefs of the Shawanese then held a consultation, the result..was, that they would, after four weeks, send an answer to Vincennes. But the promised answer was never sent, and in the course of only a few months afterwards, more than one hundred persons were killed upon the Ohio, and in the district of Kentucky. ...

(36) Boston, Oct. 10. .. Chilicothe, October 25. .. By the Scioto Gazette, we learn Col. BURR will return to Chilicothe in a few days, on his way to Pittsburgh, to meet Comfort TYLER and his retinue, and that his son-in-law ALSTON, a few weeks ago, with his wife descended the Ohio river.

The following is worthy of notice. Nashville was made the head-quarters of Zach. COX's treasonable expedition to take the Yazoo lands a few years ago: "Col. Aaron BURR, the steady and firm friend of the State of Tennessee, arrived in this

10

(36) (Cont.) place on Friday the 28th Sept. and on the next day a dinner was given him at TALBOT's hotel..." (Nashville paper.)

(37) Norfolk, Nov. 15. .. November 18. Daniel CLARKE, Esq. Member of Congress, who arrived at Philadelphia on Thursday last..from N. Orleans, informs, that Gen. WILKINSON having taken the command of the U. S. army at Nachitoches, had opened a conference with the commander of the Spanish troops, in consequence of which, matters were adjusted, and the Spaniards had crossed, or at least agreed to recross the Sabine immediately. (Bal. Even. Post.)

(38) A letter from Gov. Wm. C. C. CLAIBORNE, to Captain John SHAW, commander of the U. S. marine force in New-Orleans. (Copy.) New Orleans, 7th Oct. 1806. Sir, .. For the present, Sir, I cannot say what particular duty will be exacted of the navy, but I am solicitous that you should make every possible exertion to have the boats in port prepared for a cruize..since in two or three days some military stores will be shipped for Nachitoches, and I am desirous that the gun-boats should give them convoy by the fort of Baton Rouge. ... (Signed) Wm. C. C. CLAIBORNE.

(39) Edenton, November 26, 1806. .. State of North-Carolina. Perquimans county Nov. Term, 1806. Jno. & Thos. GRANBERY, vs. Thomas JONES, sen.} original attachment, Returned, levied on the lands of said Thomas JONES, in the county aforesaid. It being represented to the court that the defendant in this suit is an inhabitant of the state of Virginia; It is ordered, That three months public notice be given in the Edenton Gazette, to said Thomas JONES, sen. that he appear at the end thereof, viz. at February term, 1807, replevy his property, and plead to issue, or that final judgment will be entered against him. Test, Thomas H. HARVEY, Clk.

(40) On Wednesday, the 3d day of December next, will be Sold at public auction, on a credit of four months, the schooner Mary Turner, with her tackle and apparel; the one half of which is to foreclose a mortgage given to me by Capt. Alexander FERGUSON; the other half to discharge a debt due me by Capt. Daniel BELL... Henry FLURY. November 25th, 1806.

(41) On Saturday, the 6th of December next, will be Sold on HATHAWAY's wharf, in the forenoon, sundry articles of Rigging, a Main-Sail and Flying Jib, belonging to the sch'r. Jane; for the benefit of the Underwriters and all others concerned, by James HATHAWAY, sen. Edenton, Nov. 26, 1806.

(42) State of N. Carolina, Camden County,)ss. Nov. Term, 1806. James NASH, having sued out an original attachment against the estate of _sa FERGUSON, late of the county aforesaid, mariner, returnable before the court of said County;—And the sheriff having returned thereon, that he had levied the same on the surplus of property levied on by Thomas GORDON's attachment;"-it is therefore ordered, that three months public notice thereof be given to the said Asa FERGUSON, (by advertisement in the Edenton Gazette)..that unless he appear at the next term of the said Court..the first Monday in February next, replevies his estate, and pleads to the said action, final judgment will be entered up against him. By Order, Malachi SAWYER, C. C. C.

(43) Ten Dollars Reward. On Sunday evening, the 9th inst. the Subscriber's store was broken into, and the following property stolen therefrom, viz. A Silver Watch, with a double case, maker's name James SCHOLEFIELD, No. 153, London, the handle of which turns very easy. That part of the case which holds the christal is remarkably high and rounding, and uncommonly thick. She is an old fashioned watch, and

(43) (Cont.) the face numbered with letters. One other very large double cas'd pinch back Watch, having no number nor name.. A Small Trunk, containing bills of sale, letters, &c... An old Pocket-Book, containing Notes, Accepted Accounts, Receipts, &c. one of which was given to Myles HASSELL, for the sum of 450 dollars, payable in 22 inch shingles; and dated the 13th of May, 1805, endorsed to me. One other, given by John CREECY, to William MILLER, endorsed to me, date not recollected.-Also, sundry pieces of Goods, amounting, together with the Watches, to near 70 dollars. I will give the above reward and all reasonable expences for the recovery of the above property; or Five Dollars for the Trunk and Pocket-Book, and no questions asked. ... Benjamin HASSELL. Edenton, Nov. 11th, 1806.

(44) The Subscriber Begs leave to inform his customers that he has just opened a large and general assortment of Goods, suitable to the season, which he offers for sale, by wholesale or retail..for cash or country produce. Henry KING. He has also on hand, French Brandy, Rum, Wine, Molasses, Loaf Sugar, Hyson & Imperial Teas, Bar-Iron, &c. November 18th, 1806.

(45) State of N. Carolina, Camden county,}ss. Nov. Term, 1806. Thomas GORDON, having sued out an original attachment against the estate of Asa FERGUSON, late of the county aforesaid, mariner, returnable before the court of said county:—And the sheriff having returned thereon, that he had levied the same on the "Land lying at SPENCE's landing, and the Houses thereon, also two Mohogany Tables, one Juniper Table, two old Chests, two small Trunks, six Windsor Chairs, one Bed and Furniture, one small Pot, one Dutch-Oven, and one Tea-Kettle:"—it is ordered, that three months public notice thereof be given to the said Asa FERGUSON, (by advertisement in the Edenton Gazette)..that unless he appears at the next term of the said court..at the Court-House in Camden, on the first Monday in February next, replevies his estate, and pleads to the said action, final judgment will be entered up against him. By Order, Malachi SAWYER, C. C. C.

(46) The Subscriber Will expose at Public Sale at his Farm in DURANT's Neck, on the 20th of December next, all his Stock of Cattle, Horses, Hogs, and Farming Utensils, on a credit of twelve months.. He is also desirous to let his said Farm on a Lease for years, either in whole or in parcels. Wm. LITTLEJOHN. Edenton, Nov. 18th, 1806.

(47) For Sale, One Third of that most valuable Estate, held in common by Josiah COLLINS, and the Heirs of Nathaniel ALLEN, and those of Samuel DICKINSON, deceased commonly called the "Lake Company."—The said Estate consists of 53,000 Acres of Land, in Washington county, North-Carolina, lying between the Canal and Long Acre, binding on Lake PHELPS, Pungo Lake, and the head of Pungo river. Also, 5000 Acres of Land on Gum Neck, near Little Alligator river, in Tyrrel County. .. This Canal, formerly cut by the Company to join the waters of Lake PHELPS to Scuppernong River, is 20 feet wide and 6 feet deep, and affords an excellent navigation the distance of 6 miles on one side of the first tract, on it and on the Lake is the plantation, containing about 300 Acres of cleared Land; in a high state of cultivation. .. On the plantation is a Rice Machine in complete order, in a building of 72 feet long, 44? feet wide, and four stories high. Also, a Grist-Mill, with a pair of Stones for Corn, and a pair for Wheat, with two ____ing-Cloths (blot), &c.-Also, a T_____ing (blot) Machine in excellent order. There is a Saw-Mill in good repair-There is also a good Dwelling House two stories high, and all convenient Out-Houses, besides two Barns and Stable, &c. There are upwards of Sixty Negroes above 12 years of age, amongst them are tradesmen of different kinds, and upwards of 36 under 12 years old. There are Carpenter's, Coopers', and Blacksmiths' Tools, besides every kind of Plantation Utensils in good

(47) (Cont.) order. Horses, Mules, Hogs, Sheep and Cattle; three large Flats for the use of the Canal, &c.

The Subscriber, executor of the last will of Nathaniel ALLEN, deceased, offers the before mentioned property for Sale, on a credit of 6, 12, and 18 months, the purchaser giving bond with approved security. Any person inclined to purchase this most valuable property may see a map of it, and the country adjoining, with the Rivers and Lakes, by applying to John GRANBERY, Esq. of Norfolk, or to Josiah COLLINS, Esq. at Edenton. If the above property is not disposed of at Private Sale before the 11th of December ensuing, it will on that day be sold at Public Vendue, in the town of Edenton. ... Samuel TREDWLL, Ex'r. Edenton, July 23, 1806.

(48) The Subscriber respectfully informs the public, that he has lately arrived from New-York with a new assortment of Dry Goods..--Also, Cogniac Brandy, Holland Gin, Wine, Loaf-Sugar, best Hyson Tea..all of which he will sell low for Cash, or approved produce at his store, opposite the dwelling-house of the late Nath'l. ALLEN, Esq. dec. ... Edmond HOSKINS. November 11th, 1806.

(49) The Subscribers Take this method of informing..that they have just received from New York their Fall & Winter Goods... M'COTTER & MUIL. November 11?th, 1806.

(50) Valuable Property for Sale. Determined to remove with my family to the Northward in the course of the ensuing year, I will sell, on reasonable terms, the following property, viz.--my Wharf and Lotts, in Edenton, and my Farm, in HARVEY's Neck:--with the Farm may be had, all the stock of Horses, Cattle, Sheep and Hogs with all the Farming Utensils. Also, from fifteen to twenty very likely and valuable Negroes..or, I will sell the Farm where I live, with the Stock, &c. ... John SKINNER. November 1st, 1806.

1807 - Filmed from originals in the North Carolina State Library-September 17-December 30. All other issues are missing.
Edenton: Printed by Ja___
Vol. II. Thursday, Septem_____
[Note: The upper one-third of the two right columns of this and the following page have been torn away.]

(51) Trial of Aaron BURR. Examination of Jacob ALLBRIGHT. Mr. HAY. Our object is to prove by his testimony the actual assemblage of men on BLANNERHASSETT's island. .. Jacob ALLBRIGHT. The first I knew of this business was; I was hired on the island to help? to build a kiln for drying corn; and after working some time, Mrs. BLANNERHASSETT told me, that Mr. BLANNERHASSETT and Col. B. were going to lay in provisions for an army for a year. .. In a few days after the boats came and landed at the island. The snow was about three inches deep, and I went out a hunting. I was on the Ohio side. I met two men.. As we were talking together, they named themselves Col. BURR's men, belonging to the boats, landed at the island. .. I went to the island the day the Proclamation came out. But before I went to BLANNERHASSETT's house, I heard he was not at home, but at Marietta. .. I waited at the house till BLANNERHASSETT came home. .. When night came on, I was among the men, and also in the kitchen, and saw the boat-men running bullets. .. Then BLANNERHASSETT came down..he had four or five trunks. .. When we got down, some person..asked me to stand by the trunks, till they were put in the boats. When the last of them went off, I saw men standing in a circle on the shore. .. The first thing I heard was, they laying plans how BLANNERHASSETT and Comfort TYLER should get safe by Galliapolis. One Nahum BENT was called forward, and when he came, BLANNERHASSETT asked him, whether he had not two smart horses.. Then a

(51) (Cont.) man by the name of TUPPER, laid his hands upon BLANNERHASSETT; and said: "Your body is in my hands in the name of the Commonwealth;" or such a word as that. As quick as TUPPER made that motion, there were 7 or 8 muskets levelled down at him.. TUPPER then changed his speech, and said he wished him luck and safe down the river. ..

Examined by the Counsel for the Prosecution. Mr. WIRT. Had you seen Col. BURR on the island? A. Yes. Was he there before BLANNERHASSETT went to Kentucky: A. He was. Q. Did you speak of the boats under the command of TYLER? A. I did. Q. Did the boats quit the island, at the time of hearing about the proclamation? A. Yes--Mr. BURR. Did you see Peter TAYLOR converse with BLANNER-HASSETT that night? I do not recollect. Q. How long was he there before the departure of the boats? A. About 6 weeks. ..

Examination of William LOVE. Mr. HAY. Were you on BLANNERHASSETT's island; A. Yes; but not there at the time when Col. TYLER's boats arrived there. .. Q. Did you see TAYLOR and ALLBRIGHT there? A. I knew Peter TAYLOR very well and I saw ALLBRIGHT. I saw Mr. WOODBRIDGE too. .. Q. Did you see the prisoner on the island? A. I never saw Col. BURR on the island. I first saw him at Natchez about 2 and an half years ago. ..

Examination of Dudley WOODBRIDGE. Mr. HAY. Were you on the island when BLAN-NERHASSETT's party left it? A. I went there that night. Mr. WIRT. What party do you mean? A. I allude to the 4 boats, with Mr. Isreal SMITH, Comfort TYLER and others. .. Mr. HAY. Will you inform us of what you know on this subject? Mr. WOODBRIDGE. About the beginning of September or the last of August, Mr. BLAN-NERHASSETT in company with Col. BURR called at our compting house at Marietta. I had been connected in commerial business with Mr. BLANNERHASSETT for 6 or 8 years past, under the firm of Dudley WOODBRIDGE, & Co. Mr. BLANNERHASSETT observed, that Col BURR wished us to purchase a quantity of provisions.--Col. BURR went into the enquiry about the price of different kinds of provisions, and the expence of boats best calculated to carry those provisions up and down the river. After his making a number of enquiries and my giving him all the information that I could, he left a memorandum of such provisions as he wanted and of the boats that he wished to have built. .. Q. What provisions were ordered? A. Pork, Flour, Whiskey, Bacon and kiln-dried Meal..

Thursday, August 20. Examination of Simeon POOLE. I never was on the island on that time; but was opposite to it. I saw boats and men there; if I mistake not about the 10th December. .. Boats were passing and repassing during the night, from the island to the mainland..small craft. I did not speak to them.--I stood as much undiscovered as possible, as I was authorised by the Governor of Ohio to apprehend BLANNERHASSETT, and I went for that purpose. ..

Examination of Maurice P. BELLNAP. Mr. HAY. Will you tell us, sir, what you saw on the island? Mr. BELLNAP. On the evening of the 10th of December I was at the island of Mr. BLANNERHASSETT. ..I met with Mr. WOODBRIDGE, who returned to the house with me. When I went into the house, I observed a number of men..about 20. The 2 or 3 I noticed near the door had rifles, and appeared to be cleaning them. These were all the arms I saw. ..

Examination of Edmund P. DANA. On the evening of the 10th December, I understood that the boats were to start, with Comfort TYLER and his men down the river. The other young men and myself were determined to cross over from Bel-Pre, where I live. .. We went into the hall.. I was then introduced into a chamber, where there were TYLER, BLANNERHASSETT, Col. SMITH of New-York, and several other gentlemen. I was introduced to Mr. SMITH and Dr. MC CASTLE, who had his lady there.--Col. TYLER, I had seen the day before. ..

Friday, August 21. Examination of Israel MILLER. Mr. MILLER stated, that he had arrived on the island between the 7th and 10th December last, in company with Col. TYLER and Israel SMITH; with 4 boats and 32 men, with 5 rifles and about 3 or

(51) (Cont.) 4 pair of pistols in all..that he had joined them at Beaver and gone down with them at BLANNERHASSETT's island.. He saw but one man running bullets.
    Examination of Purley HOWE. Mr. HOWE stated, that he had not been on the island..he had been applied to by BLANNERHASSETT to make ____ (blot) boat poles--and that on the evening of the 10th Dec. he went to the landing (Ohio side) to deliver them from his shop; that BLANNERHASSETT had sent his flat to receive them.. One of his neighbours Mr. ALLENWOOD wanted to go over in the flat; but they refused to take him, saying that they had orders to take no person from the Ohio side. ...

(52) Baltimore, September 2. Official. Baltimore, August 31st, 1807. Sir, We have the honour to report to you, the proceedings of the detachments from the Independent Company, and United Volunteers, under our command, who offered their services to take the Pirate that was lately molesting the commerce of the Chesapeake. ... Samuel STERETT, Capt. Independent Company. Joseph STERETT, Captain, Of Baltimore United Volunteers. Col. John STRICKER, 5th Mary'd. Reg.

(53) Norfolk, September 9. Proceedings of the Court at Richmond. .. The court having decided that the assemblage of persons on BLANNERHASSETT's island, as before noticed, did not amount to an overt act of levying war against the United States, the attorney-general has entered a nolle prosequi, as to BLANNERHASSETT and SMITH, on the indictments against them for treason. Jonathan DAYTON, by his counsel appeared in court, when the attorney-general entered a nolle prosequi on the indictment against him for treason. These three last named persons, will be proceeded against as soon as Col. B's trial is over.

(54) The Gazette. Edenton, September 17, 1807. .. Died, on the (blank) inst. at the Bar, on his way from this port to Boston, Capt. Thomas ENGLAND, master of the schooner Washington, of this port.

(55) ARROWSMITH's Grand Map of the World. Proposals of Thomas L. PLOWMAN, for publishing by subscription, ARROWSMITH's Map of the World, on a globular projection, Containing all the new discoveries to the present time.. Subscriptions received by the publisher, corner of Seventh and George-street; by? John BIOREN, No. 28, Ch____ street; the principal booksellers in the ____ at the office of the Philadelphia Gazette and by Henry WILLS, Edenton.

(56) Notice. The subscriber having qualified as executor to the last will and testament of Captain Samuel BUTLER, dec. at the last term of Chowan County Court; requests all persons indebted to the estate of said deceased, to make immediate payment; and those having demands against it are hereby notified to exhibit them within the time prescribed by law. Frederick CREECY, Ex'r. Sept. 16, 1807.

(57) Notice. The subscriber having qualifed as executor to the last will and testament of John WILDER, dec. at the last term of Chowan County Court; requests all persons indebted to the estate of said deceased, to make immediate payment; and those having demands against it are hereby notified to exhibit them within the time prescribed by law. Francis WILDER, Ex'r. Sept. 16, 1807.

(58) Notice. The subscriber, having qualified as administrator to the estate of William WORSTER, dec. at the last term of Chowan County Court; requests all persons indebted to the estate of said deceased, to make immediate payment; and those having demands against it are hereby notified to exhibit them within the time prescribed by law. William NICHOLS, Adm. Sept. 16, 1807.

(59) Notice. The subscriber having qualified as administrator to the estate of

17 September 1807

(59) (Cont.) Capt. Alexander A. FREEMAN, dec. at the last term of Chowan County Court; requests all persons indebted to the estate of said deceased, to make immediate payment; and those having demands against it are hereby notified to exhibit them within the time prescribed by law. King LUTON, Adm. Sept. 16, 1807.

(60) On Monday, the 28th inst. will be Sold, to the highest bidder, at a credit of six months, all the Perishable Estate of Capt. Alexander A. FREEMAN, dec. consisting of a variety of handsome Household and Kitchen Furniture. ... Administrator. Sept. 16, 1807.

(61) Notice. All persons indebted to the subscriber are earnestly requested to come forward & make immediate payment, in order that he may be enabled to pay those to whom he is indebted; which is his most ardent desire. He hopes those that have had accounts standing with him for upwards of two years, will not fail to come forward and close them by paying the cash, or..notes--as they ought to know that he cannot live on the wind alone.. He continues to carry on his business as usual, at his shop in King-street, opposite the store of LITTLEJOHN and BOND... Joseph MANNING, Tailor. Sept. 16, 1807.

(62) Ran-away in the forenoon of yesterday, Two Negro Fellows, MINGO and TOM,* the property of Willis WILDER. I suppose they will be lurking about Edenton, or in this neighbourhood. .. A generous reward will be given to any person taking up said fellows and delivering them to me, James SAUNDERS, Agent for Willis WILDER. Yeoppim, Sept. 5th, 1807. *TOM has since been taken.

(63) Notice. Will be Sold, before the Court-House door in Tyrrell County, on Saturday, the 19th day of September next, The following Lands, not enlisted for taxation, for 1806, or so much thereof as will discharge the taxes due for said year, with all such extra charges as are allowed by law in like cases: viz. 91600 Acres, belonging to the heirs of Thos. FITT, dec. lying on the east side of Alligator and Scuppernong Rivers. 22500 Acres, the property of Generals JONES and DAVIE, near Lake PHELPS. 640 Acres, the property of Demsey JACKSON's heirs, lying on Milltan, east side of Alligator River. 100 Acres, the property of Nathaniel WILLIAMS, joining the lands of William BRICKHOUSE, sen. 400 Acres, lying on the east side of Alligator River, belonging to the heirs of Joseph LEACH. 5080 Acres lying on the east side of Alligator river, the property of John FIELD and Son, merchants, Philadelphia. James HOSKINS, Sh'ff. July 10, 1807.

(64) Notice. The subscribers having qualified as Executors of the last Will and Testament of Alexander MILLEN, dec. at the last term of Chowan County Court; request all persons indebted to the estate of said deceased, to make immediate payment; and those having demands..to exhibit them within the time prescribed by law. Josiah COLLINS, Jun. John LITTLE, Henry KING, Who offer for Sale, belonging to said Estate, on a credit of 6 and 12 months, several Negroes; among whom is a good Bricklayer about 26 years of age; and on a credit of 1 and 2 years, the House and Lot occupied by Dr. KNOX, and the House and Lot formerly occupied by Capt. Thomas COX. Edenton, 30th June, 1807.

(65) For Sale, On a very liberal credit, a Tract of Land, near this place, containing about 360 Acres; and a Wharf with a good Warehouse thereon, both lately the property of Mr. King LUTON--Apply to Josiah COLLINS, Jun. or the EX'rs. of A. MILLEN. Edenton, 30th June, 1807.

(66) Notice. The subscriber intending to leave this state for a short time,

17 September 1807

(66) (Cont.) earnestly requests those indebted to him to make speedy payment. Those who do not settle their accounts in the course of two months from this date, must excuse him for putting them into the hands of the proper officers for collection. .. He keeps on hand Gold and Silver Work as usual--Watches cleaned, repaired, and warranted, and the smallest favours gratefully acknowledged. Martin NOXON. Edenton, June 30, 1807.

(67) William MANNING, Cabinet Maker, Begs leave to inform the public, that the partnership of HANKINS and MANNING is, in consequence of the death of Thomas HANKINS, dissolved. The Cabinet-Making-Business in all its various branches, will be carried on at his shop, formerly occupied by Joseph CHILDRES, Windsor-Chair Maker, in Market-Street. ... May 16th, 1807.

(68) Daniel DAVENPORT, vs Arthur JONES.) Attachment. Whereas the plaintiff in the above suit brought into Washington County Court his attachment, returned levied on the Lands of the defendant in the aforesaid County:--And the Court being satisfied that the said defendant was not a resident of said County, have ordered, That the Clerk advertise the proceedings in the Edenton Gazette, so that he, the said defendant, may appear at the next term..on the third Monday in September next, to replevy and plead if he chuses; otherwise final judgment will be taken, and the Land sold. Test, Martin R. BYRD, Cl'k. June Term, 1807. A copy from the Minutes.

(69) Notice. All persons having demands against the estate of James DEANE, formerly of this state, and late of the Bahama Islands, Merchant, deceased, are requested to render attested statements of the same; and those indebted, to make payment without delay, to Josiah COLLINS, jun. Esq. William DEANE, Ex'r. Sept. 2, 1807.

(70) Notice. On the 14th day of October next, at the Court-House in Gates County, will be Sold, at 6 months credit, the valuable and new Schooner, just launched, the property of Charles POWELL, dec. of 100 tons burthen, by the Executors. September 9th, 1807.

(71) Ten Dollars Reward. Run-Away from the subscriber on Wednesday last, a short thick negro man by the name of PARIS, formerly the property of Dr. Frederick RAMCKE dec. about thirty five years of age. He has thick lips, a smiling countenance. and long wool. The above reward will be given to any person who will deliver him to me at Sandy-Run, Cross-Roads; or should it be inconvenient to bring the negro entire, 20 Dollars will be given for his head alone. Matthias B. DICKINSON. Sandy-Run, Cross-Roads, July 28th, 1807.

(72) Stop Thief! Stolen from the subscriber, on Friday night, the 24th inst. a large black Horse, about 7 years old.. The villain who I suppose took him away, left a small sorrel horse in the road almost starved and fatigued to death. He broke into a dairy and took what refreshments he wanted. Whosoever should apprehend and secure the thief, shall, on his conviction, receive the reward of 50 Dollars, or 10 Dollars for the horse, delivered at this place. David SHARROCK. Bertie, New-Market, July 16th, 1807.

(73) 50 Dollars Reward. Runaway from the subscriber, living in Bertie County, a negro fellow, named HARRY, Who runaway the 10th of March, 1798. He is about 33 years of age, 5 feet 8 or 9 inches high, remarkable black, thin visage, bow-legged and has a scar on his left shoulder blade about 6 inches in length, occasioned, as he informed me, by the cut of a knife, in battle with another negro. He was

(73) (Cont.) raised in Perquimans County, near Hertford, in the family of the
SKINNERs, and sold by them to William ARCHIL, and from William ARCHIL to Capt.
PENRICE, of whom I purchased him. .. Since advertising said fellow, together
with TONEY and PETER, who has since been taken, I have been informed that said negro HARRY has got a free pass, and passes for a free man, by some name as yet unknown to me. He is sometimes lurking about Norfolk, and works occasionally at the
blacksmith's, carpenter's, and shoe-making business. Any person who will take up
said fellow, and convey him to me in Bertie county, near Colerain, or secure him
in any gaol so that I get him again, shall receive the above reward..and all reasonable expences. John HOLLEY. Bertie county, July 22, 1807.

Edenton: Printed by James WILLS.
Vol. II. Thursday, September 24, 1807. Num. 83.

(74) New-York, September 4. .. Five persons, named NOBLES, BLOIS, KIMBALL,
NILES and ROBERTS, were lately committed to goal in Woodstock, state of Vermont,
charging (sic) with counterfeiting bank notes. It appears that some persons in
Rutland..became suspicious of KIMBALL, who resided in Plymouth, formerly Saltash;
and having collected 2?6 gentlemen, and put themselves under the command or direction of Gen. Isaac CLARK, they then proceeded to KIMBALL's house, where they immediately secured him. They then went in pursuit of the gang.. After a tedious
search of some hours, they were discovered on a mountain, about 2 miles from any
house, in a kind of cave.. The whole party..surrendered. .. NOBLES is the fellow who engraved so much for the noted Stephen BURROUGHS.

(75) The Gazette. Edenton, September 24, 1807. .. Trial Of Aaron BURR. Wed-
nesday, September 9. The pannel of the jury was at length completed, after having
excused several on account of their having formed and delivered opinions unfavour-
able to the accused. The following were sworn to try the issue:--Orris PAINE,
Obadiah GATHRIGHT, Robert M'KIM, Yeamans SMITH, Jesse BOWLES, Robert GORDON, James
BOOTWRIGHT, John MURPHEY, William BENTLEY, Carter B. BERKELEY, James PENN, Thomas
LEWIS. After the indictment was read, Mr. HAY produced the return of the
President to the subpoena duces tecum, requiring the exhibition of the letter of
Gen. WILKINSON to him of the 12th of November, 1806, which has before been no-
ticed. .. The return is in the following words: "On re-examination of a letter
of Nov. 12th, 1806, from Gen. WILKINSON to myself..I find in it some passages entirely confidential given for my information in the discharge of my executive
functions, and which my duties and the public interest forbid me to make public..
I have, therefore, given above a correct copy of all those parts which I ought to
permit to make public. .. Given under my hand this 7th day of September, 1807.
Th: JEFFERSON." .. Yesterday, it was expected, the Judge would deliver his opinion.

(76) Deaths. On Thursday last, Mr. Francis MAURICE, teacher of the French Lan-
guage, Dancing, Music, &c. On the same day, Mr. John CHESSON, overseer for Mr.
Wm. ROBERTS. On Friday, Mr. Andrew ELLMORE, Boot and Shoe-Maker. On Saturday,
Mrs. Martha BROWN.

(77) Notice. The Subscriber who has been an instructor of youth several years in
this county, in correct English Reading, Writing and Arithmetic, now offers his
service in that vocation, to engage for a year in some eligible neighbourhood
where there is a comfortable school-house, and board can be had convenient to it.-
-A present engagement will conclude early in November. In the interim, application may be made to me by letter, and left at the store of Mr. Henry WILLS; or if
sent by post and directed to his care, will be forwarded, and receive due atten-

(77) (Cont.) tion. ... Charles SHORT. Chowan county, Sept. 22, 1807.

(78) 40 Dollars Reward. Run-away from the Plantation of the Subscriber near this Town, on the 29th of August, a Negro Man, named ISAAC. He is about 45 years of age, 5 feet 9 or 10 inches high, very much knock-kneed, the joints of his great toes are unusually large, and he has lost two of his upper fore teeth. He is a cooper by trade, and was lately the property of Mr. James GRANBERY, dec. of this place. He has lived with the late Mr. Josiah GRANBERY, at Sunsberry, in Gates county, at Winton, in Northampton county, with Mr. Josiah GRANBERY, at the Cross-Roads, in Bertie county, with the late Mr. John D. WHITE, at the White Marsh, and at Suffolk, in Virginia; it is supposed he is well known at all those places. ... Josiah COLLINS. Edenton, Sept. 19, 1807.

(79) A Camp-Meeting, Will commence at St. John's, in Hertford County, about 12 miles from Murfreesborough and the same distance from Winton, on the road that leads from Winton to Halifax, on Friday, the 25th of September next; and will continue 4 days, or as much longer as the spirit of God, evidenced by acts of devotion and piety among the people, may direct. ... Philip BRUCE, P. E. Bridges ARUNDELL, Ast. August 5th, 1807.

Vol. II. Thursday, October 1, 1807. Num. 84.

(80) The Gazette. Edenton, October 1, 1807. The Court of Enquiry on Commodore BARRON is ordered to convene, at Hampton, on the 5th of October, Captain Alexander MURRAY, President. True Am.

(81) Died, on the evening of the 22d ult. in childbed, Mrs. (blank) BELL, wife of Capt. Daniel BELL, of this town. On Saturday last, after a lingering indisposition, Mrs. Margaret BARCO, wife of Mr. John W. BARCO, of this place.

(82) 10 Dollars Reward. Run away from the Subscriber on the 16th of March last, a Negro Man, named SAMPSON, belonging to the estate of Richard BENBURY, dec. He is about 21 or 22 years of age, five feet 9 or 10 inches high, very black, and walks very upright. ... Solomon ELLIOTT. Chowan county, Sept. 12, 1807.

Vol. II. Thursday, October 8, 1807. Num. 85.

(83) Halifax Trial. Trial of WILSON. .. A pamphlet has been published at Halifax, of the trial of John WILSON, alias Jenkins RATFORD, for mutiny, desertion and contempt. It will be recollected that this was one of the seamen found on board the Chesapeake. .. To John Erskine DOUGLAS, Esq. Captain of his Majesty's ship Bellona, and Senior Officer, &c. &c, Chesapeake, His Majesty's ship Leopard, at Sea, 22d June, 1807. Sir, In obedience to your signal this morning, to weigh anchor and reconnoitre, S. E. by E., I have the honour to acquaint you, that having arrived off Cape Henry..about 4 or 5 leagues, I bore up, pursuant to orders from the Commander in Chief, to search for deserters on board the U. States frigate Chesapeake. On arriving within hail, an officer was dispatched..to shew the order to the commander, together with the following note from myself: "The Captain of his Brittanic Majesty's ship Leopard, has the honour to enclose to the Captain of the United States' frigate Chesapeake, an order from the Hon. Vice-Admiral BERKE-LEY..respecting some deserters from the ships (therein mentioned) under his command, and supposed now to be serving as part of the crew of the Chesapeake. .." The boat..returned with the following answer: "I know of no such men as you describe; the officers that were on the recruiting service for this ship, were particularly instructed by the government..not to enter? any deserters from his Brit-

8 October 1807

(83) (Cont.) tanic Majesty's ships; nor do I know of any being here. I am also instructed, never to permit the crew of any ship that I command, to be mustered by any other but her own officers; it is my disposition to preserve harmony; and I hope this answer to your dispatch will prove satisfactory. James BARRON. Commander of the U. S. ship Chesapeake."

On the receipt of this letter, motives of humanity, and an ardent desire to prevent bloodshed, induced me if possible to endeavour to make the search without recurring to more serious measures, by repeatedly hailing and remonstrating without effect. I then directed a shot to be fired across the bow; after which he was again hailed, the answers again were equally evasive; conceiving then, therefore, that my orders would not admit of deviation, I lament to state that I felt under the necessity of enforcing them by firing into the United States ship; a few shot were returned, but none struck this ship—at the expiration of ten minutes from the first shot being fired, the pendant and ensign of the Chesapeake were lowered. I then gave the necessary direction for her being searched, and herewith send you a statement* of the number and names of the deserters found on board. .. After the search had been made, and previous to separation, the Captain sent me the annexed note... S. P. HUMPHREYS.
*William WARE, Daniel MARTIN, John STRACHAN, alias STORY—H. M. S. Melampus. John WILSON, alias Jenkins RATFORD—H. M. S. Halifax.

Copy of a letter from Commodore BARRON, to Captain HUMPHREYS, after the Chesapeake had struck. "Sir, I consider the frigate Chesapeake as your prize, and am ready to deliver her to any officer authorized to receive her—by the return of the boat I shall expect your answer... James BARRON. At Sea, 22d June, 1807."

Answer. His Majesty's ship Leopard, at Sea, June 22, 1807. "Sir, Having, to the utmost of my power, fulfilled the instructions of my Commander in Chief, I have nothing more to desire... S. P. HUMPHREYS."

(84) Norfolk, September 28. .. October 5. This day the Court appointed by the government, to inquire into the conduct of Commodore BARRON, met on board the Chesapeake, present Captains MURRAY, CHAUNCEY, HULL. The Court adjourned without doing any business until to-morrow. Littleton W. TAZEWELL, Esq. has been appointed Judge-Advocate. Commodore BARRON is, we understand, very much indisposed, and Mr. TAZEWELL is at Richmond, a witness in the case of Col. BURR.

(85) The Gazette. Edenton, October 8, 1807. .. The ship United States, Capt. MOORE, of and bound to Baltimore, from the Isle of France, owned by Wm. WILSON and Sons, was captured on Sunday off the Cape, by the British ship of war Leopard and sent to Halifax. ...

(86) Elder William BROWN will preach in the Court-House, on Sunday, the 11th instant.

(87) Married, on Sunday evening last, Mr. Joshua CREECY, to Miss Polly BENBURY, daughter of Richard BENBURY, Esq. dec.

(88) Died, on Wednesday evening last, Mrs. Winnifred HOSKINS, a very old and respectable inhabitant of this County. On Thursday evening, of the prevailing influenza, William ROBERTS, Esq. High Sheriff of this County. On Sunday evening, very suddenly, at Colerain, Bertie county, Mr. Edward REED, son of George REED, Esq. of that county. On Monday morning, in this town, Master Solomon JONES, Clerk to Mr. James R. BENT, merchant. On Tuesday, Mrs. Lydia BENNETT, wife of Major William BENNETT, dec. of this county.

(89) Federal District Court Adjourned. To all whom it may concern, Be it known,

20

8 October 1807

(89) (Cont.) that the Hon. Henry POTTER, Esq. Judge of the United States, in and for the North-Carolina District, in consequence of his indisposition, has given me orders to adjourn the District Court of said United States, which agreeably to law should be held at Edenton, on the Friday after the Friday following the first Monday in October, 1807, to the Tuesday after the Friday following the third Monday in said month of October, 1807. John S. WEST, Marshal N. C. D. September 30, 1807.

(90) Notice. An advertisement, subscribed Arthur JONES, made its appearance in the Edenton Gazette of the 27th of August last, fraught throughout with misrepresentation and abuse, which I shall attempt to answer.

Mr. JONES..says, "I have conversed with a good honest old man Benj. WYNNS, who says, that he contracted a debt with me for pipe staves on account of Daniel DAVENPORT, &c."--That statement is not correct, neither will that honest good old man support it.--I sold the staves to Mr. JONES myself, and delivered them to him, and was to have received payment for them at the time of delivery.

Mr. JONES further says, "I wish Mr. DAVENPORT had demanded it before process." If the gentleman means by that side-way mode of delivering his sentiments to deny that payment was demanded before process, I reply to that statement, that it is also entirely incorrect, and I can prove it to be so. I have myself, and persons for me, called on Mr. JONES for payment oftentimes before process was had, and have been as often disappointed.

Mr. JONES also says, "The rascally ignorant stupid boobies of Magistrates who issued the attachment ought to blush, if they had feeling enough to know shame, &c."--Had not Mr. JONES been very ignorant himself, he would have known, that the Magistrates of Washington County Court had nothing to do in issuing the attachment; they only advertised that such an attachment issued by a single Magistrate out of Court, was returned to the Court, &c.

As to the indecent epithets before recited, so liberally bestowed by that gentleman on the Court, nothing can account for the use of them, but that Mr. JONES was conscious he had the benefit of an Irishman's protection, Impudence and Ignorance, and that he might shield himself by the benignity of it. Daniel DAVENPORT. Washington County, Sept. 30, 1807.

(91) To Be Sold. That valuable Plantation late the residence of the Subscriber, situate on the west bank of Chowan river, in Bertie County, State of North-Carolina, 15 miles from the town of Edenton, containing from 1000 to 1200 Acres of Land, 200 of which is cleared and under good fence, on which is a large comfortable brick Dwelling House, with 6 rooms on the first floor, surrounded with piazzas, situate 200 yards from the river, a court yard enclosed in handsome railed fencing, near two acres of garden, also enclosed by paling, a two story Kitchen, brick Store-House, large Barn, Stable, Corn Crib, &c. &c. There is also two good Fisheries in sight of the river piazza, one of which is exceeded by none on the river, 2000 barrels of fish having been put up in one season. If not sold by January 1st, 1808, it will be Let for one or more years. For further particulars and terms of Sale, enquire of Elisha NORFLEET, Edenton. Joseph A. BROWN. October 8th, 1807.

Vol. II. Thursday, October 15, 1807. Num. 86.

(92) Norfolk, October 7. .. The proceeding of the Court of Inquiry, which assembled on board the Chesapeake on Monday last, have not been correctly stated. The court was formed at 10 o'clock in the morning. Present, Alexander MURRAY, Esq. Capt. in the navy, President; Capts. Isaac HULL and Isaac CHAUNCEY, members. Littleton W. TAZEWELL, Esq. had been appointed judge advocate by the secretary of

(92) (Cont.) the navy; but being absent from Norfolk on public business, Richard RUSH, Esq. was appointed judge advocate pro tempore. The court sat two hours, and adjourned to Thursday 10 o'clock in the morning.

(93) MONROE's Treaty. .. [Copy.] London, December 27, 1806. Sir, We have the pleasure to acquaint you that we have this day agreed with the British commissioners to conclude a treaty On All The Points Which Have Formed The Object Of Our Negotiation, and on terms which we trust our government will approve. ... Your most obedient servants, James MONROE, Wm. PINCKNEY. James MADISON, Sec. State, Washington.

(94) The Gazette. Edenton, October 15, 1807. .. Died, on the 1st. inst. Gen. Peter MUHLENBURG, Collector of the port of Philadelphia.

(95) Communicated. Died in this place on the 10th inst. Mrs. Sarah LITTLEJOHN, the virtuous consort of William LITTLEJOHN, Esq. aged 60 years.--The life of this truly excellent and pious woman, was one uniform display, of all the moral, social and christian virtues. .. Tender and affectionate, to a degree of enthusiasm, towards her now afflicted husband and weeping children, sincere, affable, and sympathetic towards her numerous acquaintance...

(96) (Circular.) To the Physicians in different parts of the U. States. The recording of epidemick diseases having been long observed by Physicians to be useful in developing their history, prevention and cure, a request is made of the Physicians throughout the Union, to collect from actual observation, and transmit to me in New York, an account of the Influenza, which has lately prevailed in this city, and which is now rapidly spreading in different parts of the Continent. ... Shadrack RICKETSON. New-York, 8 mo. 25th, 1807.

Vol. II. Thursday, October 22, 1807. Num. 87.

(97) Another Insurrection. Pittsburgh, (Pennsylvania,) Sept. 9. Early last week Mr. William B. IRISH, deputy Marshal, left this place for Beaver county, to execute several writs of Habere Facias P_____esto?nem, Issued out of the circuit court of the U. States for the district of Pennsylvania, for lands recovered by the Population Company against various settlers in that county. On Wednesday the 22d inst. Mr. IRISH was proceeding to the house of William FOULKES, one of the persons against whom judgment had been obtained in said court, in company with Enion? WILLIAMS, agent of the company, George HOLDSHIP, Esq. and James HAMILTON; when having just entered the lane leading to FOULKES' house, three or four guns were fired from a thicket of bushes close by the road side, and two balls struck Mr. HAMILTON who fell from his horse and expired in a few minutes--the others made their escape immediately thro' the woods to Greersburg. Mr. HAMILTON had that morning been put in possession of a tract of land held by contract with the company, about two miles from the place where the horrid deed was perpetrated, and no doubt but the villains knew him well when they fired at him. Some neighbours collected in the afternoon to remove the body of Mr. HAMILTON; Mr. FOULKES, it is said, came to them, and expressed great sorrow at the unfortunate accident, although he had threatened a day or two before, that if the marshall would come to dispossess him, blood would be spilt on the occasion. ...

(98) The Gazette. Edenton, October 22, 1807. .. Died--on Friday last, very suddenly, Mr. Richard JONES, a native of Ireland. On Friday evening, in Hertford County, Mr. Christopher H. GALE, for many years a resident of that County. On the 14th inst. at Elizabeth-City, Mrs. Elizabeth HAMILTON, consort of Col. John HAMIL-

(98) (Cont.) TON.

(99) List of Letters remaining in the Post-Office, October 1, 1807. Agness ALEX-
ANDER, Charles ATKINSON, Hannah ARKILL, Nathl. ALLEN, William BLAIR, Jacob BLOUNT,
Wm. BUXTON, John BEVER, Richard BLACKMAN, Andrew BATES, William CLARK, Benjamin
COBB, Ira CROCKER, John CALLENDER, William COPELAND, Lemuel COTTON, Job CUNSTOCK,
William DEANE, Francis DOZIER, Capt. EASTON, William GILBY, John GOELET, Mary
GREGORY, Samuel HEDRICK, Margaret HARIOT, BURROWS and HOWELL, Thomas HARRISON,
John HOLLOWELL, Esther HERICK, Ethan HAMMOND, Thos. JONES, Uriah JOHNSON, Solomon
JONES, James HATHAWAY, Francis JONES, John MOODY, Doctor James Q. MARES, Miss
Eliza MARE, Chevalier de ST. MAURICE, Polly M'DONALD, Hugh MILLEN, Martha M'GLAUK-
LIN, James MIRICK, Dr. M'FARLANE, Exum NEWBY, Wm. ROBERTS, Deborah STEEL, Sheriff
of Chowan, Henry STARR, James TAYLOR, Mrs. Mary VAIL, Abner VAIL, Angel WARNIER,
Benners VAIL, George WILKINSON, Elizabeth WILLIAMS, Willis WILDER, Michael WILDER,
Nathaniel WILDER. Hend. STANDIN, P. M.

(100) Mr. Printer, In order to acquire that truth and justice which every person
is entitled to and ought to receive, and to unmask the features of certain persons
and furnish them with a retrospective view of themselves, I beg leave to publish
the following advertisement, and its effect, together with a small addition of
consequence thereto annexed: Notice. That whereas there is yet some small balances of old debts which appears to be due from the subscriber to his creditors, and
the worst constructions have been thrown on them that possibly could be, by those
who had rather rejoice at the downfall of a fellow creature, than to see them rise
again in the world—Therefore, he requests the favour of each and every person who
may have any just demands against him, to present them on the first day of Perquimans Court, and on the first day of Chowan County Court next, when and where he
will attend, if permitted, to ascertain their amount, and see if the ulcer is of
so great consequence as to be altogether incurable. As it was determined at the
last Superior Court at Edenton, that the subscriber's negroes, in the County of
Gates, should stand over, in the hands of Job REDDICK, for the benefit of creditors, he is anxious to know the result, and see the balance, if any. All those who
fails to exhibit their demands on them days, will be considered that they have
none, and will be thereafter prohibited from a recovery thereof. All unjust demands are hereby exempt from the trouble of appearing on the aforesaid days, as
they will likely be treated according to their merits. None is requested to
appear but such as did not come in for any part of the property given up by the
subscriber to his creditors. A true copy from the original, Edward HALL. July
14th, 1806.
     By virtue of the above notice, I have received a list of those debts from the
creditors, and that in their own hand writing, which may be seen if requested--the
amount of which is 200 hundred dollars..and for which sum there stands confined or
withheld from me, 8 valuable negroes. And as I am something at a loss to know
their intention, who contrived these things to be done, I will ask the public one
question, and thank them for their information. Suppose it was to take one half
of these negroes to pay my debts, to whom is the other half given? ... Edward
HALL.

(101) Shocking Murder. Carlisle, August 21. On Monday last, a man of the name
of F. DONNELLY, was committed to the jail of this county, on suspicion of a most
horrid murder of his own wife. .. He is said to bear a very bad character, to
possess a brutal temper, and was considered a dangerous man in his neighbourhood.
He is also said to have been long in the habit of beating and ill-treating his
wife. On Saturday the 9th inst. her screams were heard by the neighbours, supposed to be on account of his beating her, but since that time she has not been

(101) (Cont.) seen by any one. He says she ran off, but it is extraordinary and unaccountable how she could have so completely disappeared, especially as she was far gone with child; & also passing relations in this town, to whom she would most likely come if she had left her husband. These presumptions have been confirmed by others still stronger: on examining the fire place of his house, a number of bones, among which are two teeth, were found.. Physicians and a dentist, who have examined the bones, and teeth, declare..that they are those of a human being. He appears to have been in a kind of phrensy on the day this abominable murder was committed. .. He cut his eldest boy in the head with a scythe, in a shocking manner; the scull was laid bare for some inches. ...

Vol. II. Thursday, October 29, 1807. Num. 88.

(102) Norfolk, October 21. .. October 23. Washington City, Oct. 19. By the President of the United States of America, A Proclamation. Whereas information has been received that a number of individuals who have deserted from the army of the United States, and sought shelter without the jurisdiction thereof, have become sensible of their offence, and are desirous of returning to their duty, a full pardon is hereby proclaimed to each and all of such individuals as shall, within four months from the date hereof, surrender themselves to the commanding officer of any military post within the United States, or the territories thereof. In testimony whereof, I have caused the seal of the United States to be affixed to these presents, and signed the same with my hand. Done at the City of Washington, the fifteenth day of October, in the year of our Lord one thousand eight hundred and seven, and of the Independence of the United States of America the thirty-second. Th: JEFFERSON. By the President, James MADISON, Secretary of State.

(103) Gideon GRANGER, Esq. the Post-Master General, has it is said, resigned.

(104) The Gazette. Edenton, October 29, 1807. Elder WRIGHT's appointments to Preach at the following places, in November, 1807:--Thursday 5th, KNOB's-Crook. Friday 6th, Salem. Saturday 7th, Bethlehem. Sunday 8th, Widow PERRY's. Monday 9th, Hertford. Tuesday 10th, Bethel. Wednesday 11th, Yeoppim. Thursday 12th, Edenton. Friday 13th, BALLARD's-Bridge.

(105) New Pamphlet.--We have just received by mail (says the New-York Evening Post) a highly interesting pamphlet, written by Joseph Hamilton DAVEISS, Esq. of Kentucky, the object of which is to convict Mr. JEFFERSON of extreme remissness in regard to the BURR and WILKINSON conspiracy. We have no room here for extracts; but the following one is too interesting to be omitted. "To General WILKINSON, You feel deeply aggrieved, no doubt, by this pamphlet. Sir, the courts are open to you; and that you may have no difficulty in selecting the actionable words, I now state, "That you have been for years a pensioner of Spain, and have held secret intelligence with that power; and you were engaged in BURR's conspiracy and deserted him." Joseph Hamilton DAVEISS." Cornland, 22d May, 1807.

(106) Federal Circuit Court. Tuesday, Oct. 20. The Court has just delivered a long and elaborate opinion, in which it determines, that "it would be improper to commit the accused on the charge of treason." The conclusion of the opinion is as follows: "I shall commit Aaron BURR and Herman BLANNERHASSET for preparing and providing the means for a military expedition against the territories of a foreign Prince with whom the United States were at peace. If those whose province and duty it is to prosecute offenders against the laws of the United States shall be of opinion that a crime of a deeper die has been committed, it is not their choice to act in conformity with that opinion.--Israel SMITH is not proved to have provi-

29 October 1807

(106) (Cont.) ded or prepared any means whatever, and therefore I shall not commit him. .. Mr. HAY moved to have A. B. and H. B. committed for trial in the district of Ohio.

(107) On the 25th of November next, will be Sold, on 6 months credit, at the late dwelling-house of Lemuel BURKITT, dec. all the Perishable part of his estate, consisting of about 100 barrels Corn, a quantity of excellent blade Fodder, 2 or 3 very good Horses, some likely Cattle and Hogs, a good yoke of Oxen, a compleat sett of House-Carpenter's and Joiner's Tools, household and kitchen Furniture, plantation Utensils, &c. &c. All persons indebted to the estate, are requested to make immediate payment, or their Notes and Accounts will be put into the hands of an officer to collect--All persons having demands..are requested to make them known... John SKINNER, Adm. October 27, 1807.

(108) Notice. The subscriber having qualified as executrix to the last will and testament of Samuel CHESSON, dec. at the last term of Washington County Court; requests all persons indebted to the estate of said deceased, to make immediate payment; and those having demands against it, are hereby notified to exhibit them within the time prescribed by law. Elizabeth CHESSON, Ex'rx.

Vol. II. Thursday, November 5, 1807. Num. 89.

(109) New-York, September 24. Extract of a letter from a gentleman of veracity and honour, to his friend in this city, dated Richmond, 17th Sept. 1807. .. "Sometime between the 20th and 27th of August, Mr. DUNCAN, formerly one of Gen. WILKINSON's aids, at New-Orleans, and now a witness here on the part of the government, discovered a plot to poison him, by mixing laudanum with his porter, of which he usually drank when going to bed. A negro man, the property and servant of Mr. D. was apprehended, committed, and confessed the fact. On further examination before a Magistrate, he charged a person by the name of KINNEY, as his accomplice, whom he said had incited him to the act by the promise of a reward of seven hundred dollars, and a horse, if he succeeded. KINNEY, however, has never been examined.. This KINNEY was brought from New-Orleans by WILKINSON as a witness against BURR; and the circumstance of their being frequently seen together in private and earnest conversation..caused suspicion to attach to the General.

(110) Extract of a letter from Jonathan THOMPSON to his friend in this city, dated New-York, October 6, 1807. "About 1 o'clock p. m. of Tuesday the 6th October, called on Messrs. LANG & TURNER at the office of the New-York Gazette-- several persons being present..when Mr. THOMPSON remarked to Mr. LANG he wished to speak a few words with him & Mr. TURNER..we adjourned to an adjoining room. Mr. THOMPSON introduced the subsequent conversation by observing--Messrs. LANG and TURNER: there appeared in your paper, a few days since, an extract of a letter from Richmond respecting General WILKINSON. Mr. THOMPSON continued, I am authorised to ask of you the name of the person who handed it to you for publication. .. Mr. LANG asked, if authorised by Gen. WILKINSON, and was answered in the affirmative: Mr. TURNER said he was of opinion that they..were at liberty to give the name: Mr. LANG conceded, and gave the name of Robert SWART-WOUT, who, he said, was responsible for its publication. Mr. TURNER..said it was in Mr. Robert SWARTWOUT's hand writing. Mr. THOMPSON then asked for the name of the author of the letter, who, Mr. LANG said, was Mr. Samuel SWARTWOUT, Robert's brother. .. After having obtained the foregoing particulars we took our leave."

(111) Having seen in the New-York Gazette and General Advertiser of the 24th September last, a letter from some person dated in Richmond, 17th of the same month,

(111) (Cont.) directed to his correspondent in New-York, wherein he describes
circumstances, attending the attempt made by Mr. DUNCAN's ser'vt, to administer
laudanum to his master in a glass of porter; the description..is so evidently
calculated to prejudice Gen. WILKINSON in the estimation of those who are acquainted with the circumstances, that I think it my duty to state the facts as
they appeared before me, who examined the servant in my character as a Justice of
Peace for the county of Henrico; the examination took place in the room of Mr.
DUNCAN.

Upon being shewn the tumbler glass which contained the mixture; it was evident
that it was strongly impregnated with laudanum.--Doctor GREENHOW was called in,
who gave it as his opinion, that it contained a great portion of laudanum; and two
gentlemen who lodged in the room with Mr. DUNCAN, proved the attempt to have been
made in their presence by the servant of Mr. DUNCAN, I inquired of the servant
what he had to say in his defence. After some prevarication, he confessed to have
been prevailed on to do it by the offers of a man who called himself KINNEY, that
the said KINNEY at sundry times had given him money and offered him seven hundred
dollars if he would effect it, which would purchase his freedom, to which he said
to have consented, but that he had not put all the laudanum into the glass..I committed him to gaol, to be tried by the court of the county. He was accordingly
tried in court; but Mr. DUNCAN having left Richmond, and the confession of the
servant before the examining magistrate, being considered by the court inadmis-
sible testimony on his trial, he was acquitted. Some days after the examination
of the servant before me, I was applied to by Mr. DUNCAN for a warrant against
KINNEY, but as there were no testimony, save that of the slave, I refused to grant
a warrant. .. General WILKINSON was not examined before me, because not lodging
in the room with DUNCAN but in another part of the house, he could say nothing as
to the attempt made by the servant, nor was he present at the examination, so that
he could not say any thing as to the confession of the servant, consequently he
was not called on by the court of Henrico... Given under my hand this 3d of October, 1807. (Signed) Miles SELDEN. City of Richmond, to wit: Sworn before me
this 7th day of October, 1807. (Signed) Wm. RICHARDSON, Mayor.

Some time in the month of August last, I was informed by Abner L. DUNCAN, Esq.
of New-Orleans (then in the city) that a few evenings before, an attempt had been
made on his life, with a large quantity of laudanum, which was handed him by his
own servant in a glass of Porter.. Mr. DUNCAN observed, his servant had confessed
the fact..and said he had been influenced to commit the act, by..a man by the name
of KINNEY.

On hearing this statement, I received of Mr. DUNCAN the phial containing the
remainder of the laudanum, and undertook to trace from whence it came, by going to
the several apothecary shops in this city. I was generally informed, that
laudanum which I presented, did not agree with that of the apothecary, for that
mine was made of apple and their's of French brandy. ..I found but at one apothecary's (Mr. DUVAL's) where it was admitted their laudanum to have been made with
apple brandy. On renewing my enquiries, one of the young gentlemen in the shop,
remarked, that since my first enquiries, he had recollected selling, but a few
evenings before, an ounce of laudanum to a man, whose name he did not know, but
that he had frequently seen him since in company with a man by the name of LOVE..
The evening of the day of this enquiry, I was walking down the street below Dr.
DUVAL's shop, in company with Capt. WALBACT, when we passed an ill-looking man,
and..the Capt. observed, that man was KINNEY, and requested of me to return to
DUVAL's shop and get the young gentleman to say if that was the man he alluded to;
I did so, and was within ten yards of KINNEY when he passed the shop; the young
gentleman..came to the door, and was viewing him, when I came up, and before I had
time to speak, he observed (pointing at KINNEY) "that is the man I sold the phial
of laudanum to." This same man has frequently since been pointed out to me as a

5 November 1807

(111) (Cont.) witness in the charges of the U. States against Aaron BURR, and by the name of KINNEY. To these facts I am willing to swear, and now give them from under my hand at Richmond, this tenth day of October one thousand eight hundred and seven. Wm. PRICE. Gen. James WILKINSON.

(112) Territory of Orleans, &c. John MERCER, jun. of the city of New Orleans, being duly sworn, maketh oath, that he was one of the clerks in the office of the Gov. in the time of the Spanish dominion during a period of nine years from the year 1792 to the year 1801. That whilst..employed in the said office, to wit, in the years 1795 and 1796, a secret correspondence was carried on in cypher between the said Governor..and some person of note, who then was in the western part of the waters of the Ohio. That this deponent had no certain knowledge of the name of the said person, but that it was a matter of notoriety..that the said person was Gen. WILKINSON. That this deponent was entrusted with the care or charge of decyphering some of the letters..and of copying some of the answers..made to them by the Governor. .. That this deponent very well recollects that the project treated of in the said correspondence was the dismembering of the Western States and Territories from the union, but that he is not able to recollect the particulars. And..that some time towards the end of..1795, Mr. Thomas POWER, who was employed as the confidential agent of the Spanish government for this secret negociation, was entrusted with a sum of nine thousand dollars or thereabouts, destined for the said person, which sum was delivered to the said POWER in the office of the Governor in the presence of this deponent. ... J. MERCIER. Sworn before me at New-Orleans, the 31st of August, 1807. As: BONAMY, Justice of the Peace.

(113) Territory of Orleans, &c. John MC DONAUGH, jun. being duly sworn, doth depose, that sometime in the month of March, in the year 1804, Gen. WILKINSON consulted with this deponent as a commission merchant, on the probability of sugar and cotton shipped from this country to the Atlantick ports, turning to advantage. The advice of this deponent was to ship sugars in preference, upon which the General requested this deponent to purchase for him sugars to the amount of nine or ten thousand dollars, payable in cash. This deponent accordingly purchased for the General, through Messrs. DUSAN and DUBOURG, Brokers, one hundred and seven hogsheads of sugar, and chartered the ship Louisiana (in which the General took his passage) to transport it to New York. That the amount of the said sugars as invoiced was eight thousand and forty-five dollars and thirty-five cents, and this deponent gave the General a bill of exchange on New-York for one thousand dollars, the sugars not amounting to the sum which the General risked to be invested in them. That the amount of the said two sums being $9045 35 cents, was paid to this deponent by the General in Mexican dollars, and that some of the bags containing the said money were Mexican bags, such as come from Vera Cruz... John MC DONAUGH, jun. Sworn before me this 4th September, 1807, at the city of New Orleans. John LYND, Justice of Peace.

(114) Territory of Orleans, City of New Orleans, &c. Peter DERBIGNEY, of New-Orleans, Counsellor at Law, being sworn on the holy evangelists of Almighty God, deposeth, that some time in the year 1796, this deponent being then a resident at New Madrid, on the Mississippi, Mr. Thomas POWER, then employed by the Spanish government on a private agency, went up the Ohio as far as Cincinnati, as this deponent was told, and returned some time afterwards to New Madrid in quest of a sum of money which was delivered to him by Dr. Thomas PORTALL, the then commandant of that post. That this deponent was informed by a Spanish officer..that the said money was destined for Gen. WILKINSON, who was in secret correspondence with the Spanish government. That Mr. Thomas POWER, in order to conceal the said money, which was as far as this deponent can recollect, a sum of nine thousand dollars or

(114) (Cont.) thereabouts, bought from this deponent some barrels of sugar and coffee, in the centre of which the said money was packed up in small bags, which were made for that purpose in this deponent's family. That..Mr. T. POWER set off on his way to Cincinnati; and that, on..return from thence, this deponent was told that the said money had arrived safe and had been delivered to Gen. WILKINSON. And this deponent further saith, that shortly after the surrender of Louisiana to the U. States, a rumour having circulated that Gen. WILKINSON, had shipped in the vessel in which he returned to the Atlantick States, a large quantity of sugar, the price of which he had paid him in dollars lately coined, contained in bags not yet unsewed, and such as they are when sent from the Spanish mint..and felt it his duty towards the government to whom he had of late sworn allegiance, to inform the Governor of this province of the facts to him known concerning the money sent up to Gen. WILKINSON in 1796; that Governor CLAIBORNE then requested this deponent to write to the President of the United States on this subject..

And this deponent further swears, that in the winter of 1804 to 1805, this deponent being then at Washington City, in the capacity of a deputy from the inhabitants of Louisiana to Congress, jointly with Mess. DOSTREHAN & SAWIS, he was introduced to Col. BURR, then Vice-President of the United States, by Gen. WILKINSON, who strongly recommended to this deponent..to cultivate the acquaintance of Col. BURR, whom he used to call "the first gentleman in America," telling them that he was a man of the most eminent talents both as a politician and as a military character; and..that Col. BURR, so soon as his Vice-Presidency would be at an end, would go to Louisiana, where he had certain projects..and inviting this deponent to give him all the information in his power respecting that country... P. DERBIGNEY. Sworn before me at New-Orleans the 27th of August, 1807. As: BONAMY, Justice of Peace for the Parish of New-Orleans, Copies, Teste, Wm. MARSHALL, Clk.

(115) To his Excellency Brigadier General James WILKINSON. Sir, When once the chain of infamy grapples to a Knave, every new link creates a fresh sensation of detestation and horror. .. I could not have supposed, that you would have completed the catalogue of your crimes, by adding to the guilt of treachery, forgery and perjury, the accomplishment of Cowardice. .. Having failed in two different attempts, to procure an interview with you, such as no gentleman of honour could refuse, I have only to pronounce and publish you to the world as a Coward and Poltron. ... S SWARTWOUT. Richmond, 21st Oct. 1807.

(116) I Certify, that on the 20th of October 1807, between the hours of four and five P. M. at the Washington tavern in the City of Richmond, I was on the point of walking out from my lodgings, when a knock was heard at the door; I asked the person to walk in, who proved to be Israel SMITH who was this day discharged from the circuit court for Virginia. He asked for Gen. WILKINSON, who was in the room and to whom I shewed him. .. SMITH drew a letter from his pocket and handed it to the General, who asked from whom it came. .. SMITH said from Mr. SWARTWOUT— The General handed back the letter unopened, and requested Mr. SMITH to inform Mr. SWARTWOUT that he held no correspondence with Traitors and Conspirators. At this moment I stepped out of the room and heard no more. Silas DINSMORE.

We Certify, that we were present at the interview between Mr. SMITH and Gen. WILKINSON as stated above by Mr. DINSMORE, and pledge ourselves that his narrative is literally correct so far as it goes.—We further certify, that when DINSMORE left the room, Mr. SMITH asked Gen. WILKINSON if he meant his observations to apply to himself—The General observed that he (SMITH) might do as he pleased—and added these are my quarters, and there is the door; please to walk out—Mr. SMITH retired. T. H. CUSHING, John FOWLER.

(117) The Gazette. Edenton, November 5, 1807. .. Federal Circuit Court.

5 November 1807

(117) (Cont.) Latest proceedings. After the delivery of the opinion of the court, on Tuesday, the Chief Justice observed, that he had not specified..the particular district to which the prisoners were to be committed. He thought it best that there should be only one trial for them; but if BURR was sent to Kentucky, BLANNERHASSETT could not, because he had provided no means for the expedition but in the district of Ohio. Mr. HAY then moved for their commitment to Ohio, which was ordered. Mr. WICKHAM then moved for an attachment against Mr. Benjamin HAWKINS, an Indian agent, for detaining Dr. CUMMINGS, a witness in this prosecution, and breaking open certain papers in his care belonging to Mr. BLANNERHASSETT one of the accused; a Rule ordered. Messrs. BURR and BLANNERHASSETT were admitted to bail in the sum of $3,000 each. Luther MARTIN and Dr. CUMMINGS, securities for A. BURR; Dr. CUMMINGS and Israel SMITH, for H. BLANNERHASSETT. The court then adjourned till their court in course.

(118) Died—On Thursday last, at the house of William ROBERTS, Esq. dec. Mr. John B. BENNETT, of this County. On Friday, in Bertie County, Capt. William WILLIAMS, of that County. Communicated. Died—On the 21st ult. in Tyrrell County, after a long and painful sickness of near 3 months, Mrs. Mary SPRUILL, wife of Col. Charles SPRUILL, of that County.

(119) Notice. The subscriber will attend at the Court-House on Saturday of November (sic), to commence the second quarter's singing, where he wishes none but the treble to attend; and on Sunday he wishes all to attend.—He further begs leave to inform the public, that he intends to try to make up a Music Society, in this town..the Ladies to attend Wednesday and Saturday evenings, from 2 o'clock until sunset; and the gentlemen and boys from 7 or candle light, to 10 or 11; and on Sunday, all to join in concert together, beginning at 9 in the morning, and break at 4 in the afternoon. The Ladies will not be admitted after sunset of evenings. John NORCOM.

(120) State of North-Carolina, Chowan County Court,} September Term, 1807. King LUTON, vs Powers ETHERIDGE,} Original Attachment. The Sheriff having returned, that he had levied the same on 4 Mahogany Tables, 14 Chairs, 1 due bill, 1 Carpet, 1 Bed, Bed-Stead and Furniture, 6 silver Tea-Spoons, 1 Looking-Glass, Kitchen Furniture, 1 Gold Watch, 2 Tea-Boards, 1 Cow and Calf, 2 Bee-Hives, 1 Mahogany Stand, 1 Safe, 1 Negro Girl PHILLIS; it is Ordered, That 3 months public notice thereof be given to the said Powers ETHERIDGE, in the Edenton Gazette..that unless he appears at the next term of the said Court, on the second Monday in December next, and pleads to the said action, final judgment will be entered thereon against him. By Order, Test, Elisha NORFLEET, Cl'k.

Vol. II. Wednesday, November 11, 1807. Num. 90.

(121) We have given insertion this day to sundry publications, if not written by General WILKINSON himself, written on his behalf, we shall make no comment on them. Mr. POWER's certificate deserves notice. .. (No. D.) New-Orleans, 16th May 1807. Sir, I cannot, in silence, behold my name employed to sanction the calumnies levelled at any man's character; and therefore, Sir, I make you a tender of the enclosed... Thomas POWER. Gen. James WILKINSON.
I, Thomas POWER, of the city of New-Orleans, lately an officer in the service of Spain, moved solely by a sense of justice, and the desire to prevent my name from being employed to sanction groundless slanders, do most solemnly declare that I have at no time carried or delivered to Gen. James WILKINSON, from the government of Spain, or from any person in the service of said government, cash, bills or property of any species. I do most solemnly declare, that said WILKINSON, to

(121) (Cont.) the best of my knowledge and belief, had no participation, and was a perfect stranger to the mission on which I visited Kentucky in the year 1797, and do furthermore most solemnly declare, that my business at Detroit, was to deliver an official letter from the Baron CARONDOLET to Gen. WILKINSON; that on my arrival at Detroit the General was absent, and I found the place under the command of Col. STRONG, by whom I was received... Given in New-Orleans this 16th day of May, 1807. Thomas POWER.

(122) Congress. House of Representatives. Monday, October 26. This being the day fixed by the Proclamation of the President..for the meeting of Congress, a majority of both Houses convened at the Capitol. The assistant Clerk of the House of Representatives having called over the names of the Members, announced 117 Members and one Delegate to be present. He then enquired if it were the pleasure of the House to proceed to the appointment of a Speaker, which being determined in the affirmative, the Members proceeded to ballot for that officer, Messrs. CUTTS, HELMS, & John CAMPBELL being named tellers. The tellers, after examining the votes, reported that 117 were received, and Joseph B. VARNUM, a Representative from..Massachusetts, having 59 of them, was declared to be duly elected.
    The votes were given as follows, viz. Joseph B. VARNUM, 59 Charles GOLDS-BOROUGH, 17 Burwell BASSETT, 17 John MASTERS, 8 Thomas BLOUNT, 7 John DAWSON, 4 John SMILIE, 2 Benjamin TALMADGE, 1 Timothy PITKIN, 1 Roger NELSON, 1 .. The House then proceeded to the election of a Clerk. Nicholas B. VANZANDT, 37 votes. Patrick MAGRUDER, 26 James ELLIOT, 16 J. W. KING, 16 (blank) 14 (blank) 5 (blank) 1. No person having a majority of votes, another balloting took place.. N. B. VANZANDT, 52 P. MAGRUDER, 28 J. ELLIOT, 15 J. W. KING, 10 W. LAMBERT, 7 T. HANSFORD, 4 C. MANISLE?, 1. .. The House proceeded to another balloting for Clerk, the result of which was, Patrick M'GRUDER, 52 James ELLIOT, 27 Nicholas B. VANZANDT, 16 Josias W. KING, 9 Theodesius HANSFORD, 5 William LAMBERT 8 — 117 Fifty-nine votes being necessary to a choice, another balloting was immediately had, when Patrick M'GRUDER was..elected, he having 72 votes.
    Tuesday, October 27. .. An election took place for a Serjeant at Arms, which, after two ballotings, issued in favour of Thomas DUNN. Thomas CLAXTON was appointed door-keeper without opposition, and Jesse EDWARDS, assistant door-keeper at the first ballot.

(123) The Gazette. Edenton, November 11, 1807. .. Mr. DAUCE Has just arrived in town with a handsome assortment of Jewellery, consisting of Ear-Rings, Combs, Watches, &c. &c.—together with a few handsome Counterpins, which he offers for Sale, at his lodgings, at Mrs. HORNIBLOW's. Nov. 10th, 1807.

Vol. II. Wednesday, November 18, 1807. Num. 91.

(124) Congress. House of Representatives. .. Monday, November 2. .. Mr. GARDNER presented the petition of Nathan BABBITT, of New-Hampshire, stating that he served some time as a physician in the military hospital at Providence, for which he had never received compensation, praying relief. Referred to the committee of claims. Mr. QUINCY moved that the petition of Paul REVERE and J. M. REVERE, of Boston, (presented at a former session) be now referred to the committee of Commerce and Manufactures. The petitioners are manufactures of copper, and pray that a duty may be laid on imported copper in sheets, in order to encourage the works established by them with great labour and expence. Agreed. Mr. QUINCY also moved that the petition of Thomas LEACH, Levi TOWER, and Ab. TOWER, owners of the sch'r. Phoenix, (presented at the last session) praying to be allowed a bounty on a quantity of salt saved from said vessel, which the Collector had refused to allow, from some irregularity in the application, be referred to the committee of

18 November 1807

(124) (Cont.) Commerce and Manufactures. Agreed. Mr. FISK moved that the petition of William KINCAID, presented at a former session, praying for compensation as a soldier in the revolutionary war, referred to the committee of claims. Agreed. Mr. DAWSON moved that the petition of Robert PETERS and others, respecting the titles to certain lots in the City of Washington, presented last session, and referred to a select committee..be now referred to a select committee, with power to report thereon by bill or otherwise. .. The Speaker laid before the House the memorial of Duncan M'FARLAND of North-Carolina, accompanied by several documents, complaining of the undue election of John CULPEPPER, and praying that his seat may be vacated in his favour.--Referred to the committee of Elections. .. Mr. PORTER moved that the petition of Mary F. HIBBS, of Pennsylvania, presented at a former session, be referred to the committee of claims.

(125) Washington, Nov. 2. At the request of Mr. VANZANDT, the following Circular, addressed to the members of the House of Representatives of the U. S. is inserted. Washington-City, 29th Oct. 1807. Sir, I feel compelled from the duty I owe to myself and family, to answer the charges which were on Monday last so unexpectedly andvanced against my character, of having improperly divulged the secret proceedings of the House, during the first session of the ninth Congress. .. But I might have expected that the gentleman from Virginia, who made them, would at least have shewn some respect for my feelings in the manner in which he introduced them to the knowledge of the House. .. I shall briefly state the circumstances which gave rise to Mr. RANDOLPH's impressions. At the commencement of the secret proceedings of the first session of the ninth Congress, no precaution was taken by the House to have door keepers stationed at each of the passages leading to the hall of the House to prevent persons from listening. .. A gentleman of the name of Charles EVANS did discover what was the subject of those debates, and heard the speeches of Messrs. RANDOLPH and EPPES. He communicated the substance of them publickly, and I immediately afterwards communicated what I had heard from him to Mr. BEDINGER, then a member from Kentucky, with the express view of convincing him how easy it was for the proceedings of the House to become public, notwithstanding the order for closing the doors; and it is highly probable that Mr. BEDINGER repeated it to other members, without being particular in relating also the manner in which I became possessed of a knowledge of the debates. .. Had I met with an adversary against whom I could have been permitted to contend on equal grounds, or had he given me notice of his intended attack, I might perhaps have been your choice as clerk of the House, and enjoyed an elegible situation for the support of my family. .. Nicholas B. VANZANDT. October 28th, 1807.
I, Charles EVANS, of George-town, in the district of Columbia, do hereby certify and declare, that the foregoing ssatement by Mr. VANZANDT, as far as the same respects my public communication, is strictly true. Charles EVANS. Witness, John THOMPSON.
City of Washington, October 28, 1807.) I do hereby certify that on the day alluded to yesterday, by the Hon. John RANDOLPH, I myself went into the committee room adjoining the Representatives room, in consequence of the door being open, and without key, with Mr. J. W. KING, and stood by the fire, to prevent strangers from entering; that I asked Mr. KING if he could hear any thing said in the House; he said no not a word. We then sat down by the fire. Soon after came in Mr. VANZANDT and Mr. BURCH, and went to a map near the door entering the Representatives room, when I informed them the House was on confidential business, and they immediately left the committee room. Joseph WHEATON, Sergeant-at-arms.

(126) The Gazette. Edenton, November 18, 1807. .. Fall & Winter Goods. The Subscriber has just opened a large assortment of Fall & Winter Goods, which he offers for Sale on low Terms. Henry KING. November 16, 1807.

(127) Fall & Winter Goods. The subscriber begs leave to inform..that he has just received a handsome assortment of Dry Goods, Groceries, Hardware, Crockery, Ship-Chandlery and Iron-Mongery, which he offers for Sale..for Cash or Country Produce. Henry A. DONALDSON. November 17th, 1807.

(128) Mr. BEASTALL Presents his respectful and sincere thanks to the Ladies and Gentlemen of Edenton, who have already favoured him with their patronage, and proposes (should a sufficient number of Pupils offer) to give lessons in Drawing... November 17th, 1807.

(129) Law Books. The Subscriber has just arrived from New-York, with..valuable assortment of Law Books, which he will dispose of for Cash, at the New-York prices .. Francis JONES. Edenton, Nov. 16, 1807. ...

(130) Notice Is hereby given, that John CHESTER holds a Note, signed by me for $120, payable this day, conditioned to pay $150 at 6 months, if payment is refused when demanded. All persons are cautioned against trading for said Note, as I was grossly cheated in the Horse for which it was given, and shall not pay the same until compelled by law. Joseph BLOUNT. Windsor, Oct. 26, 1807.

(131) Notice. Lost on the 15th inst. between Edenton and Capt. Richard MITCHELL's, an old red Morocco Pocket Book, containing the following papers, viz. Nath'l. WILLARD's Note, for $30 Townsend ELLIOTT's do. & judgement together, for about 40 Baker HOSKINS' ditto, sum not recollected. Zacheriah WEBB's for 6 William MILLER's ditto, sum not recollected..and about $30 in paper money. Whoever will bring the said Pocket-Book and contents to me, in Edenton, shall be handsomely rewarded. All persons are hereby cautioned against trading for said Notes and Papers. Edward REILEY. Edenton, Nov. 16, 1807.

(132) Notice. The Subscriber having met with some difficulties in his contracts; and wishing to settle his business amicably, earnestly solicits persons indebted to him to make payment on or before Friday, the 18th day of December next: As on that day he will expose to Sale, at public auction, at his house, on a liberal credit, all his Moveable Property, consisting of Beds and Furniture, Tables, Chairs, &c. &c. together with the small Stock of Goods he has now on hand—Likewise, will be Rented out, for one or more years, the House, with a Store adjoining, well finished. Any of the above property may be had by application to Jesse HASSEL, or the Subscriber. Benjamin HASSEL. Edenton, Nov. 16, 1807.

(133) Notice. The Subscriber wishes to Rent or Lease, for one two or more years, his Plantation, In DURANT's-Neck, Perquimans County. .. The Subscriber being desirous to Rent, will let the Plantation and Stock at so low a rate, that it may be an object to any person to Rent it. There is now sown with wheat a field of 80,000 corn hills. ... William LITTLEJOHN. November 15th, 1807.

(134) New-York, October 28. .. From the New-York Evening Post. Mr. COLEMAN, As I am informed some dispute has taken place between James CHEETHAM editor of the N. Y. American Citizen, and J. FRANK, one of the editors of the N. Y. Public Advertiser, about a piece written by me, and published in the Public Advertiser of Saturday the 26th September, and as you are unconnected with the parties and the dispute, I will be obliged to you to give the following a place in your paper.
CHEETHAM, following the footsteps of the emissary CULLEN, had frequently put out abusive paragraphs against France, a nation with which we have no dispute.. The piece alluded to, written by me, was on these subjects, and contained several expressions of reproof to CHEETHAM for his improper and abusive paragraphs. The

(134) (Cont.) morning after the piece was published FRANK called upon me and told me that CHEETHAM had sent a message to him demanding that he would make an apology for that publication. I immediately said to FRANK, Tell CHEETHAM from me that I am the writer of that piece, and if he has any thing to say, he must say it to me. ... Thomas PAINE.

(135) CHEETHAM v. PAINE. From CHEETHAM's American Citizen. The following note was handed to me yesterday. My reply to the bearer through the medium of my Clerk was, that I had no answer to make to such insolence. As to the second paragraph of old Tom's note..I will just remark, that one of the suits of Maturin LIVINGSTON against me, which was tried at Albany, and in which the jury gave 300 dollars damages, was for some poetick lines sent to me from the country; the other was for an article written I believe by myself. Both were, however, in every thing material, true, although..it was not in my power to adduce testimony to prove the truth. The suits of Morgan LEWIS against me, nine in number, are instituted merely to get money..and not because the publications on which they are predicated are false. In 4 of the nine suits, and of the 4, 2 are for writings of my own..one for a pindarick ode written by an ingenious friend, which appeared in my paper during the fever of 1805, and the other for an able communication under the signature of Cato on the subject of ARNOLD's murder of little Betsey VAN AMBERGH. ...

(136) The following is a complete List of the Tenth Congress. Senate. New-Hampshire--*Nahum PARKER, Nicholas GILMAN. Massachusetts--Timothy PICKERING, John Q. ADAMS. Rhode-Island--Benjamin HOWLAND, one vacancy. Connecticut--James HILLHOUSE, *Chauncey GOODRICH. Vermont--S. R. BRADLEY, *Jonathan ROBINSON. New-York--S. L. MITCHELL, John SMITH. New-Jersey--J. CONDIT, Aaron KITCHELL. Pennsylvania--Samuel MACLAY, *Andrew GREGG. Delaware--Jas. A BAYARD, Saml. WHITE. Maryland--Philip REED, Samuel SMITH. Virginia--Andrew MOORE, Wm. B. GILES. North-Carolina--*Jessee FRANKLIN, James TURNER. South-Carolina--John GUILLIARD, Thomas SUMPTER. Georgia--John MILLEDGE, *George JONES. Kentucky--Buckner THRUSTON, *John POPE. Tennessee--Daniel SMITH, Jos. ANDERSON. Ohio--John SMITH, *Edward TIFFIN.

House of Representatives. New-Hampshire--*Peter CARLTON, *Daniel M. DURELL, *Francis GARDNER, *Jedediah H. SMITH, *Clement STORER. Massachusetts--Ezekiel BACON, Joseph BARKER, John CHANDLER, Orchard COOK, Jacob CROWNINSHIELD, Richard CUTTS, *Josiah DEANE, Wm. ELEY, Isaiah L? GREEN, *Daniel ISLEY, *Ed. S. I. LIVERMORE, Josiah QUINCEY, Ebenezer SEAVER, Wm. STEDMON, Jos. B. VARNUM, Sam. TAGGART, *Jabez UPHAM. Rhode-Island--Nehemiah KNIGHT *Isaac WILBOURN. Connecticut--*E. CHAMPION, Saml. W. DANA, J. DAVENPORT, Jonathan O. MOSELEY, Timothy PITKIN, jun. Lewis B. STURGES, Benjamin TALLMADGE. Vermont--Martin CHITTENDEN, Jas. ELLIOT, Jas. FISK, *James WITHERALL. New-York--John BLAKE, jun. George CLINTON, jun. *Barent GARDNER, *John HARRIS, *Wm. KIRKPATRICK, Josiah MASTERS, Gurdon S. MUMFORD, Saml. RIKER, J. RUSSELL, *Peter SWART, David THOMAS, *J. THOMPSON, *Jas. J. VAN ALLEN, P. VAN CORTLAND, Kilian K. VAN RENSSELEAR, Daniel C. VERPLANK, *Reuben HUMPHREYS. New-Jersey--Ezra DARBY, Wm. HELMS, J. LAMBERT, *Thos. NEWBOLD, James SLOANE, Henry SOUTHARD. Pennsylvania--David BARD, Robert BROWN, Jos. CLAY, Wm. FINDLEY, *J. HEISTER, *Wm. HOGE, *Robert JENKINS, James KELLEY, *Wm. MILNER, *Daniel MONTGOMERY, J. PORTER, J. PUGH, John REA, Jacob RICHARDS, *Matthias RICHARDS, John SMILIE, Saml. SMITH, Robert WHITEHILL. Delaware--*Nicholas VANDYKE. Maryland--J. CAMPBELL, Chas. GOLDSBOROUGH, *Philip B. KEY, Edward LLOYD, Wm. M'CREERY, *John MONTGOMERY, Nicholas R. MOORE, Roger NELSON, Archibald VAN HORNE. Virginia--Burwell BASSET, Wm. A. BURWELL, J. CLAIBORNE, Matthew CLAY, J. CLOPTON, John W. EPPES, Jas. M. GARNETT, Peterson GOODWYN, Edwin GRAY, David HOLMES, J. G. JACKSON, Walter JONES, Jos. LEWIS, *J. LOVE, J. MORROW, Thos. NEWTON, jun. *Wilson C. NICHOLAS, J. RANDOLPH, J. SMITH, Abraham T?RIGG, Alexander WILSON. North-Carolina--Evan ALEXANDER, Wm. ALSTON, jun. Wm. BLACKLEDGE, Thos. BLOUNT, *J.

(136) (Cont.) CULPEPPER, Jas. HOLLAND, Thos. KENAN, Nathl. MACON, *Lemuel SAWYER, Richard STANFORD, Marmaduke WILLIAMS, *Meshack FRANKLIN. South-Carolina—*Lemuel J. AHE?RN, Wm. BUTLER, *Jos. COLHOUN, Robert MARION, Thos. MOORE, *J. TAYLOR, D. R. WILLIAMS, Richard WYNN. Georgia—Wm. W. BIBB, *Howell COBB, Dennis SMELT, George M. TROUP. Kentucky—J. ROYLE, *Jos. DESHA, Benj. HOWARD, *Rich'd. M. JOHNSON, Matthew LYON, *John ROWAN. Tennessee—G. W. CAMPELL, John RHEA, *Jesse WHARTON. Ohio—Jeremiah MORROW. Indiana Territory—*Geo. POINDEXTER. Orleans Territory—Daniel CLARK. *New Members...

(137) The Subscriber Informs..that his Cut-Nail Manufactory is now in motion; and have a good stock of Iron on hand, and am determined to keep a constant supply of Nails, Flooring Brads and Sprigs... Thomas BISSEL.

Vol. II. Wednesday, November 25, 1807. Num. 92.

(138) The Gazette. Edenton, November 25, 1807. Thomas WILLING, Esq. having resigned the appointment of President of the Bank of the United States, David LENOX, Esq. has been unanimously elected to that office. Herald.

(139) State of North-Carolina, Perquimans County,) November Term, 1807. Samuel NIXON, vs. Nathan DRAPER,) Original Attachment. The Officer having made return, levied on the Lands whereon the said DRAPER formerly lived, adjoining the Land of Joseph DRAPER, jun. It is Ordered, by the Court, that 3 months notice be given, in the Edenton Gazette, to the said DRAPER, that unless he appears at this Court, next term, and replevy the said property, it will be proceeded against as the law directs. By Order, Thomas H. HARVEY, Cl'k.

(140) Notice. The subscriber intending to break up house-keeping at the close of the year, will expose for Sale, at public vendue, at her dwelling-house, on the 2d day of Chowan County Court next, at 3 and 6 months credit, sundry Household and Kitchen Furniture, viz. 1 Bed Bedstead and Furniture, 2 Desks, Tables, Chairs, and Beaufat, a quantity of Books, and a number of other articles too tedious to enumerate. Notes and security will be required, for all sums over Forty Shillings. Miriam CARPENTER. Edenton, Nov. 24, 1807.

(141) For Sale, The Plantation whereon the Subscriber now lives, containing from 120 to 150 Acres of Land, of which there is 50,000 corn hills cleared and under good fence, and a very comfortable Dwelling-House, with two brick chimnies, shed, piazza, store, and every necessary out house:—Also on the Plantation there is 1000 Fruit Trees, 500 of which are Apple, the other Peach. Also, my Plantation in Green-Hall, joining Reuben SMALL and Lewis BOND, containing from 60 to 70 Acres of Land, about 30,000 corn hills cleared, and under good fence, with a tolerable good Dwelling-House, and some out houses; and a small quantity of excellent white oak timber and cypress. For terms, apply to Philip M'GUIRE. Chowan, Nov. 24, 1807.

(142) Asa CHAMBERLAIN, Boot & Shoe Manufacturer, Respectfully informs the inhabitants of Edenton and its vicinity, that he has taken a stand joining the store of Mr. John POPELSTON, on the wharf, where he has on hand a handsome assortment of Gentleman's Boots & Shoes, Ladies' Shoes, Children's Ditto..also, negro Ditto, of various sizes. ... Edenton, Nov. 24, 1807.

(143) Baltimore, Nov. 4, 1807. Mr. HEWES, Through the channel of your paper, permit me to express to the mayor and to the other civil authorities, as also to the military, particularly Captain William BARNEY and the first Baltimore Hussars, and Capt. Samuel HOLLINGSWORTH, and the first Baltimore Troop of Horse, my

(143) (Cont.) approbation, for their exertions last evening to preserve the persons and property of myself and others from lawless violence. ... Luther MARTIN.

Vol. II. Wednesday, December 2, 1807. Num. 93.

(144) Treason! .. Extract of a letter from a gentleman in N. Orleans, dated September 17, 1807. "We have been for some days in a state of confusion, and, I might say, rebellion. A piece of ground called the Batture or alluvion ground, fronting the upper suburbs of this city, has been in dispute for about two years between John GRAVIER, and the city. In May last, the Superior Court entered up a decree in favour of John GRAVIER, who was then put in peaceable possession of his property. Mr. Edward LIVINGSTON has since purchased the property, and on the 14th inst. got a parcel of negroes to work to dig a canal. A posse of Frenchmen, headed by Colonels BELLECHASSE and MACARTY repaired to the place and drove off the negroes—threatened to throw the constables, who were sent there to keep the peace, in the river. .. On the day following, at about 4 o'clock in the afternoon, the disorganizers were summoned to the ground by the beat of the drum, in the very teeth of the Governor, who was repairing to the spot to endeavour to pacify them. The Governor, after some conversation with the leaders, addressed them as follows: .. Fellow Citizens, Permit me to claim your attention..to submit to your consideration a few observations. Whatever may be the redress desired, believe me the mode you have adopted is improper.. It is the duty of us all to yield submission to the laws. The Supreme Court of the territory has pronounced this Batture to be the property of Mr. John GRAVIER, and he, and Mr. LIVINGSTON (who claims under GRAVIER) have been put peaceably in possession thereof by the sheriff. ... William C. C. CLAIBORNE.

(145) At a Court of Enquiry assembled on board the United States ship Chesapeake, in the harbour of Norfolk, and State of Virginia, by order of the Hon. Robert SMITH, Secretary of the Navy of the United States, and continued by adjournment from day to day, from Monday the 5th day of October, 1807, until Wednesday the 4?th day of November, 1807. Present, Captain Alexander MURRAY, President, and Captain Isaac HULL, and Isaac CHAUNCEY,} Members thereof. The following Opinion and Report was unanimously given, and directed by the Court to be transmitted to the Honourable the Secretary of the Navy of the United States.
 Pursuant to an order from the Hon. Robert SMITH, Secretary of the Navy of the United States, to Capt. Alexander MURRAY directed, dated the 12th day of September..1807, the Court proceeded to enquire into the causes of the surrender of the Chesapeake, a frigate of the United States, then under the command of James BARRON, Esq. a Captain in the Navy of the United States, to a British vessel of war..without defence being made which might have been expected from the known valor of Americans; and having heard all the evidence adduced, as well by the Judge Advocate, as by the said Captain James BARRON, and having maturely and thoroughly considered the same, (Capt. James BARRON having declined to offer any defence) Report to the Honourable the Secretary of the Navy..a state of the matters touching the said surrender, together with their opinion thereon.. 6. It appears to the Court, that antecedent to the sailing of the Chesapeake, there had been received on board of her some persons ___ (blot) had been claimed by the British govern____ (blot) as deserters from their service, but who were not ordered to be delivered up by the American officers. .. That Commodore BARRON had full knowledge of the facts that such men were on board his ship, that they had been demanded by the British government, and had not been delivered up.. 18. It appears to the Court, that when the Leopard came along side of the Chesapeake, an officer was sent from her, with a communication from Capt. HUMPHRIES, the

2 December 1807

(145) (Cont.) Captain of the Leopard, to Commodore BARRON, which the latter could not & did not misunderstand, but very correctly concluded to be a demand with which he ought not and could not comply, and..if refused would be enforced if possible. .. 22. It appears to the Court, that the conduct of Commodore BARRON during the attack of the Leopard manifested great indecision, and a disposition to negociate, rather than a determination bravely to defend his ship. ... A true copy, L. W. TAZEWELL, Judge Advocate.

(146) The Gazette. Edenton, December 2, 1807. .. Died, on the 5th ult. in Northampton county, the Rev. Lemuel BURKITT, a respectable clergyman of the Baptist Church.

(147) Raleigh, Nov. 19. The Legislature of North-Carolina, met in this city on Monday the 16th. In the Senate, General RIDDICK was re-elected Speaker; General STOKES, Clerk, and Major WILLIAMS, Assistant Clerk. Nicholas MURPHEY and Merrit DILLIARD, Door-keepers. In the Commons, Joshua G. WRIGHT, Esq. of Wilmington, was chosen unanimously Speaker; Pleasant HENDERSON, Esq. Clerk, and William LOCKHART of Northampton, Assistant Clerk. Thomas POUND and John LUMSDEN, Door-keepers. .. Benjamin H. COVINGTON, is elected Engrossing-Clerk.

(148) Benjamin WILLIAMS, Esq. is elected Governor of this State, in the room of N. ALEXANDER, Esq. ...

(149) Henry KING Has just received in addition to his assortment of Fall & Winter Goods, the following articles..for Sale, on low terms: Cogniac Brandy, Colemenar Wine, Jamaica Rum, Loaf & brown Sugar, Hyson and Imperial Tea, Coffee, Molasses, Allum Salt, Goshun Butter, by the keg, Raisons..Northern Cheese, Saltpetre, Pepper, Nutmegs, Spanish Segars..Snuff..Nails, Bar Iron, Steel, Narrow Axes, Glass Ware, And a few Crates of well assorted Earthenware. December 1, 1807.

(150) Will Be Sold, At Public Sale, on Thursday, the 7th of January, 1808. agreeable to the last will of Gen. Lawrence BAKER, dec. on the premises, Two Tracts of Land, the property of said deceased, lying on the east side of BENNETT's Creek, and known by the name of GIBSON's tract, containing 238 Acres, well timbered, fertile Land, supposed to be equal to any in the County of Gates for the production of Corn, &c.--The other known by the name of the WEBB tract, containing 500 Acres; on this there are no improvements. ... John B. BAKER, Ex'r. or Wm. GOODMAN, sen. Agent.
    Notice. All persons indebted to the estate of Gen. Lawrence BAKER, dec. are requested to come forward and make immediate payment; and all those who have claims..to bring in their accounts... John B. BAKER, Ex'r. December 1, 1807.

(151) For Rent, For one or more years, and possession given the first day of January next, that well known and commodious Tavern, in this Town, at present occupied by the subscriber, in King-Street. Should said Tavern not be rented before the 1st of January, it will on that day be put up at public auction, to the highest bidder. The person renting, it is supposed, would wish to be furnished with Servants and Furniture; if not, the Furniture belonging to the Tavern will, on that day be Sold.. The Servants..will be hired out separately, if required. There will be let with the Tavern, an excellent Mahogany Billiard-Table..with good Balls, Maces and Queus. ... Myles O'MALLEY. Edenton, Dec. 2, 1807.

Vol. II. Wednesday, December 9, 1807. Num. 94.

(152) Documents relative to the attack on the Chesapeake. British Consul's Of-

(152) (Cont.) fice, Norfolk, Virginia, 6th March, 1807. Sir--The men named in the margin deserted some time since from his Majesty's ship Melampus, in Hampton Roads, by running away with her gig, and the three first are stated to have entered at the rendezvous now open here, for the enlistment of seamen in the service of the United states. As the Melampus is at present in Hampton Roads, I submit to you, sir, the propriety of directing these men, (should they have entered for your service) to be returned to their duty on board his Majesty's ship before mentioned. .. John HAMILTON. William WARE, Daniel MARTIN, John STRACHAN, John LITTLE. Captain DECATUR. ..

Navy Yard Washington, April 7, 1807. Sir--I have the honour to inclose you the result of my enquiries relating to the men mentioned in your letter of yesterday... James BARRON.

The Honourable Robert SMITH, Secretary of the Navy. William WARE, pressed from on board the brig Neptune, Capt. CRAFTS, by the British frigate Melampus, in the Bay of Biscay, and has served on board the said frigate fifteen months. William WARE is a native American, born on Pipe Creek, Frederick county, state of Maryland, at BRUCE's mills, and served his time at said mills. He also lived at ELLICOT's mills, near Baltimore, and drove a waggon several years between HAGER's-Town and Baltimore. He also served 18 months on board the U. S. frigate Chesapeake, under the command of Commodore MORRIS and Captain James BARRON.--He is an Indian looking man. Daniel MARTIN was pressed at the same time and place. He is a native of West-Port, in Massachusetts, about 30 miles to the easward of New-Port, Rhode-Island, served his time out of New-York, with Capt. MORROWBY, in the Caledonia--refers to Mr. Benjamin DAVIS, merchant, and Mr. Benjamin COREE, of West-Port. He is a coloured man. John STRACHAN, born on the Eastern shore of Maryland, Queen Anne's county, between Centerville and Queen's Town--refers to Mr. John PRICE and (blank) PRATT, Esq. on KENT Island, who knows his relations. STRACHAN sailed in the brig Martha Bland, Capt. WYVILL, from Norfolk to Dublin and from thence to Liverpool. He there left the brig and shipped on board an English Guineaman. He was pressed on board the Melampus off Cape Finestere; to better his situation he consented to enter, being determined to make his escape when opportunity offered. He served on board the frigate two years. He is a white man, about 5 feet 7 inches high. Wm. WARE and John STRACHAN have protections. Daniel MARTIN says he lost his after leaving the frigate.

John LITTLE, alias FRANCIS, and Ambrose WATTS, escaped from the Melampus at the same time, known to the above persons to be Americans, but has not been entered by my recruiting officer. ...

(153) The Gazette. Edenton, December 9, 1807. .. General Assembly. House of Commons. Wednesday, Nov. 18. .. Thursday, Nov. 19. Mr. W. WILLIAMS, from the balloting for engrossing clerks, reported that Robert W. GOODMAN was elected .. A message received from the Senate yesterday, proposing to ballot for the Public Printer, and nominating Joseph GALES for that appointment, was taken up and agreed to. A ballot took place accordingly, when Mr. MOODY reported that Joseph GALES was duly elected.. A message was sent to the Senate, proposing to ballot for a Solicitor of the 5th circuit, to supply the vacancy occasioned by the death of Robert TROY, and nominating for the appointment, Mess. Edwin J. OSBORN, Everard HALL, Arch. M'BRIDE and Reuben WOOD. .. A message was sent to the Senate, proposing to ballot to-morrow morning for a Governor..and nominating..N. ALEXANDER. .. Friday, Nov. 20. A message was sent to the Senate, adding the names of Benj. WILLIAMS and Jos. WINSTON to the nomination for Governor. .. Mr. W. HILL was..elected engrossing clerk.

Saturday, Nov. 21. .. The Speaker laid before the house a letter from Gavin ALVES, Secretary to the Trustees of the University, stating that there are 8 Trustees wanting of the number authorised by law, owing to deaths, &c.. The letter

(153) (Cont.) being read, was sent to the Senate, with a proposal to ballot for Trustees..a ballot took place, and the following gentlemen were elected: Mess. Jas. RHODES, B. WOODS, W. W. JONES, R. WILLIAMS, J. D. HAWKINS, Jos. WINSTON, Arch. M'BRIDE and F. NASH. .. Monday, Nov. 23. .. A message was received from the Governor, inclosing a letter from Josiah COLLINS, of Edenton, which was referred to a select committee. .. Tuesday, Nov. 24. Mr. GLISSON, from the balloting for Governor, reported that Benj. WILLIAMS was duly elected. On the 3d balloting for a Solicitor of the 5th district, A. M'BRIDE was declared elected. .. The following bills were presented: .. Mr. Blake BAKER, a bill to amend an act concerning old titles of lands, for limitations of actions, and for avoiding suits at law.. .. Mr. DANIEL, a bill to confirm the marriage of James SMITH and Mary NORFLEET. ...

(154) Died--Some time since, in Hertford County, at his residence on the banks of Chowan River, Mr. Joshua SIMONS, an opulent and respectable planter of that county.

(155) Boarding House. Mrs. SMALL Begs leave to inform..that she has taken that commodious and airy house, late the residence of Capt. Samuel BUTLER, dec. a few doors below where she formerly lived, where she can accommodate a number of constant and transient Boarders, by the week, month or year, upon as good terms as can be procured in Edenton. A few children, students at the Academy, can also be accommodated, upon moderate terms. Edenton, Dec. 9, 1807.

(156) Notice Is hereby given, that on Wednesday, the 30th of December next, will be Sold, at the late dwelling house of Joshua SIMONS, dec. in Hertford County, near Mount-Pleasant, all the Perishable Estate of said deceased, consisting of Horses, Cattle, Sheep, Hogs, household and kitchen Furniture, Plantation Tools, &c. &c. Also, about 400 barrels Corn, a considerable quantity of excellent blade Fodder, one or two hundred bushels of Peas, and upwards of twenty barrels of Brandy. ... James JONES, Daniel VANPELT,} Adm's. November 26, 1807.

Vol. II. Wednesday, December 16, 1807. Num. 95.

(157) Documents respecting the affair of the Chesapeake--(Concluded.) .. A true copy taken from the United States frigate Chesapeake's Log Book, James BARRON, Esq. commander, Charles GORDON, Esq. Captain, and Samuel BROCK, Sailing-Master. Monday June 22d.--Commences with light breezes from the S., and W. and clear weather. .. ..at 9 passed two of H. B. Majesty's ships at anchor.. Tuesday 23d--Commences with light breezes from the South and West..a ship in sight apparently standing for us..and at half past 3 the ship came up with us, backed the main topsail and spoke her, was boarded by her. She proved to be the British ship Leopard, of 50 guns; she came on board to demand some men who had deserted from the English navy, the Commodore refusing to give them up, the boat returned, they ranged along side of us and commenced a heavy fire. We being unprepared, and the ship much lumbered, it was impossible to clear ship for action in proper time.. In about 30 minutes, after receiving much damage in our hull, rigging and spars, and having three men killed, viz. Joseph ARNOLD, Peter SHAKELY, and John LAWRENCE, and 16 wounded, viz. Commodore BARRON, Mr. BROOM, John HUDDEN, Cotton BROWN, Peter ELLISON, John PARKER, George PERSEVAL, Peter SUMMERS, William HENDRICK, Robert M'DONALD, Francis CONHOVEN, Thos. SHORT, Wm. MOODY, David CREIGHTON, John MARTYR, James EPPS, Emanuel HENDRICK, John WILSON, William WARREN, and John BATES. And having one gun ready, fired, and hauled down our colours. The Leopard ceased firing, and sent her boat on board, mustered the ship's company. At sun down they left the ship, taking with them four men, viz. John STRAWN, Daniel MARTIN, William

(157) (Cont.) WARE, and John WILSON, who had deserted from their service, at the same time Lieut. ALLEN went on board, and returned at 8 o'clock. The Leopard left us and stood in. ..

(158)   Norfolk, June 29th, 1807. Sir, The enclosed papers No. 1 and 2, you will perceive are from the committee of the people of Norfolk, calling on me for aid with the gun boats under my command, to prevent an invasion..threatened by the commanding officer of the British squadron lying in the vicinity of this place. .. Stephen DECATUR, jun. The Hon. Robert SMITH, Sec'ry of the Navy.

Sir—We take pleasure in presenting to you the resolution of the committee ap- pointed by the inhabitants of this borough now enclosed. Requesting your answer to the resolution, we are with the highest respect, sir, your obedient humble ser- vants. Signed (Thos. BLANCHARD, Seth FOSTER, J. W. MURDAUGH.

Norfolk, 28th June, 1807. Captain DECATUR. Whereas the committee have re- ceived information from various sources that the commander of the British ships of war have menaced the inhabitants of Hampton with an invasion for the purpose of procuring water. It is resolved that application be made to Capt. Stephen DECA- TUR, commander of the United States naval force at this place to equip the gun boats by availing himself of the services of the Captains and seamen who have proffered them, to proceed to Hampton or as near it as he may judge proper to co- operate with the people in their defence in any manner he may judge most expedient or to act as circumstances may dictate in preventing the execution of their threat.   Resolved, that Thomas BLANCHARD, Seth FOSTER, and J. W. MURDAUGH be a committee to wait on Captain DECATUR with this application. Extract from the min- utes. Signed Theo. ARMISTEAD, Sec'ry of the committee.

Norfolk, June 28, 1807. I have received your letter of this day..to equip and resist with the gun boats under my command, a threatened invasion of the territory of the United States, by the British now lying in the waters of the Chesapeake. Having the fullest confidence that the committee would not have made a request of this nature unless they were fully impressed with a belief that the hostility..was certainly intended, I feel it my duty to repel as far as I have power any such at- tempt..if a sufficient number of volunteers can be procured... Stephen DECATUR. To Thomas BLANCHARD, Seth FOSTER, J. W. MURDAUGH, Esqs. Norfolk, 28th June, 1807.

(159) Congress. House of Representatives, Thursday, Nov. 12. Debate on the re- port of the committee of elections, on the contested election of Wm. M'CREERY. .. The report of the committee of elections as follows: Report. The committee of elections, to whom was committed the petition of Joshua BARNEY, of the city of Baltimore, praying to be admitted to a seat in the House, he having, in his opin- ion, the highest number of votes given..qualified to represent the said city of Baltimore, having carefully examined the facts stated on both sides, and compared the laws of Maryland, under which the said election was held, with the constitu- tion of the U. States. Report..it is required, that the member shall be an inhabitant of his district at the time of his election, and shall have resided therein twelve calender months immediately before. .. By another act of the as- sembly of Maryland..it is enacted that Baltimore town and county shall be fifth district..entitled to send two representatives to Congress, one of which shall be a resident of Baltimore county, and the other a resident of Baltimore city.   That Joshua BARNEY is a citizen of Maryland, and has been a resident of the city of Baltimore for many years.

That William M'CREERY has been, for many years, a citizen of Maryland, and a resident of the city of Baltimore; but that in..1803, he removed himself and his family to his estate in Baltimore county; that from that time, though he himself has occasionally resided in Baltimore, yet he, with his wife & family have not made the city of Baltimore their settled residence. .. At the election in that

(159) (Cont.) district for the Congress now in session, Nicholas R. MOORE had 6,164 votes; he is a resident in Baltimore county; and William M'CREERY, against whose right to a seat in this house objection is made on account of residence, had 3,559 votes; and Joshua BARNEY who claims a seat in this house, and it is admitted is a resident in Baltimore city, had 2,060 votes; and John SEAT, also, a resident in Baltimore city, had 353 votes. .. Resolved, That Wm. M'CREERY, is entitled to his seat in this house.

(160) November 30. Mr. ADAMS from the committee appointed in the case of Mr. SMITH, made a report, recommending the adoption of the following resolutions, which were agreed to: Resolved, that the committee appointed on the 27th instant, to enquire and report the facts, respecting the conduct of John SMITH, a senator from the state of Ohio, as an alledged associate of Aaron BURR, be authorised to extend their enquiries to any other facts, which..would be incompatible with his duty as a Senator..and that they be authorised to send for persons, papers and records. ...

(161) The Gazette. Edenton, December 16, 1807. .. General Assembly. .. House of Commons, Wednesday, Nov. 25. .. Thursday, Nov. 26. .. The following bills were presented:--Mr. HUDGINS, a bill securing to Jame HOFFLER of Gates, such property as he now has, or may hereafter acquire. .. Mr. SKINNER, a bill empowering the Commissioners of the town of Edenton to convey part of the town commons to the Trustees of the Edenton Academy. .. Saturday, Nov. 28. .. Mr. YANCEY, a bill to confirm the privileges of an act passed by the legislature of Virginia, authorising Thomas WILSON to erect a wing dam from his land in Mecklenburg county, extending from the south bank of the Roanoke into the same. .. Mr. HOSKINS, a bill to enable the executors of Charles and William ROBERTS, dec. late Sheriffs of Chowan county, to collect arrears of taxes. ...

(162) Edmond HOSKINS, is elected Sheriff of this County, in the room of William ROBERTS, Esq. deceased.

(163) Married—on Sunday, the 6th instant, in Hertford County, Mr. Starkey S. HARRELL, to Miss Elizabeth SIMONS, daughter of the late Joshua SIMONS, all of that County. Died—on Tuesday evening last, in this town, Mr. Charles SHORT, a native of Ireland, and for many years a school-master of considerable eminence, in this, and the neighbouring counties.

Vol. II. Wednesday, December 23, 1807. Num. 96.

(164) The Gazette. Edenton, December 23, 1807. The Legislature of this State adjourned on Friday last. Benj. SMITH of Brunswick, and Thomas WYNNS, of Hertford, have been elected Major-Generals; and Kedar BALLARD, of Gates, J. T. RHODES, of Duplin, and Benj. LEE of Robeson, Brigadier-Generals.

(165) General Assembly. House of Commons, Wednesday, Dec. 2. .. Thursday, Dec. 3. .. Mr. FORSYTH, from the balloting committee for two Councillors, reported, that Jonathan JACOCKS was elected, but that another balloting was necessary for the 7th. .. Friday, Dec. 4. Mr. HOWELL, from the balloting for a Councillor, reported, that Jordan HILL was elected. .. Saturday, Dec. 5. Mr. GOODWIN, from the balloting committee for a Public Treasurer, Comptroller and Secretary of State, reported, that J. HAYWOOD, J. CRAVEN and Wm. WHITE, were elected. ...

(166) The Subscribers Have just received from New-York, a general assortment of Dry Goods, Hardware, Cutlery & Groceries... LITTLEJOHN & BOND.

(167) Literature. The Subscribers inform..that the Classical School formerly taught on MANEY's-Neck by Mr. Samuel NICHOLSON, will be removed to Murfreesborough, in Hertford County, the ensuing year, and will commence on the first Monday in January next; terms of Tuition as follows: For the Latin, Greek, and French Languages, Mathematics, English Grammar, and Geography, $25, to be paid quarterly. For Reading, Writing, and Arithmetic, $12, to be paid quarterly. Good accommodations for Students may be had in respectable families; and accommodations for a few good orderly boys may be had in the house where the school is to be taught. Henry RAMSAY, Sharpe BLOUNT. December 15, 1807.

(168) I Have For Sale, Low for Cash, or good Obligations, 6 Hhds. of excellent Brown Sugar. For terms, apply to Samuel M'GUIRE. Dec. 22, 1807.

(169) Notice. On Saturday, the 9th of January, 1808, at Mr. NIEL's wharf, will be Sold, at public auction, (if not sold before at private Sale) the schooner Rainbow, with her tackle and furniture as she came from sea.—Also, the schooner Delight, as she now lays at the Subscriber's wharf.. I will also sell my Wharf, which has two good Ware-Houses on it, nearly new. Likewise, a young Negro Woman and Two Children. For terms, apply to James HATHAWAY, sen. Edenton, Dec. 22, 1807.

Vol. II. Wednesday, December 30, 1807. Num. 97.

(170) Congress. House of Representatives. Thursday, December 10. .. Friday, December 11. Mr. FINDLEY, from the committee of elections, presented a report on the contested election of Mr. KEY. The report concludes with the following regulation: Resolved, That Philip B. KEY, having the greatest number of votes, and being duly qualified by the constiution of the United States is entitled to a seat in this house. Referred to committee of the whole on Tuesday. ..

(171) Norfolk, December 21. .. A Court-Martial has been ordered by the Secretary of the Navy, to sit on the 4th of January next, for the trial of Commodore J. BARRON, Capt. Charles GORDON, Wm. HOOK, gunner, and Capt. John HALL, of the marine corps, late officers of the frigate Chesapeake. Alex. D. Adv.

(172) The Gazette. Edenton, December 30, 1807. .. Married—on Thursday evening last, Mr. William L. GRIMES, of Tarborough, to Mrs. Eliza FREEMAN, widow of the late Captain Alexander A. FREEMAN, of this town. On Sunday evening, Capt. Benjamin BISSELL, to Miss Elizabeth ROMBOUGH, eldest daughter of Mr. William ROMBOUGH, all of this town. On Thursday evening, in the county of Perquimans, William JONES, Esq. to the amiable Miss Parthenia NEWBY, daughter of Mr. Francis NEWBY, dec. of that county.

(173) William MANNING, Cabinet Maker, Begs leave to inform..that he has taken the house of Mrs. Miriam CARPENTER, in King-street, nearly opposite the late residence of Col. N. ALLEN, where he carries on his business as usual, and keeps on hand all kinds of Furniture, which he will sell low for cash. The subscriber also requests all those indebted to him, to come forward and settle their accounts by paying cash, or giving their notes, in order that he may be enabled to settle with those to whom he is indebted. A good Journeyman, who is sober and industrious, is wanted at the above business. December 28, 1807.

(174) For Rent. The Subscriber offers for Rent, for 1 or 2 years, that pleasant situated Plantation and Buildings, in Bertie County, with two valuable shad and herring Fisheries, called Point-Comfort, belonging to Mr. Joseph A. BROWN.. There

30 December 1807

(174) (Cont.) is some Negroes for hire and sale. Elisha NORFLEET, Agent. Edenton, December 26, 1807.

(175) Sarah ETHERIDGE, Begs leave to inform the public, that she intends teaching School the ensuing year. Any person disposed to send their children, they will be thankfully received by the subscriber.

(176) Captions of the Laws, Passed in December, 1807. .. 17. To confirm the marriage of James SMITH with Mary NORFLEET. .. 38. To establish a turnpike road from the west end of Mattamuskeet-Lake, to John JORDAN's, on the Rose-Bay, in Hyde county. .. 44. To establish a separate election at the house of William WHITE, Esq. in the county of Burke, and for other purposes therein mentioned. .. 57. To lay off a town on the lands of John WOOTEN in Bladen county and for other purposes. .. 60. To vest in America JONES of Wake county, certain rights. .. 66. To authorise Samuel MORGAN of Nottoway county, Virginia, to bring certain slaves into this State. .. 83. To authorise Barnett BEASLY of Warren county, and John RUTHERFORD, to bring into this state two negro slaves therein mentioned. .. 85. To divorce Alexander SMITH of Ashe county from his wife Sally. .. 89. To secure to David DANNELL of Rowan county against all future demands of his wife Susannah. .. 93. To restore to credit James COURTNEY of Lincoln county.

1808 - Filmed from originals in the North Carolina State Library.

Vol. II. Wednesday, January 6, 1808. Num. 98.

(177) National Intelligencer, Extra. Washington-City, December 22. Congress this day passed the following act. .. An Act Laying an Embargo on all ships and vessels in the ports and harbours of the United States. Be it enacted by the Senate and House of Representatives of the United States of America, in Congress assembled, That an embargo be and hereby is laid on all ships and vessels in the ports and places within the limits or jurisdiction of the United States, cleared or not cleared, bound to any foreign port or place; and that no clearance be furnished to any ship or vessel bound to such foreign port, except vessels under the immediate direction of the President of the United States. ...

(178) Congress. House of Representatives. Thursday, December 17. .. Mr. FINDLEY, from the committee of elections, made a report on the petition of Duncan M'FARLAND, contesting the election of John CULPEPPER, (representative from North Carolina.) The report concludes as follows: Resolved, That from the testimony laid before, and admitted by, the committee, it appears, that John CULPEPPER, (the sitting member) is not entitled to a seat in this House. Referred to a committee of the whole on Tuesday.

(179) The Gazette. Edenton, January 6, 1808. .. Dr. Edward PASTEUR, of Newbern, is appointed Adjutant-General of the Militia of this State, in the room of Gen. Benj. SMITH, resigned.
    Married—on Wednesday evening last, Mr. Henry SKINNER, to Miss Sally ROBERTS, both of this county.

(180) The Subscriber Will attend at the Academy on Sunday next, at 10 o'clock, or at the ringing of the Bell, where he expects to have an assistant to perform a few set pieces of Music, and wishes those that signed to attend. John NORCOM. January 5, 1808.

(181) Notice. All persons indebted to the estate of Thomas HANKINS, dec. are earnestly requested to come forward and make immediate payment, as the situation of the estate renders it absolutely necessary for all in arrears to pay up their respective balances. Those to whom the estate is indebted, will call for payment. Elizabeth HANKINS, Ex'r'x. January 5, 1808.

(182) Notice. The Trustees of Edenton Academy are requested to attend the annual meeting of the Board, at Joseph B. SKINNER's office, in Edenton, on Monday, the 11th inst. at 11 o'clock. ... Jos. B. SKINNER, Sec'ry. Edenton, Jan. 4, 1808.

(183) 25 Dollars Reward. Run away from the Subscriber, on Saturday, the 26th ult. a negro man named TONY, by trade a blacksmith. He is about 24 years of age, 4 feet 9 or 10 inches high, and very yellow. One of his feet (I believe the right one) has been broken a little below the instep, from a fall in straining a horse, which causes him to limp considerably. .. His aim, no doubt, is some of the Northern states. He sometimes plays on the fiddle. ... John WALKER. Plymouth, Jan. 2, 1808. Since I arrived in this place, I have been informed by the stage-driver, that he took up the above fellow on the road, between this and Suffolk, who he conceived, from his colour and appearance, was free-born. He passed by the name of Benjamin JAMES, and said he was from Newbern, where he had worked at the silver-smith's business; but finding little employ, he was determined to try some part of the Northward. He passed as a passenger in the stage, and stopped at the different inns, until he arrived within a small distance of Suffolk, when the stage-driver dropt him. J. W. Edenton, Jan. 4, 1808.

Vol. II. Wednesday, January 13, 1808. Num. 99.

(184) Congress. House of Representatives. The Secret Session. Friday, Dec. 18. .. Thursday, December 31. The bill supplementary to the act laying an Embargo was discussed in the House, when about one o'clock, on motion of Mr. RANDOLPH, it was postponed. Mr. RANDOLPH then rose for the purpose of making a motion, and giving information to the House which he had just received. .. Mr. R. then read the following documents: Translation. In the galley the Victoria, Bernardo MOLINA, Patron, there have been sent to Don Vincent FOLCH, nine thousand six hundred and forty dollars, which sum, without making the least use of it, you will hold at my disposal, to deliver it at the moment that an order may be presented to you by the American General, Don James WILKINSON. ... New-Orleans. 20th Jan. 1796. The Baron DE CARONDELET. To Senior (sic) Don Thomas PORTELL. I certify that the foregoing is a copy of its original to which I refer. (Signed) Thomas PORTELL. New Madrid, 27th June, 1807.
    Fort Washington, Sept. 22, 1796. Ill health and many pressing engagements must be my apology for a short letter. .. I must beg leave to refer you to our friend POWER.. .. I beg you to write me fully on this question in cypher by POWER. whose presence in Phil. is necessary, as well as to clear his own character, attacked by WAYNE..& to bring me either the person or the deposition of a man, now under your command who had been suborned by WAYNE to bear false witness against me, and afterwards for fear he should recant, bribed him to leave Kentucky. .. POWER will explain to you circumstances which justify the belief of the great treachery that has been practised with respect to the money lately sent me. .. Never suffer my name to be written or spoken. The suspicion of Washington is wide awake.—Beware of BRADFORD, the Fort Pitt refugee, he seeks to make peace—there are spies every where. ... W. Copy of a letter in cypher received from General WILKINSON. Natchez, 6th of February, 1807. (Signed) Manuel GAYOSO DE LEMOS. ..
    Mr. RANDOLPH stated the following to be an extract of a letter signed T.

(184) (Cont.) POWER, whose hand writing he understood could be identified: "On
the 27th of the same month (October last) appeared in the Richmond Enquirer a certificate given by myself to Gen. WILKINSON in New-Orleans, on the 16th of May preceding. Between my repeated declarations to many of my friends and acquaintances
..and this certificate there is a manifest contradiction. And between this same
certificate and the deductions to be drawn from my declaration before the Richmond court, there is an apparent inconsistency which it is now my task to clear up
and reconcile.

During Gen. WILKINSON's residence in New Orleans last winter..I waited upon
him one morning, and after some conversation on certain transactions that had
taken place at a former period in the western country, and on the delicate situation in which his conduct during the winter was likely to place him, he asked me
if I had any objection to give him a certificate that might help him to silence
that foul mouthed BRADFORD, and refute the assertions of the editor of the Western
World. I replied without hesitation that I had none, and would give him one with
pleasure, provided he promised me it should not be published. On this he assured
me that the only use he proposed to make of it, was to lay it before the President
with the view to prove the falsehood of the charges circulated against him, vindicate his character and secure the confidence of the executive. He then desired me
to sit down and write the certificate. I observed that I might not make it out
quite to his satisfaction; and as he best knew the points he wished to be embraced
in it, he had better make it out himself, and I would copy it. .. Next morning..
he presented me with the certificate, which I copied, as it has been published
with a few alterations. One a material one, is after these words "do most solemnly declare that I have at no time carried or delivered to Gen. James WILKINSON."
I erased the words "either directly or indirectly," and declared..that I could not
insert those words, he did not insist..

Now let me with the same frankness and ingeniousness..narrate the transaction
of 1796, alluded to in my certificate.. It is the same that is the subject of the
affidavits of Messrs. DERBIGNEY and MERCIER.--That of the former gentleman is
correct as to substance, for I actually did receive from Capt. Don Thomas PORTELL,
commandant of New Madred the sum of $9640 for General WILKINSON towards the latter
end of June or beginning of July, 1796, which was packed up in the manner described by Mr. DERBIGNEY, and when I was stopped and my boat searched on the Ohio by
Lieut. STEELE under the orders of Gen. Anthony WAYNE, I had other sums on board
but that was the only one I received for Gen. WILKINSON. On my arrival at Louisville..I landed my cargo, purchased a horse, and proceeded by land to Cincinnati.
As I passed thro' Lexington, I published in STEWART's Kentucky Herald my affidavit
concerning this outrage, supported by those of the spectators of the transaction,
WELSH, WHITE and SANSOM.. And I now take this opportunity of clearing Gen. WILK-
INSON of the charge of being the author of it, as is asserted by BRADFORD of New
Orleans and declare it was written by myself, and that excepting Capt. Campbell
SMITH, no person ever saw it before it was put into the hands of the printer.

At Cincinnati I acquainted Gen. WILKINSON with the circumstances that have occurred and he gave me orders to deliver the money to Mr. Philip NOLAND. These
orders I punctually executed. Mr. NOLAND conveyed the barrels of sugar and coffee, that contained the dollars to Frankfort in a waggon. I there saw them opened
in Mr. Montgomery BROWN's store. The sugar and coffee, I afterwards sold to Mr.
Abijah HUNT, of Cincinnati. ...

(185)   The Gazette. Edenton, January 13, 1808. .. Died--on Monday evening, at
the house of Mrs. HORNIBLOW, Mr. Arthur JONES, a native of Ireland, and for many
years a respectable resident of this town.

(186)   Land for Sale. Will be Sold, at public Sale, before the Court-House, in

13 January 1808

(186) (Cont.) the Town of Windsor, on Tuesday, the 9th of February next, A Tract of Land, belonging to the estate of George GRAY, dec. containing about 800 Acres, well timbered, and lying about one mile from the Town of Windsor, on the road leading to Cashie-Neck. ... Wm. Lee GRAY, Ex'r. Windsor, Jan. 12, 1808.

(187) Letters remaining in the Post-Office at Edenton, January 1, 1808. Mrs. AN-CRUM, William ARMSTRONG, Agness ALEXANDER, Miss Frances DOZIER, William BUXTON, William BLOUNT, Richard BLACKMER, William BLAIR, Mary BATEMAN, William CLARK, William DAWS, Rev. Godfrey H. DAVENISH, Capt. DANA, John DREW, Miss Elizabeth FEREBE, James S. GALLENTON, Nancy GRAY, Ebenezer HITCH, Thomas HARRISON, John HICKSTALL, Ethan HAMMOND, Thomas HARVEY, Arthur JONES, Dr. KNOX, John M'NADER, M. MORRISS, Samuel PARKER, William R. RUSSELL, Sheriff of Chowan, Reuben SMALL, John THEOBALD, Judy THATCH, Angel WARNIER, Nancy WILLIAMS, Abner VAIL. Hend. STANDIN, P. M.

Vol. II. Wednesday, January 20, 1808. Num. 100.

(188) The Gazette. Edenton, January 20, 1808. .. Philadelphia, Jan. 6. Chamber of Commerce. A committee consisting of T. W. FRANCIS, Manuel EYRE, Robert RALSTON, Danl. SMITH, and Samuel KEITH, have been appointed by the Chamber of Commerce of this city, to enquire into the situation of the unemployed Mariners now in this port, and to report a plan for their employment and subsistence. ...

(189) Married—on Thursday last, in Pasquotank County, Joseph BLOUNT, Esq. Clerk and Master in Equity for Bertie County, to Miss Fanny CONNOR, of the former place.

(190) Tavern. The Subscribers have opened Tavern in the Town of Windsor, in the house fronting the Court-House, the property of George OUTLAW, Esq.—In this undertaking they are encouraged by the hope, that merit will be rewarded.. Their rooms and beds shall be particularly attended to, liquors and meats shall be good and well provided, and stables and forage shall be surpsssed by none. The favours of a generous public will be gratefully acknowledged. James PALMER, James MORGAN. Windsor, Jan. 8, 1808.

(191) Notice is hereby given to all the creditors of Hillary and Elizabeth SANS-BURY, late of Chowan county, that the said Hillary and Elizabeth SANSBURY are dead, and that the subscriber qualified as administrator to their estates at last December term of Chowan County Court; those indebted..are requested to discharge the same immediately; and those to whom they were indebted will bring in their demands for settlement... Jeremiah MIXSON, Adm. January 19, 1808.

(192) The Subscriber Conceives it to be his duty to inform his distant customers, the reason of the delay of their work before, and since the Christmas holidays. He has been confined to his room by sickness, for some time..added to which, two of his principal Journeymen thought proper to leave him at the very time their services were most wanted. He flatters himself, however, that he has recovered from his indisposition so far as to be enabled to carry on his business again with punctuality and dispatch. ... Joseph MANNING, Tailor. January 19, 1808.

Vol II. Wednesday, January 27, 1808. Num. 101.

(193) New-York, January 13. The Committee of Seamen appointed to wait on the Mayor and Council for the purpose of making some provisions for the unemployed Seamen of New-York, received the following answer: The Committee appointed by the Common Council to provide for the support of Seamen out of employment, have adopted the following plan: They have agreed with Capt. CHAUNCY, of the United States

(193) (Cont.) Navy Yard, to receive such Seamen at the Yard, on condition of their signing articles to continue in service during their own pleasure, and perform duty subject to his orders, the Common Council defraying the expences of their maintenance, which is to include victuals, drink, fuel, candles, and accomodations for lodging. Whenever this meritorious class of citizens can do better, they are at perfect liberty to leave the Navy Yard, Capt. CHAUNCY giving notice when they are discharged. By the Committee, John BINGHAM, Chairman. Committee of Ways and Means, Jan. 12, 1808. N. B. As some may have apprehensions of being trepanned, the honourable Council pledge their honour to provide that nothing of this nature shall take place. W. PINKNEY, W. DYCKMAN, W. TRUMAN, J. CAMP.) Committee of Seamen.

(194) The Gazette. Edenton, January 27, 1808. On Sunday morning last, a little after 2 o'clock, the inhabitants of this town were aroused from their slumbers by the distressing and awful cry of Fire, which proved to issue from the northwest corner of the Balcony of the house of Mr. John B. BLOUNT;—in a short time the whole of it was wrapped in flames, and in little more than an hour entirely consumed. The calmness of the night, and the alacrity and vigilance of the inhabitants in supplying and plying the engines, prevented his out-houses, and the neighbouring dwelling-houses, from being also consumed, and thereby arrested the general destruction which would probably have ensued. Mr. BLOUNT's loss..is very considerable:--Besides his house, which was the largest and most elegant in the town, a quantity of his furniture, bedding, &c. and his desk, containg valuable papers and money, fell a prey to this all powerful element. From what we are able to ascertain, we cannot attribute this melancholy circumstance to any thing but accident--the chimney had caught fire on the evening preceding, and great care was taken to examine the roof of the house, and have every appearance of fire removed, but it is not improbable that some latent spark may have remained in the inside, which did not finally break out into a flame until the late hour we have noticed.

(195) Died--on Wednesday last, Mr. Francis BEASLEY, of this county.

(196) Advertisement. Run away from the Subscriber, on the 18th instant, a negro man named DOLPHUS. He is generally known in this county, and in the Town of Edenton. He is a large clumsy black looking fellow, stoops in his shoulders, walks sluggish and clumsy, has some scars on his face, and two of his upper fore-teeth stands inward. .. He pretends to be a carpenter, but knows nothing of the business, is very trifling at any thing he undertakes. Any person that will apprehend the said negro fellow DOLPHUS, and deliver him to me, or confine him in gaol in this county, I will give a reward of 8 Dollars: If taken in any other county in the state, and confined as above, so that I get the negro, a reward of 10 Dollars will be given. Joshua SKINNER. N. B. DOLPHUS is a very bad disposed negro, and went off without any provocation. Perquimans, Jan. 19, 1808.

Vol. II. Wednesday, February 3, 1808. Num. 102.

(197) Congress. Senate of the United States. Wednesday, January 13. This being the day appointed for the hearing of John SMITH, a Senator from the state of Ohio, the Vice-President informed Mr. SMITH that the Senate was ready to hear any thing he might have to offer, to shew why the report of the committee should not be adopted. [It will be recollected that the report is for expelling Mr. SMITH from the Senate, for an alledged participation in the conspiracy of Aaron BURR.] Mr. SMITH said he was prepared to proceed..and named as his counsel Luther MARTIN, and Francis S. KEY, Esquires. Mr. BRADLEY, said Mr. SMITH was entitled to the benefit of counsel; but that it ought to be such as would be agreeable to the Senate. For

3 February 1808

(197) (Cont.) the purpose of ascertaining whether the counsel that gentleman had named would be admitted by the Senate he would make a motion..that Mr. KEY be admitted as one of the counsel of Mr. SMITH. This motion prevailed.. He then made a similar motion with respect to Mr. MARTIN, which was negative, 17 to 14. .. Mr. KEY rose, and..supported the following application. "John SMITH having filed his affidavit, applies to the Senate for reasonable time to procure the attendance of witnesses in his favour, and proper means to compel that attendance." This application was grounded on the following affidavit.

John SMITH of Ohio, makes oath on the Holy Evangelists of Almighty God, that he can prove by legal and competent testimony, the truth of the following facts, and that he can produce such proof..if allowed a reasonable time, and the usual means for that purpose. He can prove that the testimony delivered against him before the Grand Jury at Richmond, is utterly destitute of credit—of one of those witnesses, Elias GLOVER, he can prove, that the general character is such as to render him unworthy of belief, that he has been guilty of acts of the greatest baseness, has been published as a liar, and is generally considered in the county where he resides and is known, as a person destitute of truth; this he can prove by the testimony of the most respectable persons in Cincinnati, by Dr. STALL, John SELLMAN, Stephen MACFARLAND, Judge DUNLAVY, and many others.

Of the other witnesses, Peter TAYLOR, the obscurity of his situation, as a servant of BLANNERHASSETT, his being a foreigner and scarcely known in the country, may have prevented a sufficient developement of character, to ascertain.. whether he is worthy of belief, or not—but of his statement, as also of GLOVER's, he can prove the falsehood.. These contradictions relative to these witnesses, he can prove by Capt. GORDON, Fielding LOWRY, William M'FARLAND, Colonel CHAMBERS, Gen. GAMO, Mr. (blank) LONGWORTH, and several others. He further expects to prove that the orders drawn on him by Aaron BURR, were not drawn in consequence of any participation in any of his projects.. This he can prove by Major BIGGS, Gen. CARBERY. Jacob BURNET, Gen. FINDLAY, and several other characters of unquestioned respectability. He can also prove that his seeing Col. BURR at Frankfort was merely accidental.. He can prove this by Mr. HART, the President of the bank at Lexington, Alexander PARKER, John JORDON, Dr. CHAMBERS, James CHAMBERS, and others. He can also prove the existence of the engagements which compelled him to leave home on the last of May, and occasioned his absence at the time the bills of indictment were found against him.—That he had business requiring his presence in New-Orleans; that he went thence to an estate which he holds in West Florida, and where he was then actually completing a settlement and laying out a town.. That he immediately prepared to surrender himself for trial.. These facts he can prove by A. D. ABRAHAMS, Harriss HUE, John MURDOCH, Izra C. KNEELAND, David BRADFORD, Gov. WILLIAMS, Benj. SIMMONS, and many others. ..

He expects to disclose a confederacy between the witness, Elias GLOVER, with his other enemies, particularly with Matthew NIMMO, a man (if possible) more infamous than himself, and the base means which their malevolence suggested to injure him.. On this 13th day of January, 1808, the within named John SMITH, made oath, that the facts herein stated are true as stated, to the best of his knowledge and belief. Sworn to before me, Allen B. DUCKETT. ...

(198) Statement of Daniel CLARK, Relative to General WILKINSON. Read on the 11th January in the House of Representatives.. Mr. CLARK's Statement. .. I arrived from Europe at New-Orleans in December, 1786, having been invited to the country by an uncle of considerable wealth and influence, who had long been resident in that city. Shortly after..I was employed in the office of the Secretary of the government. This office was the depository of all state papers. In 1787, General WILKINSON made his first visit to New-Orleans, and was introduced by my uncle to the Governor and other officers of the Spanish government. In..1788, much sensa-

(198) (Cont.) tion was excited by the report of his having entered into some arrangements with the government of Louisiana, to separate the western country from the United States, and this report acquired great credit upon his second visit to New-Orleans in 1789.--About this time I saw a letter from the General to a person in New-Orleans, giving an account of Col. CONNOLY's mission to him from the British government in Canada, and of proposals made to him on the part of that government, and mentioning his determination of adhering to his connection with the Spaniards.

.. The general object was, the severance of the western country from the United States, and the establishment of a separate government in the alliance and under the protection of Spain. .. I had no personal knowledge of money being paid to General WILKINSON, or to any agent for him, on account of his pension, previously to the year 1793 or 1794. .. In 1793, two gentlemen of the names of OWENS and COLLINS, friends and agents of General WILKINSON, came to New-Orleans. To the first was entrusted, as I was particularly informed by the officer of the Spanish government, the sum of six thousand dollars, to be delivered to General WILKINSON on account of his own pension and that of others. On his way, in returning to Kentucky, OWENS was murdered by his boat's crew, and the money..was made away with by them.. COLLINS, the co-agent with OWENS..fitted out a small vessel in the Bayou St. John, and shipped in her at least 11,000 dollars, which he took round to Charleston. This shipment..became known to many, and the destination of it was afterwards fully disclosed to me by the officers of the Spanish government, by COLLINS, and by Gen. WILKINSON himself..

Mr. POWER was a Spanish subject, resident in Louisiana, and the object of his visits to the western country became known to me in 1796, when he embarked..for Philadelphia, in company with Judge SEBASTIAN, in which vessel..I saw embarked under a special permission 4,000 dollars or thereabouts, which, I was informed, were for SEBASTIAN's own account, as one of those concerned in the scheme of dismemberment of the western country. Mr. POWER..on his tour through the western country, saw General WILKINSON at Greenville, and was the bearer of a letter to him for the Secretary of the government of Louisiana, dated the 7th or 8th March, 1796, advising that a sum of money had been sent to Don Thomas PORTELL, commandant of New-Ma-[End of page.] [Note: The following two pages of this issue are missing.]

Vol II. Wednesday, February 10, 1808. Num. 103.

(199) (Copy.) War Department, January 2, 1808. In compliance with a request from Brigadier General James WILKINSON, the President of the United States has directed a Court of Inquiry to be instituted, for the purpose of hearing such testimony as may be produced, in relation to the said Gen. James WILKINSON's having been, or now being, a pensioner to the Spanish government, while holding a commission under the government of the United States. Col. Henry BURBECK, as President, Col. Thomas CUSHING, and Lieut. Col. Jonathan WILLIAMS, As members are hereby directed to meet at the city of Washington, on Monday the 11th day of the present month of January, as a Court of Inquiry for the purpose above stated; and, after a full investigation..the court will report to this department a correct statement of its proceedings, together with its opinion on the amount of testimony exhibited. Walter JONES, Esq. district attorney for the district of Columbia, will be requested to act as Judge Advocate or recorder to the court. (Signed) H. DEARBORN, Secretary of War. Colonel Henry BURBECK, President, Court Enquiry.

(200) (Copy.) Richmond, May 31, 1790. Sir, The enclosed copy of a letter from the Spanish Governor of New-Orleans to a respectable gentleman in Kentucky, was handed me by Mr. BANKS of this city. As the subject of this paper appears interesting to the U. States, I have taken the liberty to forward it to you. ... Bev-

(200) (Cont.) erley RANDOLPH. To President of the United States. A true copy. Attest, J. A. COLES, Secretary of the President of the U. States.

(Copy.) New-Orleans, Sept. 16, 1789. Sir, General WILKINSON having represented to me, that you had it in contemplation to settle in this province, and that your example would have considerable influence on many good families of your country, I think it my duty..to inform you that I shall receive you and your followers with great pleasure, and that you have liberty to settle in a part of Louisiana, or any where on the east side of the Missisippi below the Yazoo river. In order to populate the province, his Majesty has been graciously pleased to authorize me to grant to the emigrants free of all expense, tracts of from 240 to 800 acres, in proportion to their property, and in particular cases of men of influence who may aid these views, I shall extend the grant as far as 3,000 acres. ... Estevan MIRO. To Benjamin SEBASTIAN, Esq. Kentucky. A copy. Attest, Sam. COLEMAN, A. C. C. A true copy. Attest, J. A. COLES, Secretary of the President of the U. States. ...

(201) Washington-City, January 25. City of Washington, Saturday, January 23d, 1808. In pursuance of notice given to the Republican Representatives of each House of Congress, the number of eighty-nine members convened in the Senate chamber..and at half past six o'clock, P. M. Stephen R. BRADLEY was appointed President, and Richard M. JOHNSON, Secretary. The meeting proceeded to recommend persons to the citizens of the United States, to fill the office of President and Vice-President of the United States. The ballot being taken first upon the recommendation for the office of President—John MILLEDGE and Joseph B. VARNUM being appointed tellers-the votes were as follow: For James MADISON, 83. For George CLINTON, 3. For James MUNROE, 3. The ballot..for Vice-President, the votes were as follows: For George CLINTON, 79. For John LANGDON, 5. For Henry DEARBORNE, 3. For John Q. ADAMS, 1. Upon motion of Wilson C. NICHOLAS, a committee of correspondence and arrangement was appointed, in case of the death or resignation of the persons recommended..

Upon motion of Mr. MONTGOMERY, the following letter was received and read: Being too unwell to attend..this evening, agreeably to notice, _ hereby constitute my friend Mr. John MONT__MERY, my proxy, to vote for me in favour __ James MADISON as President and George __INTON as Vice-President.._iven under my hand and seal this 23d of __nuary, 1808. *Lemuel SAWYER, and then the meeting adjourned. Stephen R. BRADLEY, President. Richard M. JOHNSON, Secretary. *Mr. SAWYER's proxy was not received.

(202) The Gazette. Edenton, February 10, 1808. .. The Subscriber Begs leave to inform her old Customers, as well as all transient Travellers, that she has furnished her Tavern with every accommodation in her line for their reception... Ann ROBERTS. February 9, 1808.

(203) Notice. By request, the Treasurer of North-Carolina Baptist Missionary Society, hereby notifies the Directors of said society, that the next meeting of the Board, is appointed PARKER's Meeting-House, Hertford County, N. C. on Friday before the third Sunday in March next. Hoping they will be punctual in their attendance. Geo. OUTLAW, Treas'r. February 1, 1808.

(204) Notice is hereby given, that George Archdale Low CONNOR, of the County of Pasquotank, is dead, and that the Subscriber qualified as Executor to his last will and testament at the last term of the County Court. All persons indebted to the said estate are requested to make payment; and those having claims..to exhibit them within the time limited by law. William T. MUSE. December 30, 1807.

(205)   For Sale, On a very liberal credit, A Tract of Land, well timbered with white and red Oak and Pine, containing 214 Acres, within 3 miles of the town of Edenton. ... Solomon ELLIOT. Chowan, Feb. 2, 1808.

(206)   30 Dollars Reward. Runaway from the subscriber on Monday last, the 25th inst. a negro man, named JOSHUA, 6 feet 2 or 3 inches high. He is about thirty years of age, black complexion and well made. He has very remarkable large feet, and a scar mark over his left eye. He is a cooper by trade, plays tolerably well on the fiddle, of which he is very fond. ... Stephen CABARRUS. Chowan county, Jan 26, 1808.

Vol III.   Wednesday, February 17, 1808.   Num. 104.

(207)   Providence, Jan. 31. .. War With Algiers. Arrived this evening, the fast sailing ship Honestus, Captain CLARK, 42 days from the Downs. Left London about the 11th December for the Mediterranean—off Cape Trafalgar, spoke a British ship of war, who informed that Algiers had Declared War against America, and captured a number of vessels; in consequence, went into Tangier for further information; and on application to the American Consul, the account of war was fully confirmed; and a letter handed by the Consul to Capt. CLARK—a copy of which is given below. ..
        Letter.   Tangier, 31st Dec. 1807. Sir, The belief of the Algerines having commenced hostilities on the flag of the U. States, is founded on the declaration under oath of Captain Ichabod SHEFFIELD of the schooner Mary-Ann of New-York, made at Naples; which states that his vessel and the brig Violet of Boston, was captured on the 25th of October*, by an Algerine frigate of 44 guns. .. He was fortunate enough to overpower the Turks put on board the Mary-Ann, and arrived at Naples, 4th Nov.+ ... James SIMPSON. Captain Nathan CLARK, ship Honestus, Tangier Bay. *Capt. CLARK saw Capt. SHEFFIELD's declaration, and is confident that there is a mistake in this date, and that it was the 26th of November.   +December 4th in the original.

(208)   The Gazette. Edenton, February 17, 1808. .. Under the Marine Memoranda head in the N. Ledger of the 8th inst. we notice the following:—Arrived sch'r Union, MAHON, 18 days from the City of Santo Domingo, Coffee, Moses MYERS.—December 25, on the outward bound passage, in lat. 30, 54, long. 69, saw a wreck-ahead, boarded her, supposed her to be a Nova-Scotia built schooner of about 180 tons, both masts gone by the board, rudder gone, had been stripped of sails and rigging..her anchors on her bows—loaded with coarse salt—on her after locker was written with chalk: "Think of the fate of us poor mariners, who were without spars or rigging and not a mouthful to eat, were fortunately relieved from the jaws of death by the sch'r Robert Cockrin, of Wilmington, Stephen RICHARDSON—Wrecked in lat. 52, 20, long. 77, 30—taken up by the brig Hope, of Portland, Moses HALL, master."

(209)   This paper (No. 104) completes two years of the establishment of the Edenton Gazette in this town..it is with much regret that the Printer is obliged to complain of not receiving the stipulated remuneration for his services...

(210)   Married—on Wednesday last, Mr. John M'GUIRE, to Miss Lavina MATTHIAS, both of this County.

(211)   Adjutant-General's Orders. The several Officers of Divisions of Brigades, Regiments and Battalions throughout the State, who failed to make complete Returns of the Militia under their respective commands to the late Adjutant-General are required to forward the same to the undersigned without delay. The Inspection Re-

(211) (Cont.) turns and Muster Rolls of that part of the Militia which is to constitute the Quota to be furnished by this State, as part of the detachment of the
Militia of the United States, are particularly called for... Edward PASTEUR, Adjutant-General. Newbern, Jan. 18, 1808.

(212) For Sale, Antigua Rum, by the hhd. at $1 12 1-2 Cents per Gallon. Sugar of
a good quality, at $11 per hundred.. Apply to John POPELSTON, in Edenton, or
Lemuel CREECY, at his own house. February 14, 1808.

(213) Notice. The subscriber having qualified as administrator to the estate of
Joseph BRYAN, dec. in Martin County, at last term of September Court, requests all
persons indebted to the estate..to make immediate payment; and those having demands are hereby notified to exhibit them... George OUTLAW, Adm. Windsor, Jan.
14, 1808.

(214) Notice Is hereby given, that Josiah ROBINSON, Esq. of Perquimans County, is
dead, and that the subscribers qualified as Executors to his last will and testament at November term last. All persons indebted..are requested to make immediate
payment; and those having claims..to exhibit them... James WHEDBEE, William
JONES,} Ex'rs. Perquimans, Feb. 5, 1808.

(215) Notice Is hereby given, that William ROBERTS, of the County of Chowan is
dead, and that the subscriber qualified as Executrix to his last will and testament at the last term of the County Court. All persons indebted to the said
estate, are requested to make payment to John B. BLOUNT; and those having claims
against it, to exhibit them to him..as he is authorised by me to settle the business of said estate. Mary ROBERTS. February 15, 1808.

Vol III. Wednesday, February 24, 1808. Num. 105.

(216) Congress. House of Representatives. Thursday, February 4. Mr. MONTGOM-
ERY, presented petitions from Charles GARTS and others, of Baltimore, and Edward
PENNINGTON and others, of Philadelphia, sugar refiners, praying that a drawback
may be allowed on all sugar refined in the United States from imported raw sugar,
which may be exported. Referred to the committee of commerce and manufactures...

(217) Norfolk, February 15. .. District of Portsmouth. I. Swepson WHITEHEAD,
Notary Public in and for the district aforesaid, do hereby certify, that on the
13th day of February, 1808, Isaac ANDERSON, of lawful age, personally appeared be-
fore me and made oath, that in the month of November last a certain Littleton
DAVIS, commander of the pilot-boat Jefferson received on board said boat at
Norfolk fourteen quarters of Beef, and on the succeeding day delivered it on board
a vessel called the Hope, a tender to the British squadron then at the Capes of
Virginia. That about a week after the delivery of the said Beef, the said Littleton DAVIS, in the Pilot-boat aforesaid, did put on board the British frigate
Milan, within the Capes, a quarter of Beef and a keg of Butter. The deponent
acted as a Sailor on board said Pilot-boat, at the time.. This deponent has often
heard the said DAVIS declare, that in the event of a war between Great Britain and
America. he would go the side of the British, and pilot their vessels up to
Norfolk. to destroy that town and Portsmouth. In testimony whereof, I have hereunto set my hand, and affixed my Seal of Office, the day and year within mentioned. (A true copy.)

(218) Marseilles, 21st Nov. 1807. Sir, I had the honor of addressing you on the
5th of last August and 14th ult. This, under cover of William LEE, Esq. our Con-

(218) (Cont.) sul at Bordeaux, is to remit you here inclosed a copy of a letter, I just received from our Consul at Naples, dated the 9th instant.. I have already advised the American masters and citizens of the United States in my district... (Signed) Stephen CATHALAN. James MADISON, Esq. Secretary of the United States, Washington.

Naples, 9th Nov. 1807. Sir, I have the honor to inform you, that from the report of Capt. Ishabed SHEFFIELD, of the schooner Mary-Ann of New-York, arrived on the 4th inst. in this port from America, it appears that unexpected war has taken place between the regency of Algiers and the United States. ... J. B. DA-COSTER. Stephen CATHALAN, Esq. Com. and Navy Agent for U. S. A. at Marseilles.

(219) Important News. .. Circular, (Copy) Algiers, Dec. 16, 1807. Sir—You have undoubtedly before this, heard that three American vessels had been detained by a frigate of this place, in consequence of the annuities for two years past, not having been sent from the United States, in naval and military stores, as stipulated by treaty, notwithstanding the amount thereof has been repeatedly offered in cash. These vessels are the ship Eagle of New-York; THALERS from Bristol to Palermo..brig Violet, of Boston, J. MER?ET, from Oporto to Leghorn..and and schooner Mary Ann, of New-York, I. SHEFFIELD, master from the Streights of Belle-Isle to Leghorn.. .. I have now the honor to inform you that I have adjusted this business with the Dey, who has received the amount of two years annuities due, in cash, and the vessels are liberated, and that our commerce will receive no further molestation from the cruizers of this Regency. ... Tobias LEAR. Wm. KIRKPATRICK, Esq. Consul of the U. States of America, at Malaga.

(220) The Gazette. Edenton, February 24, 1808. .. Take Notice. The subscriber, acting for the administratrix of Gregory REILLEY, dec. gave his note in settlement with Arthur JONES, dec. in the month of September, 1807, payable twelve months after date, he hereby forwarns all persons from taking the said note for the whole amount, as he has a just credit, from under Arthur JONES's hand, for three hundred dollars, for the administratrix. Henry AUSTIN. Tarborough, Feb. 17, 1808.

(221) For Sale, On a credit of six and twelve months, three Houses, standing on ground of William LITTLEJOHN, Esq. on Broad-Street; one of them is at present occupied by Mr. Benjamin WHEDBEE, as a Hatter's Shop, and the other two are adjoining. They are situated in a very centrical (sic) part of the town for business, and would be very suitable for shop-keepers, traders or mechanics. ... James CUNNINGHAM. Edenton, Feb. 23, 1808.

(222) 100 Dollars Reward. Ran away from the Subscriber on the 26th December last, a Mulatto Man named TONEY, a blacksmith by trade; he is about 24 years of age, 5 feet 10 inches high—his right foot has been broken, which causes him to limp, and is much larger than the other.—He travelled in the stage from Edenton to Suffolk, the 28th ult. I have understood he went by the name of Benjamin JAMES while in Suffolk. .. The above reward will be given to away person who will secure him in any gaol so that I get him again, and all reasonable charges paid if delivrred to me in Plymouth, North-Carolina. John WALKER. January 8, 1808.

Vol III. Wednesday, March 2, 1808. Num. 106.

(223) The Gazette. Edenton, March 2, 1808. .. Married—on the 23d ult. in Camden county, Dr. Samuel MATTHEWS, of Norfolk, to the amiable Miss Harriot C. SAWYER, daughter of Enoch SAWYER, Esq. Collector of the port of Camden.

(224)   All persons are cautioned against employing or dealing with negro JACOB, the property of Mrs. Ann BLOUNT, without a written pass from me, accompanying his certificate, at their peril. The Printer. March 2d.

(225)   Notice is hereby given, that James MANEY, of the county of Hertford, is dead, and that the subscriber qualified as administrator to his estate at the last term of Hertford County Court. All persons indebted to the said estate are requested to make payment; and those having claims..to exhibit them... Thomas WYNNS, Adm. February 28, 1808.

(226)   Notice is hereby given to all whom it may concern, that Arthur JONES, late of Edenton, is dead, and that the subscriber qualified as administrator to his estate at the last term of Hertford County Court. All persons indebted..are requested to make payment; and those having claims..to exhibit them... Jos. F. DICKINSON, Adm. March 2d, 1808.

(227)   Notice.   On Tuesday, the 15th inst. before the door of Mrs. HORNIBLOW's Tavern, in the Town of Edenton, will be Sold, to the highest bidder, among other things the property of the late Arthur JONES, a mahogany Desk, an Iron Strong Box, sundry articles of Stationary, &c. &c. ... Jos. F. DICKINSON, Adm. March 2, 1808.

(228)   I Have for Sale a Seine about 200 fathoms long, fishes 26 feet, haulyards, hauling ropes, &c. 100 fish Stands, 4 or 500 cypres barrels, and a good Batteau. For Rent, A Fishery on Chowan river, 10 or 12 miles above Edenton---as a herring fishery 'tis surpassed by none. Apply immediately. Jos. F. DICKINSON. Winton, March 2, 1808.

(229)   Two Dollars Will be paid by the Subscriber, or Mr. John COOPER, of Pitch-Landing, to any person that will, within 10 months, take up negro JACOB, in Hertford county, with, or without a pass, and give him 20 lashes, well laid on, on his bare back. He is a low, black, well-set fellow, and has a wife at Mrs. RUSSEL's, near RAYNER's Ferry. The above reward will be paid by either Mr. COOPER or myself, on satisfactory proof being given, that JACOB bears the merited marks of 20 lashes Well Laid On. James WILLS. March 2, 1808.

(230)   Henry WILLS, Invites the attention of the Public. to the following Collection of Books. It is such a one as is rarely offered for sale in Edenton...

Vol III. Wednesday, March 9, 1808. Num. 107.

(231)   The Gazette. Edenton, March 9, 1808. ARROWSMITH's map of the world, now publishing in Philadelphia by Mr. Thomas L. PLOWMAN, is, we understand, in a state of forwardness, and will be the finest thing ever published in this country. The subscription price..heretofore Eight Dollars, is now raised to Ten.

(232)   Mr. John CULPEPPER (says the Raleigh Minerva of the 18th ult.) passed through this city on Sunday last, on his way to the seat of government. We learn that he had a majority of more than 600 votes over Duncan M'FARLANE, for Member of Congress.

(233)   Departed this life, on the 2d inst. Christopher Gale CREECY, son of Col. Lemuel CREECY, of this County, and a student of the upper class in Edenton Academy.---The life of this amiable young gentleman, was truly exemplary; and his death is deeply regretted, by all who knew his worth.---To manners, peculiarly mild and

9 March 1808

(233) (Cont.) engaging, he united a mildness, and suavity of temper, a propriety of deportment and piety of life, that gave additional lustre, to a genius acute and penetrating, a judgment strong and correct, and a heart replete with "simplicity and Godly sincerity."—In every action of a life, embittered by frequent and painful disease, "the beauty of holiness" shone resplendent. His gentle and sympathetic manners, his many virtues, his early and uniform piety, endeared him to his fellow students, and acquaintance, and leave a comfortable assurance, that he now participates the joys of a happy immortality.—"O Death divine, that giv'st us to the skies!"

(234) Died—on Monday the 29th ult. Mrs. Deborah HAUGHTON, wife of Mr. Edwd. HAUGHTON, of this county. On Tuesday morning last, of a pleurisy, Mr. George HEWITSON, a native of England.

(235) The advertisements inserted in the inside of this day's paper relative to negro JACOB, is hereby countermanded; having returned him to his owner. He is no longer my property. Printer.

(236) Preserve your Rags And exchange them for Cash or Books. The subscriber having contracted with an ingenious Mechanic to erect a Paper Mill in the vicinity of Raleigh, wishes the citizens generally to preserve their Rags of every kind, that they may be converted into Paper; as there is no kind of Rags, formed of hemp, flax or cotton, which cannot be made useful in this way. The Paper Mill is to be completed by the first of June next. .. When these considerations are taken into view, it is expected that every good housewife will prepare a bag or bags, in which she will direct every piece of useful Rag to be put, which she will send..for the use of the Raleigh Paper Mill, to be delivered at the store of the subscriber, or at the house of John WHITAKER, Esq. near Raleigh, to whose grist mill, the works are to be annexed. Joseph GALES. Raleigh, Feb. 16, 1808.
Merchants in every part of the state are requested to receive white linen and cotton Rags for the Raleigh Paper Mill.. Rags for the above Mill received by Henry WILLS.

(237) For Sale, A Very valuable Tract of Land, of about eight hundred Acres, lying in Bear Swamp, in the County of Chowan, belonging to the estate of Mrs. Lydia BENNETT, deceased. The soil of this Land is esteemed of an excellent quality, and is very well stocked with good white and red oak and cypress Timber, for lumber; on it is a clearing of thirty thousand corn hills, in a state for cultivation, under a fence..with a good Barn and Negro House thereon. .. Henry P. BENNETT, Ex'r.

Vol III. Wednesday, March 16, 1808. Num. 108.

(238) Congress. House of Representatives. .. March 2. .. The Senate have, without division, sanctioned the nomination of William PINKNEY, minister resident at the court of London.

(239) List of Promotions and Appointments in the Corps of Engineers made on the 23d day of Feb. 1808. Lt. Col. Jonathan WILLIAMS promoted to the rank of Colonel. Maj. Jared MANSFIELD, do. do. Lt. Col. Capt. Alexander MACOMB, do. do. Major. Capt. Joseph G. SWIFT, do. do. Major. 1st Lt. George BANEFORD, do. do. Captain. 1st Lt. Wm. M'REE, do. do. Captain. 2d. Lt. Charles GRATIOT, do. do. Captain. 2d. Lt. Eleazer D. WOOD, do. do. 1st Lieut. 2d. Lt. Wm. PARTRIDGE, do. do. 1st. Lieut. 2d. Lt. Prentice WILLARD, do. do. 1st. Lieut. Joseph G. TOTTEN, Cadet Samuel BABCOCK, Cadet Daniel A. A. BUCK, and Cadet Sylvanus THAYER, Appointed 2d

(239) (Cont.) Lieuts.

(240) Charleston, Feb. 25. The ship Boyne, Capt. SAFFORD, sailed from this port 81 days ago, with a cargo of cotton, &c. bound to Bordeaux. On the 31st of December..was bro't to by the British frigate Tribune, Capt LEONARD, who warned Capt. S. of entering at Bordeaux; at the same time informing him, that every port of France, Spain, Portugal, or the Mediterranean, was under a state of blockade...

(241) Norfolk, March 7. .. A duel was fought on Wednesday at Washington, between the honorable Mr. GARDENIER, of New-York, and the honorable Mr. CAMPBELL, of Tennessee, in which the former was dangerously wounded. The ball had been extracted, and there were hopes of his recovery on Friday last.

(242) March 9. .. Another Traitor in Custody. We have now before us a letter from Detroit, dated January 23, 1808.. "I presume you have heard that we have hre ecompanies (sic) in this place called into actual service—two of infantry and one of riflemen. A few days ago, a complaint was lodged by the attorney general, against Stanley GRISWOLD, Esq. secretary of the Michigan territory, for enticing and procuring men to desert from this detachment. He has been arrested at the suit of the United States, and acourt of enquiry is now holding before justices M'DOUGALL, MAY, and Richard SMITH. ... N. Y. Paper.

(243) Thomas PAINE. This patriot having lately presented a memorial to Congress, having for its object some gratification for his revolutionary services, has produced an investigation into his affairs as stated by himself. ...

(244) The Gazette. Edenton, March 16, 1808. The Norfolk Herald of the 7th inst. says, Captain HERBERT, arrived last evening from Alexandria, says that Mr. GARDENIER died on Thursday morning!

(245) Report.—A gentleman of strict veracity, who arrived here yesterday, affirms on good authority, that Gen. James WILKINSON in attempting to horse-whip John RANDOLPH, Esq. received a ball from the latter which in a few moments terminated his existence! [This report is founded, we presume, on the affair of GARDINIER and CAMPBELL.] W. Gaz.

(246) Notice is hereby given to all whom it may concern. that Timothy THOMPSON, late of Chowan county, is dead, and that the subscriber qualified as administrator to ___ (torn) estate at September term, 1806. All perso__ indebted to the said estate, are requeste_ __ make payment; and those having claim_ _gainst the same, to exhibit them... William THOMPSON ___ March 15, 1808.

(247) Philadelphia, Feb. 22. .. Saturday at twelve o'clock, JOYCE and MATTHIAS, the men convicted of murdering Mrs. CROSS, were brought from prison to the county Court-House, to receive sentence of death. .. ..pronounced by Mr. Chief Justice TILGHMAN. "John JOYCE and Peter MATTHIAS! You have been convicted after an impartial trial of an offence of the blackest dye—the only offence, which by the law is punished with death. You have taken that life which can never be restored, from a harmless, industrious old woman a widow, helpless, and incapable of resistance.. "

Vol III. Wednesday, March 23, 1808. Num. 109.

(248) The following proceedings of the military court of enquiry in the case of General WILKINSON have been communicated for insertion in the National Intelligen-

(248) (Cont.) cer. The Court being formed on the 16th ult. at the particular request of General WILKINSON, for the purpose of perpetuating testimony. .. I therefore request, that lieut. SPENCE, of the navy, and Lieut. MURRAY, of the army, may be sworn. The court then proceeded to take the testimony of Lieut. SPENCE..Lieut. MURRAY..and Thomas H. WILLIAMS, secretary of the Mississippi terri- tory.

The rules of the court having prohibited the publication of the testimony as it occurs, we can barely state from a bye-stander of good authority, that Lieut. SPENCE acknowledged he had embarked at Philadelphia with madame L'AUVERGNE, BOLL- MAN, and ALEXANDER, with the privity of BURR—that he bore a letter of recommenda- tion from BURR to Daniel CLARK..that he bore letters from BOLLMAN, and madame L'AUVERGNE (alias Norah HASKELL) to BURR.. Lieut. MURRAY's testimony was we learn, of great importance. He declared that on being urged to attack Baton Rouge, he, after resisting the proposition made by Judge WORKMAN and Lewis KERR, applied to his friend, Mr. CLARK, then in New-Orleans, who advised him to attack and take the place by all means—adding, that he "was going to Congress, and would do him (M.) all the good he could"—that he would "inform the Government it would require a large force to retake the place—and that before the Government could send down troops for the purpose, he (MURRAY) would find himself in a situation to do as he pleased."

This happened in April, or May, 1806. Mr. WILLIAMS was called to prove, that Daniel CLARK and D. WADSWORTH were appointed on the part of the American commis- sioners, CLAIBORNE and WILKINSON, to receive the Spanish archives at the surrender of Louisiana—which Mr. WILLIAMS did most amply.. The military court has adjourn- ed to the 14th of March...

(249) Norfolk, March 14. .. Accounts from Washington as late as Friday state that Mr. GARDINIER is rapidly on the recovery. He was able to walk about his chamber.

(250) The Gazette. Edenton, March 23, 1808. .. Notice. The subscriber intends leaving this place in a short time, wishes to close his accounts as soon as pos- sible; requests the favor of all persons indebted to settle as speedily as possi- ble; and those who have claims..to exhibit them.. He will attend during the Sup- erior Court at his shop regularly each day for that purpose. Andrew KNOX. Eden- ton, March 19, 1808.

(251) Notice is hereby given to all the creditors of the late Lydia BENNETT, of the county of Chowan; that the said Lydia BENNETT is dead, and that the subscriber qualified as executor at December term, 1807; who earnestly requests all those in- debted to the said estate, to make payment as speedily as possible; and those to whom the estate is indebted, to exhibit their demands... Henry P. BENNETT. March 20, 1808.

(252) Philadelphia, Feb. 29. Commemoration of WASHINGTON's birthday. At the il- lumination of the house of Timothy BLAKE in Front-street, on the 22d of Feb. in celebration of the day that gave birth to the Immortal WASHINGTON, the following toasts were drank by the guests to musick. .. 5. The memory of Major Gen. Nathaniel GREEN, whose councils as a Soldier WASHINGTON always respected. .. 7. The memory of John HANCOCK, the friend of WASHINGTON, and President of the Con- gress that declared the American states, Free And Independent. .. 11. John ADAMS, and Thomas JEFFERSON the honoured successors of President WASHINGTON. ...

Vol III. Wednesday, March 30, 1808. Num. 110.

(253) Congress. House of Representatives. Friday, March 11. Mr. LEWIS from the select committee, reported "a bill for the relief of Richard Bland LEE," which was referred to a committee of the whole on Monday. Mr. MUMFORD presented a petition from a number of merchants of New-York, stating that they had on hand a large quantity of Flaxseed, which, unless exported in a short time, would be useless and lost.. Referred to the committee of the whole House to whom was referred the report of the committee of Commerce and Manufactures on the petition of William HASLETT, of Philadelphia. ...

(254) Norfolk, March 21. .. On the 16th inst. a number of the Wheelbarrow Criminals, made their escape from Baltimore, and with them the noted Thomas L. JUDGE, "fair complexion, black eyes and hair, five feet ten inches high," well known in this place. A reward of 300 dollars is offered for him.

(255) The Gazette. Edenton, March 30, 1808. We are authorised to inform the citizens composing the Electoral District of Edenton, that Gen. Joseph RIDDICK, of Gates County, offers his services as an Elector, to serve at the next Presidential election, and to assure them, if elected, he will vote for James MADISON, as President, and George CLINTON, as Vice-President.

(256) We observe by the Western papers, that the following gentlemen have offered themselves as Electoral Candidates, at the ensuing election..all of whom are determined to support James MADISON. for President: Alexander ROWLAND, Esq. for the district of Fayetteville; Kemp PLUMMER, Esq. for the district, composed of the Counties of Halifax, Warren and Northampton; and Gen. Thomas WYNNS, for the district, composed of the Counties of Hertford, Bertie and Martin.

(257) John WHERLOW, for the apprehension of whom 1000 Dollars was offered, passed through Norfolk, on the 24th inst. in the safe keeping of two men from Camden, (S. C.) in the neighborhood of which place he was taken. DOUGHERTY, one of the wheel-barrow creminals, and accomplish of Thomas L. JUDGE..is also taken. .. The keeper of the goal died of the wounds received, in attempting to prevent their escape.

(258) Married--on the 17th inst. in Pasquotank County, Col. John HAMILTON, to Miss Nancy SCOTT. Died--a few days past, in Bertie County, Capt. Willis SAWYER, of that County.

(259) Notice. Whereas, King LUTON, administrator on the estate of Alexander A. FREEMAN, dec. having a Note in his possession that I gave the said Alexander A. FREEMAN, in the year 1805, for $130, or thereabouts; the said LUTON refuses to give me up the Note, although there is not one cent due on account of it. I therefore caution all persons from receiving the said Note..as this notice will be plead in bar against it. Caleb ELLIOT. March 20, 1808.

(260) Another Duel! .. Two gentlemen of color, acting in a subordinate situation at a tavern in this city, terminated an affair in the following manner--The former. of the name of Wm. DICKSON, perceiving a pair of pistols on a table belonging to one of the boarders, called Minto FISHER, to know if he had any inclination of imitating the great folks of the present day, by entering into the field of glory, to which the latter consented. ..the fire of FISHER's pistol took effect--the contents being shot, perforated through the coat, waistcoat and linen of DICKSON, without other injury. ...

Vol III. Wednesday, April 6, 1808. Num. 111.

(261) The Gazette. Edenton, April 6, 1808. .. Blake BAKER, Esq. is elected one of the Judges of the Superior Court of Law and Equity, in this state, to fill the vacancy occasioned by the death of the Honorable Spruce M'CAY.

(262) The Rev. Wm. BROWN will preach in the Court-House on Sunday next. Married--on the 20th ult. in Hertford county, Mr. Henderson LUTON, to Miss Sarah GALE, both of that county. On Tuesday last, in the same county, Mr. George KITTREL, of Gates county, to Miss Crissy SCULL, third daughter of Capt. Elisha SCULL, dec. of the aforementioned county. Died--at Salisbury, on the 8th ult. Nathaniel ALEXAN-DER, Esq. late Governor of this state, in the 53d year of his age.

(263) Negroes for Sale. I Will sell, at a low price, for good Notes, a Negro Fellow, his Wife and Child. The fellow is an excellent hand with the broad-ax and whip-saw, is about 28 years old; the wench is about 22, and the girl 5, all healthy likely Negroes. John SKINNER. April 5, 1808.

(264) Notice Is hereby given, that Benjamin NORFLEET, of the county of Chowan, is dead, and that the subscriber qualified as administrator to his estate at the last term of Chowan county court. All persons indebted to said estate are requested to make payment; and those having claims..to exhibit them... Jas. HATHAWAY, Adm. March 31, 1808. ...

(265) Notice is hereby given to all the creditors of Luke H. WHITE, of Washington county, that the said Luke H. WHITE is dead, and that the subscriber qualified as executrix to his estate at the last term of Washington County Court. All persons indebted to said estate are requested to make immediate payment; and those having claims..to present them for payment... Priscilla WHITE, Ex'rx.

(266) Take Notice. Israel LANE, late of the County of Perquimans, is dead, and Isaac BARBER, Esq. of the aforesaid County, administered on his estate at last November term; and at February term, the subscriber administered on the estate of Robert WHITE, late of the said County, who administered on the estate of Joshua WHITE, dec. of Pasquotank County; and the said Robert WHITE having the estate in his hands unsettled at the time of his death; I therefore request all persons indebted to either of the estates above mentioned to make immediate payment; and all those having claims..are requested to exhibit them... Isaac BARBER, Adm.

(267) Collector's-Office, Edenton, 6th April, 1808. Notice is hereby given to Citizens of the United States, who have property in any port or place without the jurisdiction of the United States, and wish to obtain permission to dispatch vessels in conformity with the provisions of the 7th section of the supplementary embargo act, passed the 12th of March, that they must make application at this office within ten days from the date hereof... Sam. TREDWELL, Collector.

(268) Washington-City, March 14. A Statement of the affair between Mr. GARDENIER and Mr. CAMPBELL. On the 23d day of February, Mr. GARDENIER addressed to Mr. George W. CAMPBELL the following note: City of Washington, Feb. 23, 1808. Sir--It would be as impossible as it would be painful to me to remind you of all the expressions in which you indulged yourself concerning me, in the debate in the House of Representatives yesterday. Among them were charges of falsehood, meanness, baseness. I have allowed you one night to reflect on the intemperance of such language, and I must insist that you will either disavow the expressions..to the satisfaction of my friend, Mr. WHITE, or through him authorize me to consider them as having been avowed out of the walls of the House. ... B. GARDENIER. G. W. CAMPBELL, Esq.

(268) (Cont.) To this note Mr. George W. CAMPBELL returned the following answer: Washington, Feb. 23, 1808. Sir--Your note of this morning has just been received. In answer to which I have only to say that any expressions used by me will never be disavowed. .. The charge made on Saturday by you, that the majority of the House, of whom I was one, were governed by French influence. ... Geo. W. CAMPBELL. B. GARDENIER, Esq. ..

Mr. WHITE, The publicity given to the affair by the first unsuccessful attempt to meet on the Montgomery road, and the interposition afterwards of the civil authority of the District, delayed the second meeting a few days. A place having been fixed on without the District, the parties repaired to Bladensburg.. They met the next morning, March the 2d..took their stations, fired nearly at the same time, and Mr. GARDENIER was severely wounded. .. To prevent misrepresentations this statement is signed by the friends of the parties. Samuel WHITE, John W. EPPES.

Vol III. Wednesday, April 13, 1808. Num. 112.

(269) The Gazette. Edenton, April 13, 1808. .. Died--on Tuesday, the 22d ult. in New-York, in the 40th year of her age, Mrs. Margaret HARRISON, widow of the late Mr. John HARRISON, original proprietor of the "New-York Weekly Museum."--she has left five orphan Children, to mourn in silent sorrow, a loss never to be repaired.

(270) The subscriber on the 19th January, 1807, gave to William P. HARDY, a signed Account for 18 barrels of Corn; which said HARDY still retains and refuses to deliver to the subscriber, although the aforesaid Corn has been paid. All persons are therefore warned not to trade for said Account. James TURNER. April 6, 1808.

(271) 25 Dollars Reward. Run away from the plantation of the Subscriber on Lake-PHELPS, in Tyrrel County, on the 10th of March, a negro man named ANTHONY. He is 21 years of age, has a smooth black skin, about 5 feet high, stout made, his fore-teeth are somewhat rotten, but he has not lost any of them. .. I expect he is at this time in Edenton or its vicinity, having relations at Mrs. HORNIBLOW's and also at her plantation... Ebenezer PETTIGREW. Tyrrel County, April 12, 1808.

Edenton Gazette, Extra. [20 April 1808.]

(272) Philadelphia, April 1. .. Important. The ship Baltic, arrived on the 29th ult. at New-York.. On the 18th March, in lat. 42, 12, long. 56, 24, spoke the ship Pocahontas, Thomas HARRIS, master, of and for Boston from Liverpool; Captain H. sailed on the 24th February, and on the 1st of March was captured by two French frigates..the Commodore of the frigates permitted the Pocahontas to proceed (after discharging the crates between decks into the sea), on condition that Capt. HARRIS should take on board without any supply of provisions, the officers and crews of the ships Eliza, William and Brutus. The Eliza, Elisha DUNBAR master, of New-York, from Liverpool for Charleston (belonging to Jacob BARKER of this city), was captured on the 17th Feb. and set on fire two hours after, allowing only time for the officers and people to take their clothes from her. The William, Chas. ROCKWELL master, of N. York, from Liverpool for Savannah, was captured on the 29th of February..and set her on fire the 1st of March. ...

(273) The Gazette. Edenton, April 20, 1808. .. New Edition of Expinasses Reports.--A new edition of this valuable work, published at Hartford, and edited by Thomas DAY, Esq. is offered to the public for sale. ...

20 April 1808

[Note: The first two pages of the regular edition for 20 April 1808 are missing.]

(274) The Gazette. Edenton, April 20, 1808. .. Albert GALLATIN is reported to have resigned the office of Secretary of the Treasury, and Gabriel DUVAL of this State is said to be designed as his successor. This is rumour and wants confirmation. Balt. Amer.—April 8.

(275) Died in this place, on the 15th inst. Benjamin WOODS, Esq. of Newbern, Attorney at Law, and United States Attorney for the North—Carolina district. His remains were followed to the silent tomb by most of the respectable inhabitants of Edenton, whose unaffected grief is the best eulogy which can be paid to his memory. ...

(276) A List of Letters remaining in the Post—Office, Edenton, April 1, 1808. William ANDREWS, Clerk and Master of Equity, Chas. C. BLOUNT, Micajah BUNCH and neighbors, Asa BROOKS, John BARCO, William CLARK, Benjamin COBB, Clerk of the District Court, Clerk of the Superior Court, Capt. Belcher DANIEL, Polly M'DONALD, Oliver GREEN, Elisha HALL, John HOLLOWELL, Sheriff of Chowan, Daniel JONES, T. JONES, Richard JONES, Arthur JONES, Alexander LAW, Miss Sarah MOORE, Phillip M'GUIRE, Oliver PIERCE, Nancy PARKHAM, Wm. RUSSELL, Edward REILY, Thomas and Lieut. SATTERFIELD, George E. SPRUILL, Mr. (blank) SMILIE, Mary SUGS, Henry TITUS, John STROTHER, Mrs. Mary VAIL, Richard WOOD, Elijah WARRINGTON, Jesse VAN NEAZ. Hend. STANDIN, P. M.

(277) A Philadelphia paper contains the following singular advertisement: "An enemy has done this thing." Sacred Writ. Adverse scenes in domestic life, and the cruel interference of others in my family circle, compel me publicly to state, that the woman who is by law my wife, has been induced to abuse my family. Though I cannot consent, hereafter, to be responsible for her contracts, it is far from my feelings to wage war, with woman, or add a stain to the reputation of her with whom I had lived with affection. ... Ashael HAWLEY.

Vol III. Wednesday, April 27, 1808. Num. 114.

(278) The Gazette. Edenton, April 27, 1808. .. 20 Dollars Reward. Runaway from the subscriber, on Friday, the 15th inst. a negro woman named DINAH, about 25 years of age, 4 feet 10 or 11 inches high, of a yellowish complexion, thick bushy hair, pretty thick lips, and slim spare made. She is the wife of negro HEWS, the property of Col. John BOND, of this County, and who is well known in Edenton as a river pilot; and who, as he informed me, would keep his wife out eternally. This circumstance is mentioned to remind those who may take her, that HEWS will, at the risque of his life, rescue her, should it come to his knowledge. ... Phillip M'GUIRE. Chowan County, April 25, 1808.

Vol III. Wednesday, May 4, 1808. Num. 115.

(279) The Gazette. Edenton, May 4, 1808. .. The Rev. Wm. P. HARDY, is expected to preach in the Court-House on Sunday next.

(280) Notice. The Copartnership of Anthony COPELAND and Co. having expired, Anthony COPELAND is authorised to receive and pay the debts of said concern. Charles WHITLOCK, Anthony COPELAND. Windsor, April 23, 1808.

(281) Mr. WILLS—Please to give the following address a place in your next week's paper. To the readers of the Edenton Gazette. You have no doubt observed a piece

(281) (Cont.) in last week's paper, signed James TURNER, dated April 6, 1808, in which he asserts that he gave me a signed account, and that it is paid, and I refuse to deliver it to him; which assertions are erroneous. The contents of the paper that said TURNER gave me, is as follows:--January 19, 1807. This day settled accounts with William P. HARDY, and find a balance due said HARDY of Thirty-Six Pounds, currency, which I promise to give him 18 barrels of merchantable Corn for, delivered at my plantation, on the sound, when applied for. .. James TURNER.

On the back of which is the following receipt:--Received, at several times in the course of the spring 1807, a parcel of Corn from James TURNER's plantation, on the sound, with a large portion of rotten and shattered Corn, and trash; so that after fanning it, we could scarcely use it for bread, and had also to fan it for the horses to eat; said by James TURNER to be 18 barrels of Corn. William P. HARDY. I leave it with you to say whether a paper of the above contents can, with propriety, be called a signed account. ... William P. HARDY. Bertie, April 23, 1808.

(282) Notice. On Tuesday, the 7th day of June next, will be Sold, at Elizabeth-City, by virtue of a decree of the Court of Chancery for Chowan county, at last April term, a Tract of Land, in Pasquotank county, belonging to Charles W. HARVEY, which he purchased of Joseph HARVEY; and also another Tract of Land, in the said county, belonging to the said Charles W. HARVEY, which he purchased of William STOTT. ... John B. BLOUNT, C. M. E. C. C. April 20th, 1808.

(283) Notice. On Saturday, the 25th day of June next, will be Sold, at Gates Court-House, by virtue of a decree of the Court of Chancery for Chowan county, at last April term, a Tract of Land, in Gates county, belonging to Jeremiah SPEIGHT. ... John B. BLOUNT, C. M. E. C. C. April 20th, 1808.

Edenton Gazette. Edenton, May 11, 1808--No. 116.

(284) The Gazette. Edenton, May 11, 1808. .. The President of the United States has appointed Mr. Beverly DANIEL, of Granville county, Marshal of the North-Carolina District. Mr. D. it is said, will reside in Raleigh.

(285) We are authorized to alter the reward offered by Phillip M'GUIRE in our last, for negro wench DINAH, from 20 to 50 Dollars.

(286) Persons having business in the office of Clerk of the Superior Court of Law for the County of Chowan, are requested to apply in the absence of the subscriber to Mr. James NORFLEET, who is authorized to act. James IREDELL, Cl'k. Edenton, May 7, 1808.

(287) Cow-Pox. The Subscribers have just received a supply of genuine Vaccine Matter, and will be happy to serve those gentlemen who may wish to have their families or their children inoculated. The infection has been communicated in a few cases, and the genuineness of the matter sufficiently established. SAWYER & NOR-COM. Edenton, May 10th, 1808.

(288) Lost or Mislaid, A Gold mourning Ring, set with five diamonds, and has the following inscription in enamel on the side, viz. Ann MOSELEY--ob:29th May, 1747, etat:59.--A reward of Twenty Dollars will be given by the Editor of this paper, to any person who may return the above Ring, and no questions asked. Edenton, 10th May, 1808.

Vol III. Wednesday, May 18, 1808. Num. 117.

(289)   The Gazette. Edenton, May 18, 1808. .. Died--on Thursday evening last, at the house of Henry FLURY, Esq. Mr. William WATSON, a native of this town.

(290)   We are under the necessity again of altering our days of publication to Thursday; owing to the Northern Mail being placed on the Summer establishment, which brings it in here on Wednesday evening.

(291)   A List of Acts, Passed at the first session of the tenth Congress. .. An act to extend certain privileges as therein mentioned to Anthony BOUCHERIE. .. An act to provide for the payment of certain expences incurred in the impeachment of Samuel CHASE. An act for the relief of Oliver EVANS. .. An act to provide for the payment of certain expences incurred in the inquiry into the conduct of John SMITH, a Senator from Ohio. .. An act for the relief of Samuel WHITING. .. An act for the relief of Edward WELD, Samuel BEEBEE and John DAVIDSON. .. An act granting William WELLS the right of pre-emption. .. An act for the relief of the legal representatives of Thomas BARCLAY, dec'd. .. An act for the relief of Matthew SMITH and Darius GATES, jointly, and Darius GATES, separately. .. An act for the relief of Phillip TURNER. .. An act for the relief of George HUNTER. An act authorizing the Secretary of the Treasury, to pay to the comptroller of the Treasury in trust the amount of certain bills drawn by John ARMSTRONG, minister from the United States to the Court of France, on the Treasury of the United States. .. An act for the relief of Joseph CHASE, Jared GARDNER, and others. ...

Vol. III. Thursday, May 26, 1808. Num. 118.

(292)   At a general court martial assembled on board the U. States' ship the Chesapeake, in the harbour of Norfolk..Virginia, on Monday the fourth day of January, in the year of our Lord one thousand eight hundred and eight, and continued by adjournment from day to day, until Monday the eighth day of February in the same year. Present. Capt. John RODGERS, President. Captains William BAINBRIDGE, Hugh G. CAMPBELL, Stephen DECATUR Jun. and John SHAW. Masters' Commandant, John SMITH, and David PORTER, Lieuts. Joseph TARBELL, Jacob JONES, James LAWRENCE, and Charles LUDLOW,) Members.
     The court pursuant to an order from the Honorable Robert SMITH, Secretary of the Navy..to Captain John RODGERS directed..the seventh day of December..one thousand eight hundred and seven, proceeded..to try James BARRON Esq. a Capt. in the Navy of the United States, upon the charges in the said warrant stated..gave the following Opinion: The first charge stated against Capt. James BARRON.."For negligently performing the duty assigned him." "Specification" 1st. "In that he did not visit the frigate Chesapeake, during the period she remained in Hampton Roads, and before she proceeded to sea.." 2d. "In that when he did visit her, he did not..examine particularly into her state and condition. .. 1st. It appears to the court, that Captain James BARRON did visit the frigate..twice..before she proceeded to sea..this specification is not proved. 2d. ..this second specification is not proved. ..Not Guilty under this first charge..
     The second charge..in the warrant..is..: "For neglect on the probability of an engagement to clear his ship for action." "Specification." 1st. "In that certain threats on the part of some commander of a British vessel of war..were known to or heard by the said James BARRON, and still he neglected to clear his ship for action." 2d. "In that there were various indications of a hostile disposition towards the frigate Chesapeake, exhibited by the..Leopard..still, that not withstanding these suspicious appearances..observed by..James BARRON, he neglected to clear his ship for action." .. The court having agreed in the proceeding (sic) opinions that Capt. James BARRON although not guilty of three of the charges preferred against him, is nevertheless guilty under that wherein he is

(292) (Cont.) accused "for neglecting on the probability of an engagement to clear his ship for action," do further agree..being guilty of this charge..they do adjudge and Sentence the said Captain James BARRON to be Suspended from all command in the navy of the U. States, and this without pay or official emoluments, of any kind, for the period & term of Five Years from this eighth day of Feb. in the year of our Lord one thousand eight hundred and eight. John RODGERS, Wm. BAINBRIDGE, Hugh G. CAMPBELL, St'hn. DECATUR, jr. John SHAW, John SMITH, D. PORTER, Jos. TARBELL, J. JONES, Jas. LAWRENCE, Charles LUDLOW. Littleton W. TAZEWELL, Judge Adv. ...

Vol. III. Thursday, June 2, 1808. Num. 119.

(293) The Gazette. Edenton, June 2, 1808. .. From the Pennsylvania Correspondent. Friend MINER, I have discovered that Train-Oil is a great destroyer of Caterpillars, equal to fire. I took a bottle that had the oil in, made a swab of long wool, put in the neck of the same, and destroyed 12 nests in a short time. Done at Milton, Solebury, Bucks county, by John KNIGHT. April 28. N. B. Give this a place in your Correspondent that we may get cyder and apples this year.

(294) Married--on Saturday evening last, Mr. William SATTERFIELD, to Mrs. Elizabeth HARRIS, widow of Thomas HARRIS, dec.

(295) We learn (says the Raleigh Minerva) that the following persons are appointed to command the quota of the standing army to be raised in this state:--Edward PASTEUR, of Newbern, a Colonel, Abner PASTEUR of do. a Captain; William JOHNSTON, of do. a Lieutenant; William BLOUNT, of Tennessee, now of Tarborough, son of the late Governor BLOUNT, a Captain; Robert RUFFIN, of Warrenton, a Captain.

(296) Departed this life, greatly lamented, on the 31st ult. Mrs. Nancy NORFLEET, the amiable consort of Elisha NORFLEET, Esq. aged 44 years. In all the relations of life, as a wife a mother, a neighbor and a friend, she was truly exemplary. The pains of a long and distressing illness, she supported with uncommon fortitude, patience and resignation; and in the last hours of her mortal life, she expressed that firm, rational and unshaken belief, that lively and confident hope in the merits and mediation of her blessed Redeemer, which afford a sweet, an ineffable consolation to her numerous and sorrowing friends, and imparts a pleasing hope that she participates the joys of a happy immortality. ...

(297) Spring Goods. Henry KING, Has received a handsome assortment of Spring and Summer Goods..for Sale on low terms for Cash. ...

(298) Extract of a letter from Albany, dated April 3d, and written by an intelligent and active member of the incorporated Society for the promotion of arts. "Of late there is a great spirit of manufacturing with us. .. There is a manufactory of broad cloth set up at Poughkeepsie by a Mr. BOOTH. He brought to this city last week a piece of his own manufacturing.. ..It was made of the Merino wool, which he purchased of Mr. L. R. LIVINGSTON. ...

(299) A Camp-Meeting Is to commence on Friday, the 10th June next, in the County of Gates, within a mile of the Court-House. It is desired that those who may avail themselves of the opportunity of this convocation, would come provided with tents and the other necessary provisions, to continue on the ground during the full period. Those who come by water to BENNETT's Creek Bridge, will be furnished with land carriage from the Bridge to the Camp ground. For individuals, or those persons who come unprovided, accommodations will be furnished at the Court House

(299) (Cont.) on reasonable terms. Phillip BRUCE, Presiding Elder. Enoch JONES, Assistant. May 25, 1808.

(300) Mr. Printer, Owing to the unexpected detention which I have experienced here, and the industrious malignity of James TAYLOR and others, the most unfavorable reports have been circulated respecting my character. Every attempt that the futile imagination of TAYLOR could suggest, has been made to destroy my reputation. The formality of a legal investigation is now an instrument in the hands of TAYLOR, which undoubtedly, for a short time, will serve to prop his blasted reputation. .. Although I was led to understand at the time Mr. MAYO was appointed, how and in what manner this investigation would terminate; yet I did not believe that there were men in this community of sound judgement and good understanding, who would consider the result of this business as an evidence of TAYLOR's innocence. ... Richard TUCK. Nixonton, May 4, 1808.

(301) Notice is hereby given to all the creditors of Joseph THACH, dec. of Perquimans County, that the said Joseph THACH is dead, and that the subscriber qualified as administratrix to his estate at the last term of Perquimans Court. All persons having claims against said estate are desired to exhibit them, properly attested, within the time limited by law, or they will be barred of recovery. Rosannah THACH, Adm'rx. May 20th, 1808.

Vol. III. Thursday, June 9, 1808. Num. 120.

(302) Baltimore, May 27. Arrived last evening, Spanish sch'r St. Salvadore, 12 days from Havanna, passenger, Capt. CHALMERS, who went out supercargo of the sch'r Lovely Lucy, KNOWLES, bound from this to Savannah. Capt. C. informs that on the 22d April, off Cape Romain, they were captured by the French privateer schooner Superior, who put a prize master and 8 men on board, and ordered her to Samana. They immediately ordered all the crew below, threatening to put us all in irons if we did not remain there. On the evening of the same day, experienced a very severe gale..she broached too, capsized and filled, then they cut away the masts, when she righted..she thumped several holes through her sides. The gale continuing with increased violence, in that situation they remained three days, when the decks bursted asunder. Capt. CHALMERS, Mr. William CAMPBELL, (a passenger) and three negro sailors were fortunate enough to get on that part of the deck that floated; the others were all drowned. They remained on that part of the deck 4 days, at the mercy of the waves, without provisions or water. On the 28th one of the negroes died; part of whose body they ate. On the 29th they were providentially picked up by the brig Nancies, from Norfolk bound to Havanna. Mr. CAMPBELL died on board the brig the evening of the day they were picked up.

(303) The Gazette. Edenton, June 9, 1808. .. Died—on Sunday the 29th ult. in Camden County, Mr. John W. BARCO, late of this town.

(304) Spring & Summer Goods. Just received from New-York, and for Sale by the Subscribers, a handsome assortment of Fancy & other Goods, which they will sell at reduced prices for Cash. M'COTTOR & MUIL. June 8th 1808.

(305) Grand Lodge of Virginia. At a general Assembly of the Most Excellent Supreme Grand Royal Arch Chapter of Virginia..held in the Mason's Hall of Norfolk, on the evening of Saturday the seventh day of the fifth month, (May) A. L. 5808— R. A. M. 2800--and A. C. 1808. Resolved unanimously, That the E. S. G. Scribe cause a notification of the establishment of the Supreme Grand Royal Arch Chapter of Virginia, to be notified in several of the Newspapers of this State.. Resolved

(305) (Cont.) unanimously, That the Most Reverend Supreme Grand High Priest be requested to summon a General Assembly of the Most Excellent Supreme Grand Royal Arch Chapter of Virginia, to be held in the City of Richmond, in December next, during the sitting, or soon after the rising, of the Grand Lodge of Virginia. (Extract from the minutes.) Teste, A. C. JORDAN, E. S. G. Scribe.

Vol. III. Thursday, June 16, 1808. Num. 121.

(306) Prospectus. Of a plan for disposing of the Arlington Improved Sheep, so as to promote the Woolen Manufacture of the united States.. .. The lambs will be delivered, upon producing a receipt for twenty dollars, deposited in the hands of either of the following gentlemen: General MASON, of Analostan Island, William HERBERT, Esq. of Alexandria, and John TAYLOE, Esq; of Mount Airy, in the state of Virginia.. ... George W. P. CUSTIS. Arlington House, 4th May, 1808.

(307) From an Alexandria Paper, May 17. Mr. SNOWDEN—On Saturday last, in the presence of Laurence LEWIS, Esq. I sheared nine Ewe lambs of the Arlington long wooled race.. ..the Arlington long wooled lambs, yield a pound of wool for every 14 lb. 7 oz. gross weight; and that the old country kind yield only a pound of wool for 30 lb. of gross weight. ... Wm. H. FOOTE.

(308) The Gazette. Edenton, June 16, 1808. .. Masonic. At a regular meeting of Cement Lodge No. 19, at St. Albans, (Vermont) May 2d A. L. 5808, pursuant to a report of the committee on the complaint against James S. ALLEN, a member of said Lodge, for a flagrant violation of the principles of Masonry. Resolved, That the said James S. ALLEN be and is hereby expelled this Lodge; and that the Secretary cause this resolution to be published agreeable to an ordinance of the Grand Lodge of this state. Rosewell HUTCHINS, Secretary.

(309) Married—on Tuesday evening in Perquimans County, Mr. Charles SKINNER, to the amiable Miss Mary CREECY, eldest daughter of William CREECY, Esq. of that County.

(310) Notice. That on Friday, the 29th day of July next, will be Sold, at a credit of Six Months, as much of the Land belonging to the estate of Col. John HARVEY, dec. as will satisfy the balance of the debts. By the Guardian. June 14th, 1808.

(311) Notice. All persons having claims against the estate of Demsey PARKER, dec. are requested to bring them in before the 16th of September next, or this notice will be plead in bar against those who do not. All those who are indebted to the said estate are desired to make immediate payment, as no further indulgence can be given. Hillary WILLEY, Ex'r. Gates, June 11, 1808.

(312) 25 Dollars Reward. Run away from the Subscriber some time since, a negro fellow named DIVER, about 40 years of age, 5 feet 10 or 11 inches high, very black, stout well set, and has a very domineering manner of conducting himself when among those of his colour, chews tobacco to excess, and is extremely fond of spirits. He was formerly the property of the late Captain Samuel BUTLER, of Edenton, of whom I purchased. He is a good sawyer, pretty well acquainted with hewing with the broad-axe, and can do tolerable good work at the carpenter's business.—I expect he has by some means procured a free pass, and is lurking about among his relations; having a mother in Nansemond County, Virginia, and a brother in DURANT's-Neck, the property of a Mr. DOALS or NOALS, mill-wright; or, in the lower part of Pasquotank County, near the shingle-Swamp.—I will give the above reward

(312) (Cont.) and all reasonable expences to any person who will bring said fellow to me, on the banks of Chowan river, 13 miles from Edenton, or secure him in any goal... Stephen SMITH. Chowan county, June 14, 1808.

(313) Five Hundred Dollars Reward. Treasury Department, May 28th, 1808. It has recently been made known to this department, that on the first day of June, 1807, the first moieties of the under-mentioned Notes of the bank of the United States, were enclosed by William KEAIS, Esq. Collector of the Customs at Washington, North-Carolina, in a letter addressed to Thomas Tudor TUCKER, Esq. Tresurer of the United States, and put into the Post-Office at that place; and on the 8th day of June, 1807, the second moieties of the said Bank Notes were enclosed, addressed and put into the Post-Office as aforesaid: neither of which letters..have been received. On the back of each moiety of every Note was written the name of William KEAIS, and on one part of the back..was written the name of Lewis LEROY.. Payment of the Notes has been stopped at the Bank of the United States..and a reward of Five Hundred Dollars will be paid to any person who shall give such information to this department, as shall produce the conviction of the offender by whom the letters..were purloined or stolen. Albert GALLATIN, Secretary of the Treasury.

Description Of Notes.

No.	Date.	To whom payable.		Dollars.
1401	20th July, 1804,	Adam GILCHRIST or Bearer at Charleston, for		100
1428	20th July, 1804,	do.	do.	100
2284	12th March, 1805,	do.	do.	100
4729	27th Feb. 1807,	do.	do.	100
4790	27th Feb. 1807,	do.	do.	100
2641	19th March, 1805,	Joseph HABERSHAM, Savannah,		100
2620	Do. do. do.	do.	do.	100
2666	Do. do. do.	do.	do.	100
2774	Do. do. do.	do.	do.	100
35	2d April, 1806,	W. WARNER at the Bank of the U. States,		100
3061	16th April, 1805,	Cornelius RAY, New-York,		100
3841	22d Jan. 1802,	do.	do.	100
1973	20th July, 1804,	Adam GILCHRIST, Charleston,		50
3609	12th March, 1805,	do.	do.	50
2183	20th July, 1804,	do.	do.	50
1265	23d March, 1804,	Joseph HABERSHAM, Savannah,		50
1355	23d do. do.	do.	do.	50
5597	18th Nov. 1806,	do.	do.	50
			Dollars,	1,500

May 30.

(314) Fatal Duel.--An altercation, arising from political discussion, between Mr. Thomas LEWIS, and Mr. John M'HENRY, at Fincastle, Virg. the former challenged the latter to fight with pistols; Mr. M'HENRY declined that instrument, and they concluded to use Rifles! They met; and both fell. LEWIS was shot through the heart; M'HENRY a little below; he died the day following. They fought-and with rifles--at fifteen paces. Federal Gazette.

Vol. III. Thursday, June 23, 1808. Num. 122

(315) Charleston, May 30. The following highly important case in the Federal Circuit Court, will be read with the deepest interest.. Courier. Ex parte, Adam GILCHRIST & others, vs. The Collector of the Port of Charleston.) In the Federal Circuit Court, May 28, 1808, before Judges JOHNSON and BEE. A motion was made by

23 June 1808

(315) (Cont.) Mr. WARD for rule on the Collector to show cause why a mandamus should not be issued against him, to compel the granting of clearances for the ship Resource, MORETON; ship Two Pollies, WILDER; ship Navigator, BOWDEN; ship Rising States, ANDERSON, and ship Louisa Cicilia, FOWLER, founded on the following affidavit: "Adam GILCHRIST, and J. S. BARKER, of Charleston, merchants, being severally sworn according to law, deposeth, That the American registered Resource, arrived from a foreign voyage in the port of Charleston about six months since, owned one half by the deponent, J. S. BARKER, residing in Charleston, and the other half by American citizens residing in Baltimore; That the deponent representing the owners aforesaid, apprehensive that the bottom of the ship might, by being detained here during the Embargo, be totally destroyed by worms, did for that reason determine on sending her to Baltimore, & regularly advertised for freight to said port of Baltimore; That having obtained the promise and actually engaged the freight, of about 600 bales of cotton, it became requisite to ship either ballast or heavy freight, so as to enable the said ship to be navigated with safety; That ballast not being obtainable, these deponents, about three weeks since agreed to carry to Baltimore about 200 barrels of rice, freight free, and that the same was shipped by permit from the custom house, and under the inspection of a revenue officer, about two weeks since; That on application for a clearance of the said ship and her cargo to Simeon THEUS, Collector of the port of Charleston..he hath refused to grant a clearance..alledging..that the clearance demanded is to cover an ostensible voyage to Baltimore, __ to infringe or evade the existing laws, relative? to the Embargo..he is bound to refuse such clearance, under the directions of the Executive of the United States... Adam GILCHRIST. J. Sanford BAKER." Sworn to before me this 24th of May 1808. John WARD, Q. U. ...
Judge JOHNSON delivered the following opinion of the Court. .. We are of opinion that the act of Congress does not authorize the detention of this vessel. .. A mandamus was ordered accordingly, commanding the Collector to grant a clearance to the Resource.

(316) The Gazette. Edenton, June 23, 1808. On Saturday last, a man calling himself Richard CANNON, of Chatham County, in this state, was detected in endeavouring to pass counterfeit Bank Bills of the Branch Banks of New-York, Charleston and Savannah, and Bills of the currency of this state. .. After an impartial and patient hearing, he was committed to gaol, from thence to be conveyed in a few days to the city of Raleigh. But owing to the insufficiency of the gaol, and the lenity observed towards prisoners here, he made his escape on Sunday evening. He is a stout young man, about 25 years of age, dark complexioned, large white eyes, has a down guilty look, dark hair, and has on the back part of his head a bunch of grey hairs. ...

(317) Married--on Tuesday evening the 14th inst. in Hertford County, Mr. George CAMPBELL, of Orange County, to Miss Mary SCOTT, second daughter of Gen. John SCOTT, of the former County.
Died--on Sunday morning last in Perquimans County, Thomas H. HARVEY, Esq. Clerk of the County Court of that County.

(318) Notice is hereby given, that the subscriber qualified as executrix to the last will and testament of Willis SAWYER, deceased, of Bertie county, at last May court. All persons having claims..are notified to make them known within the time limited by law; and it is requested that this may be done as soon as possible, that provision may be made to discharge the debts as speedily as possible. It is expected that those indebted to said dec. will make immediate payment. Sarah SAWYER, Ex'rx. Bertie, June 10, 1808.

(319) Notice. On Tuesday the 12th of July next, will be Sold, at public sale, at the late dwelling house of Willis SAWYER, dec. in Bertie county, a part of the Perishable Property of said dec. consisting of Horses, Cattle, work Stears, a Herring-Seine, with ropes, &c. Fish-Stands, empty Barrels, Salt, Corn, &c. ... Executrix. Bertie, June 20, 1808.

(320) Notice. The Copartnership of Jackson S. HOYLE and Drew S. WHITMELL, trading under the firm of HOYLE and WHITMELL, is this day dissolved by mutual consent. All persons having demands against said firm are requested to present their accounts; and all those indebted..to come forward and settle their respective amounts due by them with Jackson S. HOYLE, who is duly empowered to settle said firm. Jackson S. HOYLE, Drew S. WHITMELL. Edenton, 14th June, 1808.

(321) Broke Jail On Sunday evening last, Richard CANNON, of Chatham county, committed on a charge of attempting to pass counterfeit Bills of the Branch Banks of N. York, Charleston and Savannah. He is about 6 feet high, very stout made, short black hair, with a small bunch of grey hairs on the back part of his head, white eyes, appears to be about 25 years of age. .. He has a down guilty look; and must, I expect, cut a dirty appearance, having dug out of prison with no other clothes than what he had on. He was seen on Monday morning at sun-rise, on the road leading to Hertford. The day following he was seen near this town, enquiring the way to Gates county. I expect he will endeavor to cross Chowan river, and either make for home, or saunter into the state of Virginia. He left at Plymouth, on his way to this place, an elegant bay horse, and a pair of saddle-bags containing clothes and 18 dollars, one of which was counterfeit. The clothes..being marked I. K. induces me to believe that Richard CANNON, is an assumed name. I will give a reward of Fifty Dollars to any person who will take up said Richard CANNON and deliver him to me, or safely lodge him in the jail of Wake County. Edmond HOSKINS, Sh'ff. Edenton, June 22, 1808.

(322) 100 Dollars Reward. The above reward of One Hundred Dollars will be paid for apprehending and securing in any goal within the United States, Arthur HOWE, and negro MUSTAPHA, commonly called MUSS. Arthur HOWE is a young man 19 or 20 years old, dark complexion, short yellowish hair and hazle eyes, his face is round, and his countenance ferocious and expressive of dark angry passions. He is remarkable for having a deformity in his back, which occasions him to walk nearly half bent, so that when he is in his most erect posture, he would scarcely measure 4 and a 1-2 or 5 feet high. His arms have much motion when he walks, are very long, and hang as low down if not lower than his knees. The above described young man stole or enticed off on Monday night, the 11th inst. a negro fellow called MUSS or MUSTAPHA, about 28 years old, of a darkish complexion, very long head, forehead nose and chin more prominent than persons of his colour generally have, his eyes are large, projecting, and of a reddish colour, his mouth rather large, and his teeth yellow. In his general behaviour he is polite and submissive, he is a complete body servant, and a handy fellow with most tools or about horses. .. The above felon and slave went off on a single stick chair, a large bay horse, and have been traced in company about 18 miles from Edenton.--It is conjectured that Arthur HOWE will conduct MUSS as far as Virginia, and may sell him several times on his journey; and MUSS having many acquaintances in Norfolk, Petersburg and Richmond, may endeavour through their assistance to make his escape to the northward. Arthur HOWE has relations near Wilmington, in this state, and near Nashville, in Tennessee... Matthias E. SAWYER. Edenton, June 21st, 1808.

(323) Longevity.--Died, at Cornwall, Vermont, on the 30th ult. Mrs. Rebecca CLARK, in the 106th year of her age. This is the most remarkable instance of Lon-

(323) (Cont.) gevity which has ever been known perhaps in this State. She lived to see the fifth generation in her own family. Her posterity is supposed to be between two and three thousand.

Vol. III. Thursday, June 30, 1808. Num. 123.

(324) New-York, June 13. .. Yesterday the brig Sally-Ann, Capt. DANIELS, arrived at this port from St. Croix. Off the Capes of Philadelphia, she was chased by a French privateer; shortly after Captain D. fell in with a pilot-boat, and took on board..Mr. George COWELL, of Philadelphia, pilot, and stood close along shore, to avoid meeting with other privateers. ...

(325) The Gazette. Edenton, June 30, 1808. Soon after our last week's paper was worked off Richard CANNON, alias Richard KENON, who was advertised as having broke gaol, was brought back to this place, and put in close confinement. On Friday the Sheriff proceeded with him to Raleigh.

(326) Edward PASTEUR, Esq. of Newbern, having accepted the Colonelcy in the additional army of the United States..the office of Adjutant-General of this state is again become vacant.

(327) Extract of a letter from a gentleman in St. Mary's, to his friend in Savannah, dated 24th May, 1808. "A day or two ago all the property, at least all the provisions, for sale, belonging to Josiah SMITH of Savannah was seized by the Collector of St. Mary's and the officers of the gun boat, I believe, on suspicion of his being a smuggler—he has before been detected in thus violating the laws of our country. ..."

(328) Frogs. The following curious article is copied from a letter written by Dr. WILLIAMS, of the state of Vermont to a friend: "At Castleton, in the year 1779, the inhabitants were engaged in building a fort near the centre of town. Digging into the earth five or six feet below the surface, they found many frogs apparently inactive, and supposed to be dead. Being exposed to the air, animation soon appeared, and they were found to be alive and healthy. I have this account from general CLARKE and Mr. MOULTON, who were present when those frogs were dug up.
  A more remarkable instance was at Burlington, upon Onion river. In the year 1788, Samuel LANE, Esq. was digging a well near his house. At the depth of twenty five or thirty feet from the surface of the earth, the laborers threw out with their shovels something which they suspected to be ground roots, or stones covered with earth. Upon examining..they were found to be frogs, to which the earth every where adhered. An examination was then made of the earth in the well..a large number of frogs were found.. Being exposed to the air, they soon became active; but unable to endure the direct rays of the sun most of them perished. ...

(329) Salem, June 7. .. In the Raven came passenger Mr. THOMAS, late mate of the ship Union, of Plymouth, Miller SMITH, master. ...

Vol. III. Thursday, July 7, 1808. Num. 124.

(330) Philadelphia, June 22. .. In the fall of the year 1806, a Swedish sch'r. with a cargo of considerable value, both owned by a Swedish subject, and under the care of Mr. John NAGLEE, an American supercargo, sailed from this port for the Isle of Cuba. In the voyage she was captured by the privateer Dolphin, commanded by Capt. BROUVARD. ...

(331) Charleston, June 16. .. State of Georgia, St. Mary's. Personally appeared Robert BROWNLOW, who being duly sworn, deposeth and saith—That on the 4th day
of June, in the year of our Lord one thousand eight hundred and eight, while in
the brig Charles, of Baltimore, of which this deponent is master, lying in Amelia
sound, within the province of East-Florida, he was boarded and taken possession of
by Ant. BONASSON, Louis FELLIR, and Jean Baptiste CARVINE, owners and master of
the armed schooners Exchange and Jean Estelle, and forcibly deprived of two
hundred barrels superfine flour, the property of this deponent; and this deponent
further states, that he will be entirely without redress, if the property of the
said BONASSON, FELLIR, and CARVINE, is not attached to answer the demand of this
deponent; and further, that he is endamaged to the amount of six thousand dollars,
by the loss of the..flour; by reason of the detention aforesaid, and the failure
of his voyage and sale of the said flour. Sworn to before me, this 7th day of
June, in the year of our Lord one thousand eight hundred and eight, at St. Mary's,
in the state of Georgia. Robert BROWNLOW. Hormen COURTEZ, J. P.

(332) The Gazette. Edenton, July 7, 1808. .. On Saturday afternoon the 18th
ult. a sloop going from New-York to Tinicock Point and Rye, upset, and every
person on board was lost.—Joseph BROWN was the master of the sloop.

(333) Salem, June 21. Spanish News. Mr. Peter LANDER, of this town, who came
passenger in the sch'r Hannah, which sailed from Gibraltar the 10th of May, and
arrived at Marblehead on Sunday last, has favoured us with the following minute,
which we received from Capt. Joseph YOUNG, of the ship Native, which had arrived
at Gibraltar from Malaga: "The grand duke of Berg was to be appointed Regent at
Spain, in the absence of the Royal Family at Bayonne, when a grand council was to
be held on the subject of the Confederation of the Rhine. ..."

(334) Communicated. Died much lamented by her surviving relations and numerous
acquaintance, on the 28th ult. Mrs. Julia SOUTHALL, the amiable and respectable
consort of Daniel SOUTHALL, Esq. of Gates C. House. The benefits resulting from
an early dedication of herself to God, and an uniform pious life in his sacred
service to her last hour, was manifested in her dying moments. Though severely
afflicted, which she bore with a Job-like patience, she assured her weeping
friends who attended her dying moments, that Death was no terror, and exulted in
the opening prospects of immortal joys. About 36 hours after, her Infant Daughter
about 5 months old, followed her to the Paradise of God.

(335) Died—on Saturday evening last, in Bertie County, Capt. Cornelius RYAN, an
inhabitant of that County.

(336) Notice. On Saturday, the 15th inst. the Commissioners of the town of Edenton will offer to the lowest bidder, the building of a new Market in the said
town; a plan of which can be seen on application to the Subscriber, or any one of
the Commissioners. The terms of payment will be made known on the day of Sale.
At the same time will be sold to the highest bidder, the materials of the old
Market. John B. BLOUNT, Town Clerk. Edenton, July 1, 1808.

(337) Letters remaining in the Post-Office at Edenton, 1st July, 1808. William
ANDREWS, John BARCO, Thomas BROWNRIGG, William CLARK, John BRITTON, Clerk of Su-
perior Court, Joshua CREECY, Samuel CHESSON, Isaac COLLINS, Benjamin COFFIELD,
Samuel COLLINS, Clerk of the District Court, Asa CHAMBERLAIN, Hannah DILLON,
Nathan ETHERIDGE, Russel FOWLER, Thomas GUY, Charles G. RIDGELY, Henry GREY, John
GILMORE, John HOLLOWELL, Ebenezer JESTER, William JONES, David LAW, Peter P. LAW-
RENCE, King LUTON, Wm. MEEKINS, Frederick M'COY, Mrs. M'GLAUKLIN, Alexander MIL-

7 July 1808

(337) (Cont.) LEN, John M'CRAE, John M'NIDER, Ebenezer PAINE, James POOL, John SALESBURY, Thomas SMITH, William SANDERS, Henry TITUS, Nathan TRUEBLOOD, Charity THOMPSON, James WATT, Jesse WEST. Hend. STANDIN, P. M.

(338) Nassau, (N. P.) May 21. Longevity.--Died, at Harbor Island, on the 11th inst. Flora THOMPSON, a black woman, aged 150 years; she was born in Africa in the year 1658, and carried to Jamaica, as a slave, soon after that island came into the possession of Great Britain..she was brought to Nassau, during the time this Island was in possession of the pirates, and sold to Mr. Wm. THOMPSON; on his decease she became the property of his son John THOMPSON, Esq. with whom she continued until his death, about 48 years ago, and then obtained her freedom. ...

Vol. III. Thursday, July 14, 1808. Num. 125.

(339) The Gazette. Edenton, July 14, 1808. .. Dreadful Tornado--Between the hours of one and two P. M. yesterday, the attention of the citizens of Knoxville was called to witness a scene the most awfully majestic, which has or may present itself to human eyes. .. This spectacle..was viewed with indescribable satisfaction, when the citizens of Knoxville found it had crossed the Holstein about three quarters of a mile below the town.. .. Many of the most beautiful plantations on the river, are said to be stripped entirely of their improvements--amongst others, we have heard particularly of Mr. Jas. MILLER's, five miles from this place, on the Nashville road. We have heard of only two lives..lost, but fear that is not all. Knoxville paper.

(340) Died--late on Wednesday evening last, in the 50th year of his age, Mr. William ROMBOUGH, a respectable native inhabitant of this town.

(341) State of North-Carolina, Chowan County Court,} June Term, 1808. Whereas, Franklin CORNELL and Co. hath sued out an original attachment against the estate of Charles JAUNDUS, late of Edenton, returnable before the County Court of Pleas and Quarter-Sessions for the County aforesaid--It is Ordered, That public notice be given to the said Charles JAUNDUS, by advertisement in the Edenton Gazette, for three months; that unless he appears at the next term of the said Court..at Edenton, on the second Monday in September next, replevy his estate, and plead to this action, final judgment will be entered up against him. By order, Elisha NORFLEET, Cl'k. July 13, 1808.

(342) Trial of Commodore BARRON. As soon as a sufficient number of Subscriptions are procured, to defray the cost of the Paper, Will Be Published, At The Ledger Office, Norfolk, The Whole Proceedings In The Trials of Commodore James BARRON, Capt. Charles GORDON, Commandant of the U. States' frigate Chesapake, John HALL, Esq. Capt. of Marines, and William HOOK, Gunner. ... The Editor Of The Public Ledger. Norfolk, July 1, 1808.

(343) Mammoth Children!--How sportive is nature. Sometimes adding, sometimes diminishing! As a proof of the former, we mention that Capt. John SIMPSON, in Pendleton district, S. C. has a daughter and son--the former, Eleanor SIMPSON, aged 170 years, in height 5 feet 2 inches, weighs 180 pounds; the latter, John O. SIMPSON, aged 4 years, is 4 feet high, and weighs 90 pounds. Pendleton paper.

Vol. III. Thursday, July 21, 1808. Num. 126.

(344) Washington-City, July 4. .. It has been proved to the satisfaction of this court, that Brigadier General James WILKINSON had been engaged in a tobacco

(344) (Cont.) trade with Governor MIRO of New-Orleans, before he entered the American army in 1791; that he received large sums of money for tobacco delivered in New-Orleans, in the year 1789, and that a large quantity of tobacco, belonging to him, was condemned and stored in N. Orleans in that year.. It has been stated by the General that after his damaged tobacco had laid some years in store at New-Orleans, his agent there received for it and remitted to him, the several sums, credited in the copy of an account current presented by him..and under the impression that the letters accompanying the said account were written by his said agent Philip NOLAN, the court think it highly probable that the statement is correct. .. It is therefore the opinion of this court, that there is no evidence of Brigadier Gen. James WILKINSON's having at any time received a pension from the Spanish government..and the court has no hesitation in saying, that as far as his conduct has been developed by this enquiry, he appears to have discharged the duties of his station with honor to himself and fidelity to his country. City of Washington, June 28, 1808. (Signed) H. BURBECK, President. T. H. CUSHING, Jona. WILLIAMS, Members. July 2, 1808. Approved, (Signed) Th: JEFFERSON.

(345) New-York, July 5. .. July 6. .. Yesterday arrived the long expected ship Osage, DUPLEX, 48 days from Falmouth, with dispatches, from France and England. Passengers, Lt. LEWIS, Wm. OLIVER, Wm. BAYARD, Jun. Hermon LE ROY, Jun. Charles BLODGET, Joshua MOSES, Wm. PINCKNEY, Jun. and Jos. HOWLAND, Jun. together with the following who belonged to American vessels detained and condemned in England, viz. Samuel KING, Abishai MACEY, Wm. P. JONES, Abishai SWAINE, Edward JENKINS, Adam CHAMPLAIN, A. FELIX, and E. MURPHY. ...

(346) The Gazette. Edenton, July 21, 1808. .. On Monday, the 4th of July, being the Anniversary of American Independence, the Citizens of Pitch-Landing and its vicinity, and a great number of respectable citizens from Bertie; with a large collection of respectable Ladies from both counties, met at the house of Mrs. HILL, for the purpose of celebrating the day; when James JONES, Esq. was chosen President, and Gen. John SCOTT, Vice-President, they sat down to an elegant Dinner, prepared for the occasion...

(347) Married--on the 10th instant, In Camden County, Capt. James HATHAWAY, Jun. of this town, to Miss Sarah WARDEN, of that county.
　　Died--on Thursday last, at the house of Mrs. SMALL, of the dropsy, Mons. Valentine AUSSANT, a native of Merseilles, in France. At his seat in Dedham, Massachusettes, on the 4th inst. the Hon. Fisher AMIS.

(348) Collector's-Office. Edenton, 19th July, 1808. The President of the United States having deemed it expedient to extend the time for granting permissions to send vessels in ballast to places in the West-Indies, or to any port of America, North of the line, for the purpose of bringing property into the United States, under the 7th section of the act of the 12th March last--Notice is hereby given, that permissions will be granted at this office, provided that application be made prior to the first day of August next; after which none will be granted. Samuel TREDWELL, Coll'r.

(349) State of North-Carolina, Chowan County Court,) June Term, 1808. Whereas, Joseph UNDERHILL, administrator of Thomas FITT, dec. hath sued out an original attachment against the estate of James DEANE, late of Turk's-Island, dec. returnable to this Court at this term--It is Ordered, That public notice be given to Mary DEANE, executrix, Benjamin BASCOME, George BASCOME, and William, James, and Michael DEANE, executors of the said James DEANE, by advertisement in the Edenton Gazette for three months; that unless they appear at the next term of the said

21 July 1808

(349) (Cont.) Court..at Edenton, on the second Monday in September next, replevy the said estate, and plead to the said action, final judgment will be entered up against them. By order, Elisha NORFLEET, Cl'k.

Edenton Gazette. Thursday, July 28, 1808. No. 127.

(350) Marry for Money. Died--Lately, in Starbrook, [Ten.] Oliver HEARD, Esq. attorney at law, aged 27.--He had just married a blooming widow of 88 years, who had led him to suppose she possessed the attractive charms of $8000 property, but who unfortunately did not possess an 8000th part of that sum--Finding he had lost his cause and mortified at the non-suit he took an affectionate leave of his tender and amiable consort--and, drinking her reformation in a bowl of poison, added suicide to the crime of rank speculation.

(351) From the New-York Gazette. From Washington, July 9. The President..made the following appointments this day--"William DUANE, Lieut. Colonel commandant of the twenty fifth regiment Pennsylvania militia, to be Lieut. Colonel of the first regiment of riflemen in the U. States Service. Jonas SYMONDS, Lieutenant Col. of the fiftieth regiment Pennsylvania militia, to the command of the sixth regiment of infantry in the U. States service."

(352) The Gazette. Edenton, July 28, 1808. The President of the U. States has appointed Robert H. JONES, Esq. of Warrenton, attorney of the U. States for this district, in the place of Benjamin WOODS, dec.

(353) Raleigh, July 14. Dr. Calvin JONES of this city, is appointed by Gov. WILLIAMS, Adjutant-General of the Militia of this state, in the room of Dr. PASTEUR of Newbern, recently appointed a Colonel of the standing army about to be raised.

(354) To the Honourable the Judges of the Superior Courts of law and Equity of the State of North Carolina. In March last, I laid before the Council of State, Petitions from the counties of Chatham, Cumberland and Martin, together with a Presentment from the Grand Jury of the County of Grenville, representing the distresses of the inhabitants of those counties in consequence of the existing Embargo, and praying that the Legislature might be convened for the purpose of suspending the process of the law with respect to executions for debt. The Council of State, after deliberately discussing the subject, deemed it inexpedient to comply with the prayer of the petitions.. Since which time, the following petitions and presentments of Grand Juries..have been received, viz: One from Duplin County, one from Caswell County, two from Granville County, three from Bladen County, one from Anson County, together with a presentment of the Grand Jury of the County Court; a presentment from the Grand Jury of the County Court of Johnston; a presentment of the Grand Jury of the Superior Court of Greene County, and a presentment of the Grand Jury of the last Federal Court.
I am disposed to infer, from these petitions, that they express the sense of the several counties..because they are signed by some of the most respectable characters in the counties respectively, and..no counter petitions have been offered. .. I now..take the liberty of applying to you for information respecting the necessity and expediency of this measure.--Your situation in the courts, your having lately visited the different parts of the State, have given you opportunities of knowing the extent of the pecuniary embarrassments under which the citizens labor, and..duly estimate the probable effects and utility of the measure which these petitions have so much at heart. ... B. WILLIAMS. Raleigh, July 4, 1808.

(355) The Judges' Reply. Raleigh, July 5, A. D. 1808. Sir, With every disposition to furnish your Excellency with the information requested..we find..that we scarcely witnessed any further indications of the public sentiment than such as are contained in the petitions..laid before you. ... John L. TAYLOR, John HALL, Frans. LOCKE, Blake BAKER. His Excellency Benj. WILLIAMS, Esq.

(356) Married--on Tuesday evening last, at Mr. BENNETT's, Capt. Nathaniel BISSEL, to Miss Mary MARE, both of this county.
   Died--a few days past, in Tyrrell County, Capt. Woolsey HATHAWAY, sen. of that county.

(357) Wells COOPER, vs. The President and Directors of the Dismal Swamp Canal Com'y.} In Equity, March Term, 1808. Walter HERON & Thomas MORRAN, surviving partners of William PLUME and Co. having failed to put in their answer in the above suit; and it being represented to the Court that they are not inhabitants of this State--It was Ordered, That four weeks public notice be given in the Edenton Gazette, that unless they appear and put in their answer before the first Monday after the fourth Monday in September next, judgement pro confesso will be entered up against them. Teste, John B. BLOUNT, C. & M. E. C. C.

(358) Lost, Some time in the month of June last, A Note of Hand, given by Dr. Andrew KNOX to James R. BENT, and endorsed by him to me, for $55 30 cts. dated the 29th of February, 1808. All persons are cautioned against trading for said note. Stephen SMITH.

Edenton Gazette. Thursday, August 4, 1808. No. 128.

(359) The Gazette. Thursday, August 4, 1808. .. Hudson, (N. Y.) July 12. Providential escape.--On Friday last, as Captain John SWIFT, of this city, was employed in depositing a quantity of flax in the Claverack creek, for the purpose of water-rotting it, influenced by the warmth of the season, and the agreeable temperature of the water, he plunged into the stream, to enjoy the pleasure of a cold bath. Having never been..an expert swimmer..he was immediately carried by the rapidity of the current, to a deep place in the river, and there went to the bottom. Being instantly sensible of his danger, he attempted, as he rose to the surface of the water, to call for assistance to a Mr. HUTCHINSON, a man in his employ, who was depositing the flax at a small distance below him. But as he was in a measure strangled, he failed to excite the attention of HUTCHINSON, and again went to the bottom. As he rose the second time he found himself too much exhausted to attempt calling for help, and went down the third time. .. Just at this critical moment, a large dog belonging to the Captain seeing his master in distress, leaped into the stream, and swam to the place where he last disappeared.-- As he rose again, he was so fortunate as to lay hold of his dog. He was immediately brought to the shore, supported, as he supposed, by his friend HUTCHINSON; but how great must have been his astonishment and gratitude when he found that he had been preserved from a watry grave..by the wonderful sagacity of his faithful dog! Balance.

(360) Just published, And for Sale at this Office, Price 30 Cents, The New-England Farrier: or A Compendium of Farriery..By Paul JEWETT.

(361) Mr. HALL, Sir, In your last paper I observed an advertisement of one Matthias E. SAWYER, offering a reward of One Hundred Dollars for apprehending and securing me in any jail within the United States, stating that I had stolen off a fellow of his named MUSS or MUSTAPHA, and that I left Edenton in the night. To

4 August 1808

(361) (Cont.) which assertion I give the lie, for I left Edenton after an early dinner in the day time—openly—and did hire his fellow for a guide, and gave him twenty-five dollars; and on my arrival at Mr. GRANGE's did discharge the fellow, and gave him a pass to return, and thought he was gone; but when I saw the advertisement, Mr. GRANGE, Mr. KEA and myself made inquiries about him, and finding he was not gone, we pursued him, took him, and lodged him in Wilmington jail. Now if my intention was as Mr. SAWYER states, would I have come immediately to Wilmington? would I not have offered him for sale, and not have discharged him as I did?

No—the fact is, that Mr. SAWYER and myself last winter had a dispute for having shot some robbins off a tree before his door. He abused me, and I made him retreat in his house. After a while he came out, shook hands, and said he was sorry for what he had said. This is all that I can at present recollect that could have made Mr. SAWYER advertise me in the rascally manner he has done. However, I shall wait until Mr. SAWYER shall come on here for me, and he shall find me at any time. Now it is well known in Edenton that this fellow has been for years in the habit of hiring himself from his master, and travelling with gentlemen from Edenton to Newbern, and often to this place as a servant. Arthur HOWE, Jun. Wilmington, July 12, 1808.

N. B. The Printer in Edenton is requested to insert this advertisement three times in his paper, and he will be paid by sending on his bill to Mr. HALL, and Mr. HOWE's friends are requested to send on depositions to clear his character, to me in Brunswick county. John GRANGE.

[Having published the advertisement of Dr. SAWYER respecting Arthur HOWE, jun. and being requested by Mr. GRANGE, a relation of said HOWE, to insert the above; we deem it but justice to Dr. SAWYER to say, that the above production, as far as comes within our knowledge, is totally unfounded. MUSTAPHA, we are informed by the Doctor, has never, since he owned him, been allowed to hire his own time. HOWE's intentions certainly were bad, having, as we are credibly informed, taken the fellow off in the night; and his having crossed Chowan river next morning a little after day-light, savors very much of roguery. We regret (on account of his respectable connections) that it is not in our power to say any thing favorable of this young man.] Ed. E. Gaz. The Printer at Wilmington is requested to give this one insertion.

Edenton Gazette. Thursday, August 11, 1808. No. 129.

(362) Indian War. St. Louis, May 26. Sir, The bearer hereof is a chief among the Delawares who reside on Apple Creek in this territory. He has been selected by the Delawares, Shawanese, Miamies, &c. in your territory the substance of speech (sic) which I lately made to the Shawanese and Delawares at this place, with respect to the Osage nation. The Osage have killed one of our citizens more than 18 months since and have failed to deliver the murderer, they have beaten, maimed, wounded and otherwise insulted and mal-treated others; they have stolen a large number of our horses, they have wantonly killed and destroyed our cattle, they have plundered our frontier inhabitants of their clothes, house hold furniture, &c... I have in several late conferences with the Shawanese, Delawares, Kipapoos, Soos, Saires, Jaways, &c. declared the Osage no longer under the protection of the United States, and set them at liberty to adjust their several differences with that abandoned nation in their own way, but have prohibited their attacking them except with a sufficient force to destroy or drive them from our neighbourhood. The WHITE HAIR the great chief of the Osage is now with me, he has found it impracticable to govern this nation, and has therefore repaired to this place for protection. .. Under these circumstances I hope that you will permit the Indians in your territory to take their own measures for attacking the Osage. ... Meriwhether LEWIS. His Excellency, Wm. H. HARRISON, Gov.

11 August 1808

(362) (Cont.) of Indiana Territory.

(363) The Gazette. Thursday, August 11, 1808. Members of Assembly chosen at the last election. Bertie.--George OUTLAW, Senate. Joseph H. BRYAN and William EASON, Commons.

(364) With the deepest regret, we have to announce the death of the Honorable Stephen CABARRUS, Esquire; during many years a distinguished Member and Speaker, of the Assembly of this State. He died, at his seat, near Edenton, on the 4th instant, aged 54 years. The perfect and undeviating rectitude, which at all times marked his conduct, in his many public and social relations, his humane and charitable disposition, his amiable manners and improved understanding, render his loss a subject of deep and universal regret. .. His mortal remains were followed to the grave by a numerous concourse of respectable inhabitants...

(365) Lands for Sale. Will be Sold, for ready money, before the Court-House door in the County of Tyrrel, on Tuesday, the 20th day of September next, the following Lands, or so much thereof as will discharge the Taxes due for 1806 and 1807, with all such extraordinary charges as are allowed by law in like cases, viz. 22,500 Acres of Land and Juniper Swamp, lying near the east end of Pungo Lake, late the property of Generals JONES and DAVIE, conveyed by them to a certain James STRANGE-WAY. 640 Acres lying on Whipping-Creek, on the east side of Great Alligator river, supposed to be the property of Philip HUNNINGS, dec. 100 Acres adjoining the Lands of William BRICKHOUSE, the property of Nathaniel WILLIAMS, dec. 400 Acres inlisted by David COOPER for Robert LEACH. 1300 Acres listed by Elisha and Abel BELANGA, late the property of Elisha BELANGA, sen. which Land was sold by the Marshal of this state to satisfy a judgment obtained in the Federal Court in favor of Smith FOSETT, against the said Elisha BELANGA, sen. 5080 Acres valuable Juniper Swamp, lying on the east side of Great Alligator river, the property of the late Arthur JONES, dec. James HOSKINS, Sh'ff. July 20th, 1808.

(366) Notice. The annual examination of the Students in Edenton Academy, will commence on Thursday, the 25th of August. On the Saturday following will be an exhibition as usual, in the Court-House by the young gentlemen of the Institution. ... Joseph B. SKINNER, Sec'ry. August 10th, 1808.

Edenton Gazette. Thursday, August 18, 1808. No. 130.

(367) The Gazette. Thursday, August 18, 1808. .. Further returns of Members of Assembly chosen at the late Elections. Chowan--Thomas BROWNRIGG, Senate. Baker HOSKINS and Samuel M'GUIRE, Commons. Town of Edenton--William A. LITTLEJOHN, Esq. and Dr. James NORCOM were candidates--After a warmly contested election, upon counting out the ballots, a doubt arose as to which of the candidates was elected. At length after a consultation of the Sheriff and Inspectors, the Sheriff declared in favor of Mr. LITTLEJOHN. We understand that Dr. NORCOM intends to contest the election. .. Perquimans--Willis RIDDICK, Senate. Isaac BARBER & Josiah TOWNS-END, Commons. Washington--Daniel DEVENPORT, Senate. John FRAZIER and Levan BOZMAN, Commons. Tyrrel--Jesse ALEXANDER, Senate. Moses E. CATOR and Levi BATE-MAN, Commons. Gates--Joseph RIDDICK, Senate. Humphrey HUDGINS & Cader BALLARD, Commons. Hertford--Robert MONTGOMERY, Senate. Lewis WALTERS and Abner PERRY, Commons. Granville--Major Thomas TAYLOR, Senate. William ROBARDS and Samuel PARKER, Commons. ROBARDS and WASHINGTON had an equal number of votes, and the Sheriff decided in favor of ROBARDS.
    This day the different Sheriffs meet at Hertford, to deliver in the number of Votes given for Member of Congress for this district. From the Counties we heard

(367) (Cont.) from Mr. SAWYER has a considerable majority; and there seems to be but little doubt..that he will be re-elected by a very large number of Votes over William H. MURFREE.

(368) Lost, On Saturday last, the 13th instant, A Note of Hand, given by William SLADE in favor of Jackson HOYLE, for $64 83 cents, dated 11th June last, & payable either one or three days after date. All persons are cautioned from receiving the said note in payment; and, whoever may have found it, will oblige the subscriber by returning it to him. Hezekiah GORHAM. Edenton, August 15, 1808.

Edenton Gazette. Thursday, Aug. 25. No. 131.

(369) Burlington, (Ver.) August 5. Melancholy event.--We have to record a melancholy event which took place in this vicinity on Wednesday last. A revenue cutter from the lines, commanded by Leiut. FARRINGTON, with a serjeant and 12 privates was dispatched by the collector of the customs in pursuit of a large batteau, called the Black-Snake, owned by persons near the lines, well known here to have been some time employed in smuggling. The Cutter pursued her up Onion river, where she was found and taken possession of by Lieut FARRINGTON, while her crew who were armed, stood on the bank of the river, and threatened to fire on the first man who went on board. ..They had not gone more than one hundred rods before they were fired on from the shore..and one man on board the cutter was shot through the head, and immediately expired. Several more shots were made, when the Lieut. ordered his men to steer for the shore.
   Scarcely had they landed when the whole contents of a large gun, called a wall piece, about ten feet in length, carrying 16 ounce balls was discharged upon them, which proved fatal to Asa MARSH another of the crew of the cutter and Mr. Jonathan ORMSBY, an inhabitant of this town, who returning from his work, happened to be present at this unfortunate moment. The Lieutenant also received a ball through his left arm and was slightly wounded in his head.--By the spirited exertions of the people of this village, eight persons were apprehended and are safely loged in the common gaol, which is guarded by a detachment of the town militia. .. Just as this paper was going to press, Capt. HARMON..arrived here with a person called Captain PEAS, one of the crew of the Black Snake. He was apprehended on Hog-Island.

(370) The Gazette. Edenton, August 25, 1808. Further returns of Members of Assembly chosen at the late elections. Currituck--Thos. WILLIAMS, Senate. Willoughby DOZIER and Willis SIMMONS, Com's. Camden--Nathan SNOWDEN, Senate. Caleb PERKINS and Thomas BELL, Commons. Pasquotank--William S. HINTON, Senate. Marmaduke SCOTT and John MULLEN, Com's. Halifax--M. C. WHITAKER, Senate. William WILLIAMS and Lewis DANIEL, Commons. Town of Halifax--William P. HALL. Northampton--William EDMUNDS, Senate. Francis A. BYNUM and Col. John HARRISON, Commons. Warren--P. HAWKINS, Senate. W. R. JOHNSON and J. HARWELL, Commons. Franklin--John FOSTER, Senate. Thomas H. ALSTON and James HILL, Commons. Beaufort--Frederick GRIST, Senate. Col. James WILLIAMS and Jonathan MARSH, Com's. Craven--Henry TILLMAN, Senate. John S. NELSON and Stephen HARRIS, Commons. Town of Newbern--William GASTON. Carteret--Elijah PIGOTT, Senate. Jacob HENRY and J. ROBERTS, Commons. Jones--Enoch FOY, Senate. Edm. HATCH and James C. BRYAN, Commons. Duplin--Joseph T. RHODES, Senate. Jas. M'INTIRE and Daniel GLISSON, Commons. Onslow--Stephen WILLIAMS, Senate. Edward WILLIAMS and John SPICER, Commons.

(371) From the returns of the different Sheriffs of this district, we are enabled to state, that Lemuel SAWYER, Esq. is re-elected a member of Congress by a majority of 1116 votes over William H. MURFREE, Esq. John STANLY, Esq. is elected for

25 August 1808

(371) (Cont.) the Newbern district, by a majority of 185 votes over William BLACKLEDGE, Esq. Mr. William KENNEDY, is elected for the Edgecomb district, by a majority of near 180 votes over Gen. Thomas BLOUNT.

(372) Married--on Sunday evening last, at the house of Henry FLURY, Esq. Capt. Edward HUNNINGS, to Miss Nancy HARRIS.

(373) A Camp-Meeting Will commence on Friday, September the 9th, at BRIDGES-Creek-Chapel, Northampton County, and end the Tuesday following. All who wish to be profited should come provided to stay on the ground. ... Philip BRUCE, Presiding Elder. Enoch JONES, Robert A. ARMISTEAD, Thomas MORE,) Ast'ts.

(374) Notice is hereby given, that Cornelius RYAN, Esq. of Bertie County, is dead, and that the subscriber administered on his estate at the last term of Bertie County Court. All persons indebted..are requested to make payment; and those having claims..to exhibit them within the time limited by law. Jehu NICHOLLS, Adm'r.

Vol. III. Thursday, September 1, 1808. Num. 132.

(375) New-York, August 13. .. August 15. While we publish with pleasure, the following Note, received this morning from Mr. ASTOR, it is proper to state, that the source of the information, on which our article was grounded, has been communicated to him.. To the Editor of the Commercial Advertiser. Mr. LEWIS, I observed in your paper of the 13th inst. a piece inviting the public attention to a transaction..of a most extraordinary complexion, relative to the ship Beaver and the Mandarin. If the author..will please to give his name, and if he is not prejudiced against every act of the Administration, nor influenced by envy arising from jealousy, he shall receive a statement of facts relative to the transaction in question... John Jacob ASTOR. New-York, August 15.

(376) The Gazette. Edenton, September 1, 1808. On Thursday instant, commenced the annual examination of the Students of Edenton Academy. The proficiency manifested by the Students..were highly honorary to themselves, and the institution of which they are members. .. The performances were concluded, by an affectionate and respectful valedictory address, to his fellow Students, the Trustees of the Academy, and to the audience, by Master Nathan NEWBY... Edenton, Aug. 30, 1808.

(377) Tuesday the 16th ult. was the day fixed for the meeting of the Council of State, agreeably to the call of the Governor. They did not form a quorum till next day, when a communication was made to them by the Governor, which is under consideration.--Mess. James MEBANE and Jordan HILL, two of the Council, had resigned their offices, the former being elected a Senator for Orange county, and the latter Clerk of the Superior court of Franklin County--Raleigh Register.

(378) Further Election Returns. Wake--Allen ROGERS, Senate. Allen GILCHRIST and Nathaniel JONES, Commons. Johnston--John WILLIAMS, Senate. Joseph BOON, jun. and Joseph RICHARDSON, Com's. Wayne--James RHODES, Senate. William SMITH and Ezekial SLOCUM, Commons. Lenoir--Simon BRUTON, Senate. William BRANTON and John WOOTEN, Commons. Duplin--Joseph T. RHODES, Senate. Daniel GLISSON and Andrew M'INTIRE, Commons. Sampson--Joab BLACKMAN, Senate. Jesse DARDEN and William KING, Commons. Cumberland--John DICKSON, Senate. Donald M'QUEEN and James CAMPBELL, Com's. Town of Fayetteville--Samuel GOODWIN. Richmond--Duncan M'FARLAND, Senate. James HARRINGTON and John SMITH, Com's. Chatham--John FARRAR, Senate. John MEBANE and Andrew HEADEN, Commons. Orange--James MEBANE, Senate. John THOMPSON and David

1 September 1808

(378) (Cont.) MEBANE, Commons. Town of Hillsborough—Catlett CAMPBELL. Nash—William ARRINGTON, Senate. Redmond BUNN and Amos GANDY, Commons. Edgecomb—Henry Irwin TOOLE, Senate. Hardy FLOWERS and Nathan STANCIL, Com's. Moore—Benjamin TYSON, Senate. Francis BULLOCK and (blank) M'NEIL, Commons. Bladen—Col. Samuel ANDERS, Senate. Jas. OWEN and Thomas BROWN, jun. Commons. Robeson—General Benjamin LEE, Senate. Hugh BROWN and Alexander ROWLAND, Com's. Anson—Thomas THREADGILL, Senate. William JOHNSTON and Lawrence MOORE, Com's. Montgomery—Edmund DEBERRY, Senate. Joseph PARSON and Clabon HARRIS, Commons. Randolph—Collen STEED, Senate. W. ARNOLD and Seth WADE, Commons. New-Hanover—T. F. BLOODWORTH, Senate. W. W. JONES and H. JAMES, Commons. Brunswick—Gen. Benj. SMITH, Senate. Thomas LEONARD and Thos. RUSS, Commons. Guilford—Jonathan PARKER, Senate. Robert HANNON and John HOWELL, Commons. Town of Wilmington—Joshua G. WRIGHT.

(379) Mr. W. ALSTON, is re-elected a member of Congress for the district of Halifax. Maj. Thomas KENAN is elected for Wilmington district, without opposition. Mr. A. M'BRIDE is elected for the district of Fayetteville by a majority of 311 votes over Mr. CULPEPPER. Mr. Richard STANFORD is elected for Hillsborough district by a large majority over D. CAMERON. Nathaniel MACON, Esq. is re-elected for the district of Warrenton, without opposition.

(380) Newbern, August 25. We have had the satisfaction to learn, that the exertions of the people of Green County to discover the murderers of the Post-Boy William WISE, have been successful. Two negroes who had escaped from the jail of this town some months since, one called Bill SMITH, apprehended as a runaway, whose owner was not known, the other called Sam JARMAN lately owned by Mr. John COLBY, were known to be lurking about Green County & were on strong grounds suspected—their place of retreat was discovered and a party placed near it; late in the evening of the 17th inst. they came forth, both armed. They were fired on, Bill fell—Sam ran a short distance and was brought down, after snapping his musket at one of the party. .. Sam was secured—part of the money of which the mail was robbed was found on him...

(381) Notice. On Thursday next will be Sold, at RYAN's Ferry, the Perishable Estate of Cornelius RYAN, Esq. dec. consisting of Stock of different kinds, Household and Kitchen Furniture, and sundry other articles. ... The Administrator. September 1, 1808.

(382) 10 Dollars Reward. Runaway from the subscriber on Monday, the 15th inst. a negro man named TOM, about 35 years of age, 5 feet 8 or 9 inches high, is quite black, and when spoken to has a smiling countenance, has a scar over one of his eyes.. I purchased him of Mr. Thomas SATTERFIELD of Edenton, about 8 years ago, at which place and Roanoke he is well known. ... Shadrach COLLINS. Tarborough, Aug. 23, 1808.

(383) Mr. Thomas GRIMSHAW of Alexandria advertises "new constructed Bed Cords" for sale which he says "are rendered superior to any other kind by their infallability in destroying and preventing those insects called Chinches, which harbor in the holes of the bedsteads." He believes they will "last 15 or 20 years and retain the same virtue." If they do not answer the purpose, on delivery of the Bed Cords the money will be returned.

(384) Horrid and unnatural Murder.—On Saturday the 23d ult. Mr. Elijah FISHER, of this county, was found dead within a few feet of his spring, where he had lain down under the shade of a tree to sleep. Upon examination it was discovered that

(384) (Cont.) he had received a large load of buck-shot in the side of his head.. The suspicions of the neighbourhood immediately fell upon his son, a boy of about fourteen years of age, who had been heard a few days before to threaten that he would kill his father. He was apprehended on the same day and committed to jail. There is very strong circumstantial evidence against him, and scarcely any doubts are entertained of his guilt. Fayetteville Pap.

(385) Articles Of a Conventional agreement between the States of South-Carolina and North-Carolina. The undersigned Joseph BLYTHE and Thomas SUMPTER, Jun. on the part of the State of South-Carolina, and James WELLBORN, John MOORE and John STEELE on the part of the State of North-Carolina, having been duly appointed Commissioners by their respective States, to settle and adjust, all and singular the differences, disputes, controversies and claims of whatsoever nature they may be concerning territory, jurisdiction and limits, and to fix and establish permanently a line of boundary between the two States. .. In testimony whereof, we have hereunto set our hands and affixed our seals as Commissioners of our respective States, at Columbia..South-Carolina, the 11th day of July, in the year of our Lord, one thousand eight hundred and eight... Joseph BLYTHE, (Seal.) Tho's SUMPTER, jun. (Seal.) John STEELE, (Seal.) John MOORE, (Seal.) James WELLBORN. (Seal.) Signed, sealed, and interchangeably delivered by the Commissioners of the two states in presence of us, who have hereunto subscribed as witnesses. John TAYLOR, Ab'm. NOTT, R. W. VANDERHORST, Henry CHAMBERS, Robert HAILS, George WARING.

(386) At A Meeting Of the General Assembly of the Presbyterian Church, &c. held in Philadelphia in May 1808. .. Whereas it is the duty of all christian churches, families, and people..to humble themselves before Almighty God, to implore his mercy and protection; and whereas our country appears to be threatened with great calamities; Resolved, therefore, That it be recommended..to the churches under the care of this assembly, to set apart the second Thursday of September next, as a day of fasting, humiliation and prayer... Certified by Jacob J. JANEWAY, Stated Clerk.

Vol. III. Thursday, September 8, 1808. Num. 133.

(387) Philadelphia, August 26. We are indebted to a respectable mercantile house of this city, for the following interesting details furnished by Captain John W. COX, of the ship John Jones. Left Lisbon on the 17th of June, 1808. At that time there was a report in circulation, that a revolution had taken place in Russia...

(388) The Gazette. Edenton, September 8, 1808. .. Further Election Returns. Rowan--Jacob FISHER, Senate. Jesse PEARSON and (blank) SMITH, Commons. Town of Salisbury-Archibald HENDERSON. Onslow--Stephen WILLIAMS, Senate, John E. SPICER and Edward WILLIAMS, Commons. Stokes--G. SHOBER, Senate. Jonathan DOLTON and Benjamin FORSYTHE, Commons. Iredell--James HART, Senate. G. L. DAVIDSON and Andrew CALDWELL, Commons. Lincoln--Andrew HOYLE, Senate. Peter HOYLE and Jones ABERNATHY, Commons. Burke--Israel PICKINS, Senate. Abraham FLEMMING and Thomas BREVARD, Commons. Pitt--Dr. Robert WILLIAMS, Senate. John MORING and Benjamin MAY, Commons. Rockingham--Nathaniel SCALES, Senate. Mark HARDEN and Thomas WORTHAM, Com's.
James COCHRAN is elected a member of Congress for the Caswell district. Joseph PEARSON is elected for the Salisbury district. Meshack FRANKLIN, Esq. is re-elected for the Salem district. Joseph WINSTON, it is believed, is elected for the Stokes district. William HOLLAND is re-elected for the Morgan district.

8 September 1808

(389) Communication.—It is believed, that William GASTON, Esq. will be a candidate for the appointment of Elector, in this district. ... Newbern Herald.

(390) Departed this life on Monday, the 5th inst. Miss Elizabeth LITTLE, infant daughter of Mr. John LITTLE, merchant. ..

Died—on Friday last, in Bertie county, Mr. Benjamin ASHBURN, an inhabitant of that county, in the 78th year of his age.

(391) Notice Is hereby given, that Woolsey HATHAWAY, sen. of the county of Tyrrel, is dead, and that the subscribers qualified as executors to his last will and testament at last Tyrrel court. All persons indebted..are requested to make payment; and those having claims..to exhibit them within the time limited by law. Burton & Woolsey HATHAWAY, Executors.

(392) Notice. Will be Sold, at public sale, on Thursday the 15th September next, at the late dwelling house of Willis SAWYER, dec'd. in Bertie county, several likely Negroes, Household Furniture, a set of Black-smith's Tools, a Cotton Gin, fixed to work by hand, Plantation Utensils, and other articles. .. I will also sell at private sale, the Land whereon the said deceased lived. It is estimated at 370 Acres, though supposed to be more; there are about 60 Acres of cleared Land, a Dwelling-House and other convenient Houses—a Saw and Grist Mill nearly built—a good Fishery, with Houses, &c. For terms apply on the premises to Sarah SAWYER, Ex'rx. Bertie, Aug. 17, 1808.

(393) Worcester, (Mass.) Aug. 17. Singular Circumstance.—Last winter a son of Mr. Eleazer HAWS, of Marlborough, about 11 years old, accidentally got a cent into the lower part of the oesophagus. A puke and other means were employed in bringing it up, without any effect. It got into his stomach. Drastick catharticks and other means, were also used, without any effect. Olive oil was the principal medicine used afterwards. It continued to lay in his stomach until the boy was sent to ride four or five miles in haste, when he immediately felt a pain in his bowels; the next day the cent passed from him, which made six months into about an hour, that it lay in him. At the time the boy swallowed it he had the hooping cough, and it immediately cured him, by the salivation of the copper, and it continued to salivate almost the whole of the time it lay in him. ...

Vol. III. Thursday, September 15, 1808. Num. 134.

(394) The Gazette. Edenton, September 15, 1808. .. Further Election Returns. Person—Richard ATKINSON, Senate, Robert VANHOOK and John PAINE, Commons. Caswell—Azariah GRAVES, Senate. Jas. BURTON and James YANCEY, Commons. Wilkes— James WELLBORN, Senate. William HULM and Edmund JONES, Commons. Hyde—Henry SELBY, Senate. David CARTER and James WATSON, Commons.

(395) Fire—On Monday evening the 5th inst. the inhabitants of Newbern were alarmed with the dreadful cry of Fire! It appeared to have began at a house on Craven street.. The brick dwelling-house of Mr. Isaac TAYLOR, was preserved with the utmost difficulty.. The following houses with nearly all the property contained in them were destroyed: One belonging to Mr. Thomas MARSHAL, occupied as a store by Mrs. Elizabeth COLE. One owned by Capt. Richard FISHER, occupied as a dwelling house. One owned by B. C. GILLESPIE, occupied by Mrs. BALL, as a shop. Two owned by F. X. MARTIN, one back and one front, occupied as dwelling-houses by HARDWICK and NOBLES. One owned by Mr. Joshua SCOTT, occupied as a dwelling-house and hatter's shop. One owned by Mr. PIGOTT, occupied as a dwelling-house. Major George ELLIS, a very worthy character, died next morning of a wound received in

(395) (Cont.)   blowing up one of the houses, deemed necessary to arrest the progress of the devouring flames.

(396)   The Boston Centinel of the 31st ult. gives the following account of the New-Hampshire Election, in 42 towns: New-Hampshire Election. On Monday last, an election of five representatives to the XIth Congress by a general ticket, was held in the state of New-Hampshire. The following names composed the two tickets--Federal. Nathaniel A. HAVEN, William HALE, John C. CHAMBERLAINE, Jas. WILSON, Daniel BLAISDELL. Democratic. Clement STORER, Daniel M. DURELL, Jedediah K. SMITH, Francis GARDNEY, Charles CUTTS. .. We are assured..that the federal ticket for national representatives, had succeeded by a handsome majority.

(397)   Rhode-Island Election. The election in this state took place on the 30th August, instant. The federal candidates are Elisha R. POTTER and Richard JACKSON. The democratic are, Jonathan RUSSEL and Isaac WILBOUR. By the packet Alonzo, WESTCOT..we learn..that the two federal members for Congress had carried their election by a handsome majority...

(398) Died--on Monday morning last, aged 70 years, Mrs. Jane MILES, a respectable inhabitant of this town. On the 29th ult. in Bertie County, Major Lewis OUTLAW, an inhabitant of that county. Near Raleigh, on the 3d instant, John CRAVEN, Esq. Comptroller of this State.

(399)   Marshal's Sales. Will be Sold, at the Court-House in Edenton, on Monday the 24th of October next, All The Lands of the late Arthur JONES, deceased, principally lying in Hertford--to satisfy a judgement obtained in the Circuit Court, North-Carolina District, by George THOMSON and Enoch PRICE, against said JONES, at June Term, 1805. The levy was made soon after judgment, as will appear upon record. John S. WEST, late Marshal. September 5th, 1808.

(400)   Notice. On the 22d instant, will be Sold, at the late dwelling-house, of Maj. Lewis OUTLAW, dec'd. in Bertie county, All The Perishable Estate of said deceased, consisting of Horses, Cattle, Hogs, Sheep, Farming Utensils, household and kitchen Furniture... Edw'd. C. OUTLAW, Adm. Bertie, Sept. 13th, 1808.

Vol. III. Thursday, September 22, 1808. Num. 135.

(401) New-York, Sept. 5. .. Protest. By this Public Instrument and Declaration of Protest be it known and made manifest to all whom it doth or may concern. That on this second day of September in the year of our Lord one thousand eight hundred and eight, before me George W. STRONG, a public notary in and for the State of New-York, duly commissioned and sworn, residing in the city of New-York, personally came and appeared David PETTY, master and commander of the schooner Speedy of Brookhaven, who..did depose, protest and say, That on the nineteenth day of August last past, he was sailing in the said schooner on the south side of Long-Island, bound from New-York to Moriches in Brookhaven, and when opposite Gilgo-Gut he was fired at and brought too by gun-boat No. 40, commanded by James RENSHAW, who sent a barge on board the Deponent's schooner, and after examining her permitted her to proceed on her voyage. That after she had proceeded about one mile to the windward he was again fired at and compelled to bear away and come under the lee of the gun-boat, when he commanded the Deponent to come on board and pilot him into Fire-Island inlet, which the Deponent consented to do for ten dollars; to which the commander replied that "he would be damned if he would give him ten cents," and added that if the Deponent did not obey, his sch'r should not be permitted to leave the gun-boat. Whereupon the Deponent persisted in his refusal the

(401) (Cont.) said commander sent his barge on board the schooner, with orders to take by force the Deponent or one of his men out of the schooner and bring him on board the gun-boat. That the Deponent was therefore compelled..to leave his own vessel and go on board the gun-boat, where he was kept and detained three days. That not being able to beat up to Fire Inlet, they were obliged to go into Gilgo Gut, with the navigation of which the Deponent was totally unacquainted, and on his mentioning that..to the commander, was told.."that if he..run the gun-boat aground, he should be shot." That having passed the gut in safety, and..anchored in the Bay, the Deponent was on the following day..put in irons with handcuffs on his legs and kept so in irons for one whole day and night, during which time he had very little refreshment, and was treated with much abuse by the said commander. ... (Signed) David PETTY. George W. STRONG, Notary Public.

(402) The Gazette. Edenton, September 22, 1808. .. A New-York paper of the 9th states, that James SULLIVAN, Governor of Massachusetts, is dead.

(403) Mr. WILLS, Will please give the following an insertion in his next paper. To The Public. Mr. James SAUNDERS having circulated a report tending to injure my character, I deem it my duty to come forward and vindicate myself from the charge. Mr. SAUNDERS some time previous to the election was at my house, with Mr. Abner N. VAIL, where some conversation took place upon political subjects, and I reprobated the administration of Mr. John ADAMS, and disapproved of the conduct of the federal party. Mr. SAUNDERS after going from my house, told several gentlemen that I had been extremely severe upon the federal party--that I had gone as far as to assert, that there were several federal characters in this County I had named in the presence of Mr. A. N. VAIL. Now, I do admit that some severe observations were made by me concerning the administration of Mr. ADAMS: But, I do declare that I never did name any person who would sell their country: And further, Mr. SAUNDERS's assertion that I did, is absolutely false and without foundation. For the truth of my declaration I refer the reader to the subjoined affidavit. John HAUGHTON. Chowan, Sept. 12, 1808.
    Personally appeared before me, Abner N. VAIL, and made oath, that he did not hear Mr. John HAUGHTON make any personal observations on the day alluded to, or at any other time, to Mr. SAUNDERS, to the best of his recollection. Abner Nash VAIL. Edenton, Sept. 12, 1808.--The above deposition was sworn to before me, Henry FLURY, J. P.

(404) In answer to the above, I beg leave to remark, first, that Mr. HAUGHTON has been very cautious to keep the colouring part of this subject out of sight, & has inserted but one expression thereof, and that for the purpose of bringing about the ill-bred expression of giving the Lie.. Now, for the explanation to the public, I think it necessary to state the conversation as it occurred, which was broached by Mr. HAUGHTON and Mr. VAIL, on the subject of the approaching election (by way of electioneering, Mr. HAUGHTON being one of the candidates) they confined their observations to the candidates for the Senate... James SAUNDERS. September 14, 1808.

(405) Some atrocious Villain Broke into my Office and drawer, on Tuesday evening last, and took therefrom a small red Morocco Pocket Book..containing..the following:--A Note of Hand, given by Arthur FOSTER, dec'd. to me, for 100 Pounds, date not recollected; which I sold to A. MILLEN, Esq. dec'd and which is now at issue in the Superior Court of this County. Several Newspaper accounts and receipts; also, two or three letters of a confidential nature, and 5 Dollars in cash.. Any person, white or black, who may discover the thief or thieves, whereby the Pocket-Book and the Note and Money contained therein, can be obtained, shall receive a

22 September 1808

(405) (Cont.) reward of 15 Dollars, and no questions asked. ... James WILLS. September 21, 1808.

Vol. III. Thursday, September 29, 1808. Num. 136.

(406) The Gazette. Edenton, September 29, 1808. Governor SULLIVAN.--The Boston papers mention nothing of the demise of Governor SULLIVAN. He has been severely indisposed, but letters state him to be recovering.

(407) A Veteran's Opinion of Duelling. The following is Gen. EATON's answer to a letter announcing to him the death of his step-son, lately killed in a duel at N. York. Brimfield, Aug. 18, 1808. Dear Sir, .. I wish DANIELSON might have lived, to the usefulness of which he was capable. .. Brave, great, and experienced men, may sometimes find it necessary to their reputation, that they meet in personal contest..but the trivial disputes which excite ardent young men to put life up at a game of hazard, cannot be reconciled to principles of morality, patriotism, nor character. ... William EATON. Lieut. Fitz H. BABBIT, U. S. Navy.

(408) President's Answer To the Boston Petition. The following answer to the petition of the inhabitants of this town..was received yesterday by the Selectmen, and is now presented to the public by their order. William COOPER, Town Clerk. Boston, Sept. 6, 1808.
August 26, 1808. Sir, I beg leave to communicate through you the inclosed answer to the representation which came to me under cover from you, and to add the assurances of my respects. Th: JEFFERSON. Charles BULFINCH, Esq. for the Selectment of Boston. .. To have submitted our rightful commerce to prohibitions, and tributary exactions from others would have been to surrender our independence. .. But while these edicts remain, the legislature alone can prescribe the course to be pursued. Th: JEFFERSON.

(409) Married--on Thursday evening last, Mr. Thomas VAIL, to Miss Elizabeth HOSKINS, both of this county.

(410) 25 Dollars Reward. Runaway on Sunday after Christmas, a small negro woman named ELCE, about 35 years of age, 4 feet 9 or 10 inches high, black complexioned, has a small scar about one of her eyes, and one ear appears as if it had a piece bit out, I believe her right ear. She obtained a pass to go to Mrs. Steuart NEARSE's in this place.. ... Benjamin FESSENDAN. Plymouth, (N. C.) Aug. 8, 1808

Vol. III. Thursday, October 5, 1808. Num. 137.

(411) The Gazette. Edenton, October 6, 1808. .. Agreeable to the order of Gov. WILLIAMS (says the Raleigh Minerva) the Council of State met in that city on the 15th ult. to advise with him in the appointment of a Comptroller. .. After balloting..they adjourned on the 18th, without making an appointment, and after receiving pay for their services, departed for their respective homes. It was understood that Col. BURTON voted for Mr. Wm. HAWKINS; Needham WHITFIELD, Esq. for Gen. James RHODES; Gideon ALSTON, Esq. for Mr. Joseph HAWKINS; James W. CLARK, Esq. for Mr. John LOCKHART; and Charles JACOCKS, Esq. for Mr. George RYAN. ...

(412) Mr. WILLS, Having observed in your paper of the 22d of September, a piece signed James SAUNDERS, in answer to a handbill of mine. I had at first concluded not to answer it, and never should if the world knew as much of his character as I have discovered since I published the handbill. .. In regard to this I have only

(412) (Cont.) to say, that my ill-breeding and depravity of heart, has never been so great at any time, as to induce me to forge checks at a loo-table; or publish to the world any thing that passed at a private house, in private conversation; much less to make an infamous falsehood and publish it, merely to curry favor and injure an individual. Perhaps this gentleman does not fully understand this allusion, as his memory is very short upon one side, and very extensive upon the other; if he does not, I will refer him to Mr. Benjamin LOWRY and Mr. Thaddeus FRESHWATER, of Pasquotank County..and they can tell him what was the cause that Col. Thomas HARVEY threatened horse-whipping him; and further said, if ever he came in his company again, he would make his negroes tie him up and whip him. The gentleman immediately after left Pasquotank County. ... John HAUGHTON. October 5th, 1808.

(413) Mr. WILLS, A report is now on the wing, circulated by Henry FLURY, Esq. &c. &c. &c. charging me of being guilty of the horrid crime of perjury, at last April term of Chowan Superior Court; I beg leave..to state the following facts, which I pledge myself to be able to prove by unquestionable testimony:--First, the said FLURY commenced a suit against me in the County Court of Washington, upon a trifling lumber contract, in which he was cast; he appealed to the Superior Court of this place, in April term 1807--the suit was continued by consent as soon as Court was opened. I then made an affidavit under the late act of Assembly, for the removal of the suit to some other County, which I informed said FLURY of in writing; but, from some circumstance unknown to me, there was nothing done further in the business until October term; where neither Mr. BROWN, Mr. HAMILTON, or Mr. HAYWOOD, the attorneys I had originally employed in the suit, were able to attend, and of course, could not know what was done, as nothing appeared of record. I then employed Mr. Thomas B. HAUGHTON to draw me another affidavit, which I swore to, without informing him of any of the former circumstances, expecting to be present when the suit would be called, and then could answer such questions as might be asked; but to my great misfortune was attacked with the influenza, which had nearly cost me my life;.. I lodged in the next room to the Court-House, where I had the windows raised and a watch fixed to know when the suit was called; but Mr. FLURY being present when the Judge announced the suit, he laid it over. At April term 1808, I made another affidavit, stating the above facts as near as I could recollect, on which he founds his accusation, so much to the prejudice of my character. .. I shall not stoop to Mr. FLURY's level of slander, but hold myself ready as a gentleman, to give him satisfaction, in a lawful way, for any injury he may think I have done him. Charles SPRUILL. Edenton, Oct. 5th, 1808.

(414) Attention! The Edenton Volunteer Company are ordered to meet, at the usual parade ground, on Thursday the 13th inst. properly equipped, at 10 o'clock A. M. By order, Henry A. DONALDSON, Lieut.

Vol. III. Thursday, October 13, 1808. Num. 138.

(415) To the Freemen of the Counties of Wayne, Green, Lenoir, Jones, Craven and Carteret. Fellow-Citizens, The period is fast approaching, when you will be called on to select some one of your body as an Elector, to vote for a President and Vice President of the United States. It has long since been announced that a very respectable gentleman, General Bryan WHITFIELD, was solicitous to receive this high and important trust. Deem me not presumptuous in expressing the wish that you would consider me also as a candidate for the appointment. .. General WHITFIELD has pledged himself, if elected, to vote for James MADISON, of Virginia, as President.. .. It is scarcely necessary to add, that if appointed an Elector, I purpose (sic) to vote for Charles Cotesworth PINCKNEY, as President... William

(415) (Cont.) GASTON. Newbern, September 19, 1808.

(416) The Gazette. Edenton, October 13, 1808. .. Married—on Tuesday evening, Mr. Samuel GREGORY, to Miss Patsey CREECY, eldest daughter of Mr. F. CREECY, all of this County.

Died—on the 5th inst. in Bertie County, much lamented, Miss Jane LENNOX, daughter of Dr. LENNOX, dec'd. of that County. On the 24th of July, at her brother's house, at Cranbrook, Eng. in the 68th year of her age, Mrs. PAINE, wife of Thomas PAINE, author of the Rights of Man.

(417) Notice is hereby given to all whom it may concern, that the Federal District Court for the District of Albemarle, will be held in this town on Tuesday, the 25th of this month. John W. LITTLEJOHN, Cl'k. Edenton, October 12, 1808.

(418) Notice is hereby given that Stephen CABARRUS, Esq. of this County, is dead, and that the subscribers qualified as his Executors at September term last of Chowan County Court. All persons indebted..are desired to make immediate payment; and those having claims..to exhibit them..to one or other of the subscribers. August CABARRUS, Samuel TREDWELL, } Ex'rs. Edenton, October 12, 1808.

(419) Notice. The creditors of Benjamin SPRUILL, jun. deceased, late of the county of Tyrrel, are hereby notified, that the said Benjamin SPRUILL, jun. is dead, and that the subscriber qualified as executrix to his last will and testament in August term last. All those indebted..are requested to make immediate payment; and such as have claims are requested to bring them forward... Lois SPRUILL, Ex'rx.

(420) Letters remaining in the Post-Office at Edenton, 1st October, 1808. William ANDERS, Wm. BLAIR, Theobold BAXTER, Jas. R. CREECY, Saml. COLLINS, Isaac COLLINS, Davezac DE CASTRA, Orlando DANA, Hannah DILLON, Caleb ELLIOTT, Robert E. EDDENS, John FOSTER, Russel FOWLER, John GOELET, Henry GRAY, John GILMORE, Thomas GUY, John GUYTHER, William F. HUNTER, Miss Jane GREGORY, Sheriff Chowan, Arthur JONES, Andrew KNOX, James W. LANGLEY, King LUTON, Members of Assembly from Chowan, Wm. K. M'KINDER, William M'NIDER, Charles G. RIDGELY, Thomas SMITH, Ann WARRING, Jesse WEST, James WATT, Ann WHITE. Hend. STANDIN, P. M.

(421) New-Orleans, Aug. 9. Report made to his Excellency the Governor, civil and military, of the Fort and Jurisdiction of Baton-Rouge, in West Florida, by the undersigned.. We, Philip HICKY, an inhabitant of this Jurisdiction, sydnic, Capt. of cavalry,—and Samuel FULTON, formerly a Col. an inhabitant of this colony, and discharging the functions of Major of militia..having been charged by his Excellency the Governor to go on board the gun-boat of the United States of America, stationed near the mouth of the Bayou or River Iberville, for the purpose of claiming..a man named ARMSTRONG, who had been living in this country for several months, and had been forcibly taken from the house of Mr. Soulliac GUIDARY, an inhabitant of this jurisdiction by the Captain or commanding officer, of said gun-boat, aided and assisted by an armed detachment of soldiers, or marines, in the service of the U. States;—this day went on board the gun-boat No. 21, commanded by Mr. John OWENS..and demanded of him the said prisoner ARMSTRONG, as having been illegally carried off by force and violence..to the great terror of the inhabitants of the house in which the said ARMSTRONG had been seized..

Whereupon the said commanding officer of gun-boat No. 21, made answer..that he neither could, nor would, restore the prisoner, without orders from his Commodore—-.. And we..make..this report..this twenty-second day of July, 1808. (Signed)

13 October 1808

(421) (Cont.) Philip HICKY, Samuel FULTON.

Vol. III. Thursday, October 20, 1808. Num. 139.

(422) Baltimore, Oct. 3. Extract from Captain CARMAN's Protest. "Samuel CARMAN master of the brig Sophia, of Baltimore..made oath..That he sailed in and with the said brig on the 9th day of July last, from Rotterdam, bound direct for this port of Baltimore; having on board the said brig, 6 pipes of gin, which he had taken in at..Rotterdam, and no other merchandize..proceeded..on the 10th day of July, being off the Isle of Schowen, having discharged his pilot..was boarded by an English gun-brig, the commander of which ordered his vessel to England to pay duties on his cargo..and on payment thereof licence was given him to enable him to pursue his voyage to Baltimore."

(423) After the polls had closed on Monday evening at FULTON's, in the midst of a crowd, the son-in-law of Luther MARTIN, Mr. KEENE, late an officer in the navy, in consequence of some previous dispute with Lieutenant John B. NICHOLSON, drew a pistol from his pocket and fired at the Lieutenant. The ball missing NICHOLSON, perforated the cheek of a gentleman, who, we are informed, lodges at Mrs. PARKER's, South-street. Mr. KEENE was immediately apprehended and carried before Esquire ASQUITH, who admitted him to bail, and took..Luther MARTIN as his security for 10,000 dollars, for his appearance. ...

(424) The Gazette. Edenton, October 20, 1808. .. Norfolk, October 10. .. October 12. .. The Department of State has lately received the following account from Cayenne in relation to the brig Littlear, Samuel W. BALCH master, which sailed from Boston on the 26th of December, 1806, bound to the River of Plate. That after the arrival of the said brig at Monteviedo, she was sold and transferred by the said BALCH to James A. BOUTCHER, who is stated to have been a citizen of the United States, belonging to Norfolk, in Virginia, or its vicinity, and to have had a family there; that soon afterwards (on the 5th July, 1807) the Littlear was carried on a coasting voyage by BOUTCHER, and she was brought back to La Plate on the 12th January, succeeding, that she again sailed (on the 15th of April, 1808,) under..BOUTCHER, bound to Rio Janeiro (sic); that on the passage BOUTCHER fell a victim to the treachery of a part of his crew, being assassinated by them; that, thenceforward, the command of the vessel, with the name of her murdered Captain, was assumed by the person who had acted as the mate; that on the 12th June last, the Littlear arrived at Cayenne under the command of the pretended Capt. BOUTCHER, who consigned both vessel and cargo to Jonathan BARRY (or BARNS) the informant of this Department; and that the Brig and her cargo have been since sold by the Tribunal 'La Premier Instance' at Cayenne." October 7th, 1808.

(425) Married—at Gates Court-House on Saturday morning last about 8 o'clock, Mr. Samuel STILLMAN, a resident of this town, to Miss Sarah REW, formerly of Newbern.
     Died—very suddenly, on Thursday afternoon last, Mr. William BEASTALL, miniature painter, native of England.

(426) Dr. BEASLEY, Has lately received from New-York a quantity of Fresh Medicines... Edenton, Oct. 18, 1808.

(427) Notice is hereby given, that the subscriber qualified as one of the Executors of William ROMBOUGH, dec. at September term last of Chowan County Court, requests all persons indebted..to make immediate payment; and those having claims..to exhibit them... Edm'd. HOSKINS, Ex'r. Edenton, October 19, 1808.

20 October 1808

[Note: The first page of this issue is missing.]
(428) Norfolk, October 19. .. October 24. .. France has declared War Against America! Office of the Federal Gazette, Sunday Morning, Oct. 23. We have just received the following letter from our correspondent, dated New-York, Oct. 21, 1808. (Twelve o'clock.) War with France. Sir--Arrived, ship Richard, ODIORNE, 28 days from Liverpool. .. Captain ODIORNE, informs, that on the 21st September, when beating down the Channel, Mr. MURRY, American Consul at Liverpool, sent one of his Clerks on board the Richard, with news of the arrival..of an express from London, advising of a Declaration of War by France against the United States of America.. Accounts were received in London the 17th September, that all the Americans in France were imprisoned. ...

(429) The Gazette. Friday. Edenton, October 28, 1808. The arrival and departure of the Northern Mail being again altered, makes it necessary for us to change our days of publication to Friday.

(430) To the Freemen in the Electoral district of Edenton, composed of the Counties of Gates, Chowan, Perquimans, Pasquotank, Camden and Currituck. The subscriber respectfully offers his services as a Candidate for an Elector.. Should he be so fortunate as to be elected, he will vote for James MONROE or Charles C. PINCKNEY for President; as he supposes only one of them will be run in opposition to James MADISON. Aaron ALBERTSON. Nixonton, Oct. 24, 1808.

(431) To Doctor Cargil MASSENBURG, of Wake County, in the State of North-Carolina. You will take notice that the Grand Jury of Bertie County Court have made a presentment against your negro man PETER, and that by virtue of a capias to me directed, attested by the Clerk of the said Court, I now hold the said negro in custody, and he will receive his trial at the next term of the said Court. to be held at the Court-House in Windsor, on the second Monday in November next.--This notice is given to you in conformity of an Act of the General Assembly, passed at Raleigh, in the year 1794, entitled "An Act to prevent the owners of slaves from hiring to them their own time, to make compensation to Patrols, and to restrain the abuses committed by free negroes and mulattoes." William H. GREEN, Sheriff of Bertie County. Windsor, Oct. 15, 1808.

(432) Asa CHAMBERLAIN, Boot & Shoe-Maker, Respectfully informs the ladies and gentlemen of Edenton..that he has just returned from the Northward and opened on the wharf, at the store of Captain Edward REILY, a general assortment of..Shoes... 26th October, 1808.

Vol. III. Thursday, October 27, 1808. Num. 140.

[Note: The last two pages of this issue are missing.]

Vol. III. Friday, November 4, 1808. Num. 141.

(433) Washington-City, Oct. 26. There is no reason to credit the information, given under the New-York head, of France having declared war against the United States. So far as it relies for credibility on any thing official received by our government, it is entirely disproved...

(434) The Gazette. Friday. Edenton, November 4, 1808. On Friday next the election for choosing an Elector to vote for President and Vice-President..will take place in this district, and throughout the state--The candidates for this district, are Gen. Joseph RIDDICK, of Gates County, and Mr. Aaron ALBERTSON, of Pas-

4 November 1808

(434) (Cont.) quotank County.

(435) Attention! The Edenton Volunteers are ordered to attend at the usual parade ground on Saturday next, at 3 o'clock, P. M. properly equipped.—In consequence of the resignation of Capt. FLURY, a Captain and other officers will then be appointed. Henry A. DONALDSON, Lieut.

(436) To Be Sold, At Public Auction, on the first Tuesday in December next..at the house of the Subscriber, at Rockahock, Four likely Negroes, 150 barrels of Corn, 100 bushels of white Peas, 5000 wt. of Fodder, two Horses and Chairs, two Cows and Calves, 3000 wt. of live Pork, two Carts and two yoke of Steers, two good Seines, with ropes, haliards and blocks for the same, the rope and twine the manufacture of Mr. COLLINS's Rope-Walk, two Flats for Seines, Salt Troughs, Fish Tubs, Hand-Barrows, Hogsheads, &c. and all my Household and Kitchen Furniture. Also the schooner Two Friends, burthen 150 barrels, with Boat, two good Anchors and Sails, now at sea, but is expected to be on the spot on the day of sale.
   At the same time, will be rented until the 5th of January, 1810, the Rockahock Plantation, on which I now live of 300 acres. ... A Dinner will be prepared for 100 persons or more, and the best Liquors that Edenton affords will be furnished, on that day. Philip M'GUIRE. October 29th, 1808.

(437) Richmond, October 18. At a meeting agreeable to notice of the Federal Republicans of the City of Richmond and Town of Manchester, held at the Bell Tavern, in the City of Richmond, on Monday, the 17th October, 1808, to decide upon the candidate whom they will support at the ensuing election of President of the U. States. Doctor James MC CLURG was unanimously chosen Chairman, and Doctor John ADAMS, Secretary to the meeting..the following resolutions were unanimously adopted. 1. Reduced by the tyranny of the General Ticket Law, to the necessity of abandoning our choice, and bestowing our suffrages on one of the democratic candidates for the Presidency..and believing that of these, the election of James MUNROE would most essentially promote the welfare of the Union; Resolved that this meeting will support the Ticket of the said James MUNROE..and that the following recommendatory address to the federal republicans of Virginia, be published in the Virginia Gazette, and in the other federal papers of this state. To The Federal Republicans Of Virginia. .. 2. Resolved, that Mr. Daniel CALL, Mr. William MARSHALL, Dr. John ADAMS, Messrs. James PENN, Robert GAMBLE; jun. Thomas WILSON, Walter MC CLURG, and Charles JOHNSTON, be appointed a Committee to correspond with the federalists throughout the State, & to adopt all proper measures to promote the succeess of the election of the said James MUNROE. James MC CLURG, Chairman. Attest, John ADAMS, Secretary.

(438) Electoral Ticket. The following is the MUNROE Electoral Ticket, republished for the information of the citizens of Virginia. Littleton W. TAZEWELL, Norfolk Borough, Arthur SMITH, Isle of Wight, Dr. James S. GILLIAM, Dinwiddie, Peter BAILEY, Mecklenburgh, Gen. Tarlton WOODSON, Prince Edward, Hill CARTER, Amherst, Thomas WATKINS, Chesterfield, Peachy R. GILMOR, Henry, Chan. Creed TAYLOR, Richmond, Col. John TAYLOR, Caroline, James HUNTER, Essex, Gen. John MINOR, Spotsylvania, Armistead MASON, Loudoun, Robert SAUNDERS, York, Chan. Samuel TYLER, Williamsburg, Gen. J. P. HUNGERFORD, Westmoreland, Richard BRENT, Prince William, Henry St. Geo. TUCKER, Frederick, James DAILY, Hampshire, John CUNNINGHAM, Pendleton, John COUITOR, Augusta, Daniel SHEFFOY, Wythe, Linah MIMS, Greenbrier, John PRUNTY, Harrison.

(439) Washington-City, Oct. 14. Appointments by the President, Wade HAMPTON, of South-Carolina, Colonel of Light Dragoons. John C. BOYD, Colonel of the 4th

(439) (Cont.) Regiment of Infantry. Joseph CONSTANT, of New-York, Lieutenant Colonel of the 6th Regiment of Infantry. Electus BACKUS, of New-York, Major of the Light Dragoons.

Vol. III. Friday, November 11, 1808. Num. 142.

(440) The Gazette. Friday. Edenton, November 11, 1808. .. Extract of a letter from Charleston, to a gentleman in Norfolk, dated Sept. 25. "A Duel was fought on Sunday between Dr. B. POWELL, and Mr. John M'MILLAN.--The former was shot through the body, and instantly expired: It was in a political discussion that the offence was passed.--The Doctor was challenged."

(441) Married--on Wednesday last, in Washington County, Mr. Enoch JONES, a minister of the Methodist church, to Miss Nancy SWAIN, daughter of Mr. Eleazor SWAIN, of the aforesaid county.
    Died--at Nixonton, on the 20th ult. Mrs. Sarah COX, wife of Mr. John COX, late of this town.

Vol. III. Friday, November 18, 1808. Num. 143.

(442) The Gazette. Friday, November 18, 1808. General Joseph RIDDICK is chosen an Elector for this district, to vote for President and Vice-President.. He has pledged himself to support James MADISON for President, and Geo. CLINTON as Vice-President.

(443) Extract of a letter from Capt. Robert COLFAX, jr. of the ship Octavian, from Charleston, bound to London, to his father in the state of New-Jersey, dated London, July 26th, 1808. "We were captured on the 27th of January last, off Dover, at 11 o'clock at night, and at two o'clock next morning were landed and put into Calais Prison, where we remained a number of days before we were released; the ship and cargo are detained under the Imperial decrees.. On a review of the subject, I think my fortune rather hard; when I left home, I took with me upwards of 4000 dollars in cash and produce, of all which I have been literally robbed, kept five months confined on prisoners allowance, marched several hundred miles barefooted through an unfriendly country, and seemingly to augment our suffering, by the orders of a government who pretend to be our friends."

(444) Communicated. Died--at Murfreesborough on the 15th ult. Bryan BENBURY, many years an approved practitioner of medicine in that place.
    At his residence in Hertford county on the 31st ult. after an illness which he bore with manly and becoming fortitude Robert MONTGOMERY, Esq.--As a statesman, a gentleman and a most amiable man in private life, he filled a large space in society. .. At his own house in Hertford county on the 1st inst. Jeremiah BROWN, Esq. long a respectable and useful man.
    Died--in Bertie county on Thursday last, Mr. John CONNOR, of Camden county.

(445) To The Lovers Of Natural History. A New and superb work, being the first of the kind ever attempted in America--Now publishing by BRADFORD and INSKEEP, Philadelphia, in imperial quarto, price 12 dollars handsomely half bound in Morocco--vol. 1, of American Ornithology;--or the natural history of the Birds of the United States..illustrated with plates, elegantly engraved and colored from original drawings taken from nature--by Alexander WILSON. Edenton, Nov. 18, 1808.

(446) For Sale, On a liberal credit, a Tract of Land, containing 144 Acres, lying in this county, near Yeoppim river. ... Nathaniel MILLER. Chowan, Nov. 11, 1808

(447)   50 Dollars Reward. Runaway from the subscriber, living in Martin county, N. C. near TAYLOR's Ferry, on the 2d of September, a negro man named HARRY, about 22 years old, supposed to be 5 feet 2 or 3 inches high, spare made, and rather more of a light than dark complexion. .. The above reward will be paid to any person for apprehending and delivering the said negro to the subscriber, provided he is taken out of the limits of N. Carolina, or 25 Dollars if taken within. John TAYLOR. October 1st, 1808.

Vol. III. Friday, November 25, 1808. Num. 144.

(448)   From the National Intelligencer. We have been favoured with the perusal of another letter recently received from Wm. MURDOCH, Esq. to George MAGRUDER, Esq. of George-Town.. "I have not had the smallest reason to alter my opinion with regard to the propriety on the continuance of your Embargo until the French decrees & British orders are annulled. ..."

(449)   The Gazette. Friday. Edenton, November 25, 1808. .. Match Race.—On Thursday las_ the Match Race, [for $1800] between Mr. Caleb BOUSH's colt Sir Solomon, by Tickle Toby, 3 years old, carrying 110 lbs. and Mr. W. WYNN's horse Gallatin. by Diomed, 4 years old, 120 lbs. four mile heats, was run over the new course, and won with ease by Sir Solomon. ...

(450)   Congress. House of Representatives. Monday, November 14. .. Wednesday, Nov. 16. .. Mr. VERPLANCK presented the memorial of certain freeholders and electors of the county of Dutchess, in the state of New-York, signed by order and in behalf of the meeting by Israel SMITH, their chairman, and attested by Jonathan HAIGHT, their secretary, praying a repeal of the law laying an Embargo. Referred to the committee of the whole house.. ...

(451)   Another Fatal Duel.—An affair of honor was, on Saturday last, determined in Maryland, between Peter V. DANIEL, Esq. and Capt. John SEDDON, both of Stafford in this state.—The latter received his antagonist's ball in his right side, languished till about 8 o'clock on Monday morning, and died. Fredericksburg paper.

(452)   William GASTON, Esq. is elected for the district of Newbern as an Elector, to vote for President and Vice-President, by a majority of 181 votes. Henry TOOLE, Esq. for the district of Washington, by a majority of 578. Thomas WYNNS, Esq. for the district of Winton or Northampton. Gov. ASHE, for the district of Wilmington, by a large majority.—The three latter gentlemen will support Mr. MADISON as President.

(453)   New-York, November 2. Mr. John PETIS, mate of the brig Juliana, Capt. LEE, of this port, that was taken by the French and sunk, informs us, that he learned from the officers of the French brig, that they had orders to burn, sink or destroy all American vessels they fell in with; that Capt. LEE, his officers and men, were plundered of all their clothes and money...

Vol. III. Friday, December 2, 1808. Num. 145.

(454)   The Gazette. Friday. Edenton, December 2, 1808. .. Died—on the 14th inst. at Frankfort (Penn.) Captain Stephen DECATUR, sen. late a Captain in the United States navy, and one of the Patriots of our revolution.

(455)   Congress of the United States. Senate, Thursday, Nov. 17. .. Mr. THURSTON gave notice, that to-morrow he would ask leave to bring in a bill to

(455) (Cont.) reward Andrew Joseph VILLARD, for an invention of public utility, when the Senate adjourned.

(456) House of Representatives. Thursday, Nov. 17. .. Mr. SAY presented the petition of John BISHOP, James CLEMENT, and Thomas SPARKS, shot manufacturers, which represents that great efforts are making by foreign manufacturers to prevent the domestic manufacture of shot, and soliciting Congress to encourage it by a duty on that article. They assert that they make shot of all kinds..that there is another shot manufactory in Philadelphia, under the direction of Paul BECK, and that either of the two are competent to supply the consumption of shot in the United States.. The petition was referred to the committee of commerce and manufactures. ...

(457) North-Carolina Legislature. Raleigh, Nov. 24. The Legislature of this State convened in the State-House..on Monday the 21st inst. .. Gen. RIDDICK was re-elected Speaker, Gen. M. STOKES, Clerk, and Maj. R. WILLIAMS, Assistant Cl'k. N. MURPHY and M. DILLIARD, door-keepers. One hundred and twenty members of the House of Commons qualified and took their seats, when Joshua G. WRIGHT, Esq. was re-elected Speaker, Maj. P. HENDERSON, Clerk, and Wm. LOCKHART, Assistant Clerk; and T. POUNDS and J. LUMSDEN, door-keepers. .. Tuesday, Nov. 22. The House passed a resolution, ordering a writ of election to issue to the Sheriff of Cumberland to hold an election on the 30th inst. for a member of this house to supply the vacancy occasioned by the death of Donald M'QUEEN, Esq.
     A message was sent to the Senate, proposing to ballot on (sic) the morning for 3 Engrossing Clerks, and nominating Daniel M. FORNEY, Robert HARRISON, Bennett BUNN, Wm. BRICKELL, Wm. HILL, Benj. H. COVINGTON, Robert W. GOODMAN, Anthony GREVILLE, Thomas A. WORD, Thomas GALES, Edw'd TROY and Edwin SATTERWHITE; which was agreed to in the Senate, and the names of John M'FARLAND & Edward LINDSAY added to the nomination. .. Mr. Thomas LOVE from the committee appointed for that purpose, reported rules of order and decorum, which were adopted and ordered to be printed. .. Wednesday, Nov. 23. Benj. H COVINGTON and R. W. GOODMAN were elected Engrossing Clerks. Mr. GLISSON presented the peititon of James NORCOM of Edenton, praying to vacate the seat of William A. LITTLEJOHN; referred to the committee of Elections. The two houses ballot in the morning for Comptroller of the Treasury. Those nominated in this house, are, Samuel GOODWIN, Wm. HAWKINS, James GAINS, John W. GUION, John LOCKHART, Joseph HAWKINS and Pleasant HENDERSON. .. The Legislature..have decided that the seat of William A. LITTLEJOHN, Esq. be vacated, and that a new election take place, which will be held to-morrow.

(458) Federal Electors. William GASTON, for Newbern district. John WINSLOW, for Fayetteville do. Murdock M'KINZIE, for Moore do. Democratic Electors. Samuel ASHE, sen. for Wilmington district. Joseph TAYLOR, for Raleigh do. Kemp PLUMMER, for Halifax do. Thomas WYNN, for Hertford do. Joseph RIDDICK, for Edenton do. Henry I. TOOLE, for Tar River do. Francis LOCKE, for Salisbury do. James RAINEY, for Caswell do. Robert CLEVELAND, for Salem do. William LOVE, for Morgan do. Peter FORNEY, for Lincoln do.

(459) Christening.—In Georgia, (Vermont) a daughter of Mr. Alpheus HARDWICK, by the name of Embargo: The reason given by the father, who is a good democrat, for imposing this ludicrous name upon his only child, is rather singular, viz. he wishes ever to have a living memorandum before his eyes of one of the best political measures to enrich the country. Mer. Adv.

(460) John POPELSTON Has just arrived from New-York, and now opening at his Store on the wharf, a handsome assortment of Fall & Winter Goods... December 1st, 1808.

2 December 1808

(461)   Notice is hereby given to all the creditors of Miles BONNER, late of the County of Bertie, that the said Miles BONNER is dead, and that administration was granted to the undersigned at the present term of Bertie County Court on his estate; who requests them to make known their demands within the time the law directs, or this notice will be plead in bar. Nancy BONNER, Adm'x. Bertie, Nov. 17, 1808.

(462)   Will be Sold, at RYAN's Ferry, on Tuesday the 13th of next month..Five or Six Hundred Barrels of Corn, a number of Hogs, Ferry Boats, 70 or 80,000 22 inch Shingles, some valuable household Furniture, &c, of the estate of Cornelius RYAN, Esq. deceased. ... Administrator. Bertie, Nov. 21, 1808.

Vol. III. Friday, December 9, 1808. Num. 146.

(463)   The Gazette. Friday. Edenton, December 9, 1808. William A. LITTLEJOHN, Esq. is elected by a majority of 3 votes, to represent this Town in the present session of the Legislature. The votes were, 48 for Dr. NORCOM, and 51 for Mr. LITTLEJOHN.

Vol. III. Friday, December 16, 1808. Num. 147.

(464)   The Gazette. Friday. Edenton, December 16, 1808. .. The Nashville (Ten.) paper of the 10th ult. says--"We have just heard that the great preacher Lorenzo DOW, died lately in the Missisippi Territory, where he had just removed his family."

(465)   North-Carolina Legislature. House of Commons. Thursday, Nov. 24. .. Monday, Nov. 28. Mr. YANCY, from the committee appointed to superintend the balloting for Governor, reported that David STONE had a majority, and that he was elected. Mr. ROBARDS, from the committee appointed to superintend the balloting for a Judge of the Superior Court, reported, that Leonard HENDERSON had a majority and was therefore duly elected. .. Joseph GALES was elected Public Printer, without opposition.

(466)   Mr. WILLS, Sir--This is the third time I have endeavoured through the medium of your paper to answer a calumnious piece in said paper of October 13, signed Henry FLURY. How the other two have miscarried is a mystery; but this being forwarded by a safe hand, I beg you will give it a place in your next num-___, and also the certificates accompany___ it. .. I will first state the cause of this great dis__te, and leave the world to judge between __. 1st. On the 23d December, 1807, I made contract with the said FLURY to amount of __out thirty pounds, which was to be dischar__d in lumber, which was tendered agreea___ to contract, but he put off the receiving __ it at that time in a friendly manner. Soon ___er a Capatin BAUM, who owed me a sum __ money, left for me in the hands of FLURY _?200, which I frequently applied for, but __uld not get a cent from him until I believe __ar two years had elapsed, and several ten___rs of the lumber had been made. Captain _AUM was then obliged to go to FLURY and a__ee to loose the interest of his money before __ could get it. FLURY finding he could not __tain the money any longer, brought suit a__inst me in Washington County Court for a __each of contract. Having stated the cause, _ _hall now proceed to answer such of his re_arks as may deserve notice. Mr. FLURY __ates that he accused me of perjury; I con__s he made use of language that no gentle_man would have done at the door cf the _ourt-House in Edenton, at last October _erm, while the Judge was onthe seat of __ice. I observed that was not a proper __ace to end such a dispute, and desired he _ould go with me and we would endeavor to __ttle it, which I

93

(466) (Cont.) suppose he construed to be _ sort of challenge, and would not leave the _oor, saying that he was protected by the _ourt, and then leaped on the steps, and with a _errible look, and in the language of a pal__oon, said his hands were tied or he could _eat out my brains with a pistol, and if I _as offended I might sue him. I replied, it _ould be poor satisfaction to prove him a lyar _t my own expence, as the world already _new that he was not able to pay the cost of _ suit—he said he would give me security for __.

FLURY states that he is not the only person _hat has accused me of perjury, which is not _rue.. He states that the jury who sat upon _he trial of his suit against me in Washing_on County Court gave him a verdict for a _uantity of shingles, and decreed, that he —hould pay the cost, which like all the rest is _alse; the verdict of the jury stands thus——_ury impannelled and sworn, find for the de_endant, which the records will prove. The _ruth respecting this trial is a certain William WATSON, who FLURY had brought up from _n infant in his own religion, came into Court and swore that the account that FLURY gave me in his own hand writing when I purchased the goods, was not the writing of _aid FLURY; and that he, said WATSON delivered all the articles contained in said account himself. But having sufficient witnesses to prove FLURY's hand writing, and also that WATSON was not present when the goods were delivered, the jury paid no attention to his evidence, as it plainly appeared that the perjury he committed was intended to add about ten pounds more than was charged in the original account, to do away the effect of the tender I had made, and compel me to pay cash. .. FLURY further states, that at October Term, 1807, I agreed to lay over the suit with him; for a proof of that falsehood I will refer the reader to the certificates hereunto annexed. ..He further says that I made another affidavit at April Term, 1808, and stated therein that I then embraced the first opportunity I had to offer an affidavit in a satisfactory manner. I would ask if I had not good reason to be dissatisfied, when, upon enquiry, I discovered my first affidavit was not to be found, the second read and rejected without my being called, though I lodged in the next room, which circumstance deprived me of the benefit that they all contemplated. FLURY further states, that he is very sorry for the loss of my first affidavit, as that would have substantiated his publication against me. ..

I now take my leave and assure Mr. FLURY that he will not hear any more from me in this way; but, should he have any communications to make to me in a private way, he shall be punctually answered. Charles SPRUILL. Tyrrel County, Dec. 6th, 1808.

Tyrrel County, Dec. 6th, 1808. We, the subscribers, being called upon by Charles SPRUILL, Esq. and sworn on the Holy Evangelists of Almighty God, depose and say, that we were in the store of Henry FLURY, Esq. in Edenton, on the 23d day of December, one thousand eight hundred and one, in company with the said SPRUILL, and saw him purchase goods of the said Henry FLURY, consisting of cloth, callicoes, and humhums; and that the said FLURY did deliver the goods with his own hands——We further depose and say, that William WATSON was not present when the above goods were delivered, nor any time that day that we saw; and the said Henry FLURY complained that he was at a loss for want of him, but he said he had sent him down the country the morning before on business——We do further depose and say, that the above named William WATSON was sworn in the Superior Court of Chowan County, on a mis-trial Henry FLURY against Charles SPRUILL, concerning the above named goods, and that he the said William WATSON did swear that he did deliver all the goods to the said Charles SPRUILL that was contained in FLURY's account with his own hands, though we at the same time knew to the contrary. William HATFIELD, John DAVENPORT. Sworn to and subscribed before B. SPRUILL.

I do hereby certify that the above testimony of William HATFIELD and John DAVENPORT is just and true, and that I was also present with them when Col. SPRUILL purchased the above mentioned goods of FLURY; and also at the time William

16 December 1808

(466) (Cont.) WATSON was sworn, and that every word contained in the above affidavit is within my knowledge just and true. Alexander his X mark OLIVER.
    Tyrrel County, Dec. 6th, 1808. The subscriber being called upon by Col.
Charles SPRUILL concerning what he may know about the continuing a suit Henry
FLURY vs. Charles SPRUILL, now at issue in the Superior Court of Chowan County--I
do certify, that the said cause was continued at October Term, 1807, by the plaintiff, as soon as the Judge announced it; and the defendant C. SPRUILL was not in
Court, nor was he called at all. I further certify, that the said Charles SPRUILL
requested me on the morning of that day to let him know when the suit was called,
as he would be ready for trial if he got well enough to attend, but he said he was
so sick that he thought himself incapable of attending the Court-House at that
time, that he had taken physic the night previous. Signed, Thomas WILLIAMS.
[Note: A narrow strip from the left side of this column is missing.]

(467) Unanimity Lodge. The Festival of St. John the Evangelist, will be celebrated, in this place, by Unanimity Lodge, on the 27th instant. ... By Order, James
WILLS, Sec'ry. Edenton, Dec. 14, 1808.

(468) Bank of Newbern. Edenton Office. Dec. 9, 1808. The President and Directors of the Bank of Newbern, having established an Office of Discount in the Town
of Edenton, Bills, Bonds and Notes will be discounted therein... John B. BLOUNT,
Agent.

(469) Will Be Sold, By order of Court..on the 3d day of January next, before Mrs.
HORNIBLOW's door, in Edenton, a very likely young Negro Fellow named MYLES. He is
a very good house-carpenter, and an orderly fellow. ... Administrator. December
14, 1808.

Vol. III. Friday, December 23, 1808. Num. 148.

(470) The Gazette. Friday. Edenton, December 23, 1808. .. Our readers will
please read in the advertisement inserted in the last page, for the sale of negro
MYLES, and after the word, MYLES, "belonging to the estate of Lemuel BURKITT,
dec'd." which the administrator accidentally omitted.

(471) On the 12th inst. David STONE, Esq. qualified as Governor of this State.

(472) North-Carolina Legislature. House of Commons. Tuesday, Nov. 29. .. Wednesday, Nov. 30. .. Received from the Senate the petition and presentation of
Dr. James NORCOM of E_enton, praying to be divorced from his wife Mary; read and
referred to the committee _ divorce and alimony. .. Monday, Dec. 5. Mr.
M'GUIRE, presented a bill to establish a separate election at the house of Mary
GREGORY, in Chowan. .. Friday, Dec. 9. Wm. A. LITTLEJOHN, the member elected to
represent the town of Edenton, in pursuance of a writ of election, appeared and
took his seat. An Attorney-General was balloted for, when Oliver FITTS was duly
elected. .. Tuesday, Dec. 13. Both houses agree to ballot to-morrow, for a
Judge of the Superior Courts of Law and Courts of Equity, and nominating for that
appointment Blake BAKER, R. WILLIAMS, J. G. WRIGHT, and Henry SEAWELL, Esqs.

(473) Norfolk, Dec. 12. .. It is stated in the last Monitor, that Gov. SULLI-
VAN, of Massachusetts, died on the 10th inst.

(474) Communicated. Died--on the 24th ult. in Tyrrel County, Orphy TARKINGTON--
And on the 26th, Milly TARKINTON, the only daughters of Col. Zebulon TARKINTON, of
that County.

95

(475)   State of North-Carolina, Chowan County,} Dec. Term, '08.   Whereas Myles HASSELL hath sued out an original attachment against the estate of Levi JONES, late of Chowan County, returnable to this Court at this term, It is Ordered, That public notice be given to the said Levi JONES, by advertisement in the Edenton Gazette for three months; that unless he appears at the next term of the said Court..at Edenton, on the second Monday in March next, replevy his estate, and plead to said action, final judgment will be entered up against him.   By Order, Elisha NORFLEET, Cl'k.

(476)   For Sale, On Five Years credit, The Turnpike & Farm At the head of Pasquotank County, with all the Cattle thereon &c. &c.—Also, a Tract of Land, lying in Chowan County, near to Mr. COLLINS's new road, and adjoining the Lands of the deceased Lemuel STANDIN, of BAINS and others, containing several hundred Acres, by patent Charles JOHNSON, Esquire. John HAMILTON. Elizabeth-City, Dec. 14, 1808.

Vol. III. Friday, December 30, 1808. Num. 149.

(477)   The Gazette. Friday. Edenton, December 30, 1808. The Legislature of this State have appointed Joshua G. WRIGHT, Esq. judge of the Superior Courts, in the room of David STONE, Esq. elected Governor.

(478)   Mr. WILLS, I cannot help regretting that the obligations I owe to you, to your readers, to decency and propriety, forbid my making such a reply to the false and scurrilous observations Charles SPRUILL as they so eminently deserve. .. However, that the world may no longer be ignorant of his villainy and malignity, I have been at the trouble of collecting a few certificates in order to place his conduct in a proper point of view.. These certificates..go directly to prove that Mr. SPRUILL has either mistaken or wilfully misrepresented the date of the transaction to which he refers; that he has impiously calumniated and insulted the memory of an unfortunate young man, whose sufferings in the closing scenes of his life ought to have exempted him from this profane and unhallowed attack..   ... Henry FLURY.
    State of N. Carolina, Chowan County, Personally appeared before me John BEASLEY, one of the Justices of the Peace for the County aforesaid, Edward GREEN, who being duly sworn..deposeth and saith, that on the 22d Dec. 1801, he arrived at Edenton with a load of lumber for Henry FLURY, Esq. and on the 23d of said Dec. in the morning, he went into said FLURY's store and requested him to let William WATSON, his clerk, receive the lumber, Mr. WATSON being then in the store—Mr. FLURY replied that Mr. WATSON was too busy in the store, and he could not spare him, but that he would get some other person—that Mr. FLURY did get a Mr. Joseph FERIBAULT, who received the said lumber—that he well remembers seeing Colonel Charles SPRUILL, of Tyrrel county, in the store of said FLURY—that this deponent was frequently in the store and remembers seeing William WATSON there on the 23d and 24th days of said December; and does not believe the said WATSON was absent from the store any longer on either of the days above mentioned than while at his meals; and further this deponent saith not. Edward his X mark. GREEN, Sworn to before me this 23d Dec. 1808. John BEASLEY, J. P.
    We, the undersigned, being called on by Henry FLURY, Esq. to examine his books for the year 1801, there find from the 4th Nov. to 30th of the same month, charges in the hand writing of William WATSON in his blotter against Charles SPRUILL, to the amount of L.23 12s.—also, on the 22d of Dec. there are entries in the same book, and an extension of figures in Charles SPRUILL's account; and on the 23d where Charles SPRUILL is charged, there are three entries in said WATSON's hand writing; and on the 24th several more: Whence it appears impossible for said WATSON to have been down the country on either of these days, as Mr. FLURY's hand

(478) (Cont.) writing and said WATSON's is in succession after each other. Given under our hands at Edenton, the 24th December, 1808. James R. BENT, James MOF-FATT, Duncan M'DONALD, Eli BARTEE, John DICKINSON.

By request of Henry FLURY, Esq. I do hereby certify, that I was present at an altercation between Henry FLURY, Esq. and Col. Chas. SPRUILL opposite the Court-House, one day in last October term, at which time, much irritating language was used by either party. Mr. FLURY accused said SPRUILL of having perjured himself in a suit depending between the parties, when SPRUILL threatened said FLURY with a prosecution for his character; but observed that he would obtain little satisfac-tion, because should damages be awarded, nothing would be received from his the said FLURY's embarrassed situation; the latter offered to furnish security; to which proposal, it is not recollected that said SPRUILL made any reply. I do not remember to have heard the said FLURY claim the protection of the Court at any time during said dispute. John M'FARLANE. Edenton, Dec. 24, 1808.

We do certify the above to be true according to the best of our recollection as we were present. John M'COTTOR, William HARRIS.

I do not recollect that Col. SPRUILL threatened Mr. FLURY with a prosecution.--but my impression is, that Mr. FLURY invited or challenged him to do so, when probably Col. SPRUILL remarked as stated in the above certificate, "that he would obtain little satisfaction, &c" To the rest of Dr. M'FARLANE's certificate I subscribe with a firm belief of its correctness. Jos. F. DICKINSON. Edenton, Dec. 28, 1808.

(479) Henry A. DONALDSON is appointed by the Legislature Colonel of this County, to supply the vacancy occasioned by the resignation of Nathaniel HOWCOTTE.

(480) Married--on Saturday evening last, Mr. William PELL, to Miss Nancy HALL, both of this Town.

(481) The Subscriber offers for Sale, on low terms, his Stock of Goods, among which are many Spring articles. Henry KING. December 28, 1808.

(482) I have for Sale, For Cash, a credit of Six months, or good paper at a dis-count, 500 bbls. of Corn.. Also, 40 or 50 bbls. of good merchantable Pork. ... Benj. COFFIELD. December 30, 1808.

(483) Notice. Agreeable to the last will of Samuel JACKSON, Esq. dec'd. late of the County of Tyrrel, Will Be Sold, before the Court-House door of said County..on Tuesday the 7th day of February next, nearly two thousand Acres of valuable Cypress and Juniper Swamp... Executors. December 26, 1808.

(484) Notice To all the creditors of Samuel JACKSON, late of the County of Tyrrel, that the said Samuel JACKSON is dead, and that the subscribers qualified as executors to his last will and testament at November term last. Those indebted to the deceased are requested to make immediate payment; and such as have demands are hereby notified, that unless they bring them forward agreeable to law, they will be barred of recovesy. Paul THEROGOOD, James HASSELL,) Ex'rs. December 26, 1808.

(485) Norfolk, Dec. 21. The electors of the states of Connecticut, Rhode Island, and New-Hampshire, have voted for Charles Cotesworth PINCKNEY as President, and Rufus KING as Vice-President, giving 20 votes for each. ..

1809 - Filmed from originals in the North Carolina State Library. Issue of 26 May is missing. [Note: The printer was out of town on personal business.]

6 January 1809

Vol. III. Friday, January 6, 1809. Num. 150.

(486)   The Gazette. Friday. Edenton, January 6, 1809. The General Assembly of
this state have closed their session. The following gentlemen are elected
Councillors of State for the ensuing year: Gideon ALSTON, Needham WHITFIELD, John
UMSTEAD, Thomas DAVIS, James KENAN, Matthew BRANDON and Wm. LANIER.

(487)   Captions of the Acts Passed last session of the Legislature. 1.   An Act
for the removal of the elections and battalion musters from Stanton HAROLDs _n the
county of Beaufort to the house of Jes_e ROBASON's on Hickory Point in the county
aforesaid. 2.   To remove the Courts of Brunswick county from LOCKWOOD's folly to
Smithsville. 3.   For the relief of the inhabitants in Capt. Jon. MERREL's company
district, in the _ourth Rowan county regiment of militia. 4.   To emancipate
Joseph BLACKWELL, in Brunswick county. .. 7.   For the removal of all
obstructions to the free passage of fish up the Six Runs as high as William
KERBY's bridge. 8.   To authorise Wm. W. JONES to erect and keep up a gate on the
road passing through _is Prospect plantation in Brunswick county. _.   To
authorise Thomas NICHOLSON to cut a _anal and make a road thereon. .. 12.   To
authorise and enable the securities of Kenneth M'IVER, Sheriff of Cumberland
county for the years 1804 and 1805 to collect the arrears of taxes due from the
inhabitants of said county for _he years aforesaid. .. 27.   To amend an act
_assed 1801, granting Philip HOODENPILE and _ob BARNETT, a turnpike in the county
of Bun_omb. .. 34.   To amend the act of 1807, to _uthorise Benj. JONES, Thos.
HARVEY, Enoch _AWYER and Fred. B. SAWYER, to cut a navi_able canal and make a road
thereon through the Great Dismal Swamp, from the Dismal _wamp Canal near the head
of the woods in Camden county, to the White Oak Spring Marsh in Gates, and to
demand and receive _oll thereon. .. 57.   To authorise Jos. H. BRYAN of Windsor,
and such other persons as may associate with him for that purpose, to raise by way
of lottery, a sum of money to enable him to carry on the manufactory of Salt. ..
70.   To restore to Philip HOLCOMBE of Buncombe county, the privileges of a citizen. .. 86.   To authorize Elisha ANDERS of Bladen county, to erect and keep up
two gates on his own land, on the road leading from Cape Fear river to South
river. .. 88.   To authorize John BLANKS of New-Hanover to build a bridge over
SMITHs creek, at the place where the bridge last stood. .. 92.   To remove the
separate election heretofore held as Jesse SCOFFIELD's in Pitt, to the house of
Palmer CANNON. .. 94.   Authorizing Silas HALEY, sen. to erect a gate on the road
leading from Rockingham in Richmond county to his ferry on Pee Dee river. ..
100.   To authorize Wilie FENNELL of Wake, to keep gates across the public road.
101.   To restore to credit John STARK of Granville. .. 108.   To emancipate
Charlotte GREEN and Leon GREEN of Chowan county. ...

(488)   Disaster At Sea. By the Blossom from Cape-Francois, we have received a
letter of the 9th inst. .. The letter confirms the narrative of the Swedish ship
Hjelton and the Venus, Capt. JELIO?FF, from Occacock to New-York, running foul of
each other on the 26th Nov. at night. Five of the Venus's people, including the
supercargo, got on board the Hjelton, and arrived in her at Cape-Francois. Such
was the state of the weather, that it was feared the Venus could not have survived
a quarter of an hour. [Balt. North Am.]
     [The Venus is the vessel, that sailed from this place with a load of Wheat for
N. York, and on board of which was James SUTTON, Esq. of this county, who,
together with the vessel and crew, were supposed to be lost.]

(489) Baltimore, Dec. 27. Marching Orders. Rumour has been busy..on the subject
of the Camp at Carlisle. The following extract of a letter from a highly
respected officer, reduces the fact to a certainty. "Carlisle Barracks, Dec. 23,

6 January 1809

(489) (Cont.) 1808. Sir, I march from this to-morrow for Pittsburgh, with two companies of Light Artillery. Report says the remaining troops here, amounting to upwards of 300, are to march to Baltimore about the first of the year, where they are to embark for New-Orleans. Very respectfully, Geo: PETERS." Mr. (blank).

(490) Married--at Buncomb-Hall, Washington County, on the 25th ult. Thomas B. HAUGHTON, Esq. Attorney at Law of this town, to Miss Eliza A. P. GOELET, daughter of John GOELET, Esq. of the former place.

(491) List of Letters remaining in the Post-Office at Edenton, 1st January, 1809. Samuel BURGES, Joel BAILEY, Capt. I. CROCKER, Michael CAPEHART, William DICKSON, John DICKINSON, Caleb ELLIOTT, William EASTON, Samuel FITT, John FOSTER, Jacob GREGG, Henry GRAY, Jesse HUNLEY, Isaac HOLLEY, Andrew HANNAH, Jonathan HARRISON, Capt. John JONES, Charles E. JOHNSON, Arthur JONES, Andrew KNOX, Frederick LUTON, King LUTON and Brothers, James W. LANGLEY, Mrs. Harriet LANGLEY, Henry MORRIS, Edward MURPHY, Nathaniel MILLER, John M'NIDER, Josiah MURDER, Duncan M'DONALD, Reuben MORGAN, Patrick O'CALLAGHAN, John PECK, Martin ROSS, Charles G. RIDGLEY, Etheridge RICHARDSON, Thomas SATTERFIELD, Thomas SMITH, John SMITH, Samuel SAUNDERSON, Mr. THOMPSON, inn-keeper, Benjamin TARKINTON, Wm. YOUNG, Mrs. Ann WHITE, Capt. John WILLIAMS, Mrs. Leah WALTON, Jesse WEST, John WOOD. Henderson STANDIN, P. M.

Vol. III. Friday, January 13, 1809. Num. 151.

(492) The Gazette. Friday. Edenton, January 13, 1809. .. Died--on the 5th inst. in this town, very suddenly, Mr. Lewis PANTIN, a native of England. At Philadelphia, on the 31st ult. in the 76th year of his age, John NIXON, Esq. President of the Bank of North-America.

(493) State of North-Carolina, Chowan County,) Superior court, Oct. Term, '08. John ALLEN vs Arthur JONES,) In Equity. The complainant having filed his bill in this Court, and the defendant having appeared and put in his answer thereto--and afterwards died before the said cause came on for hearing; and it being represented to the Court that Daniel JONES, brother and heir at law of the said Arthur JONES, dec. resides out of the state, so that process of revival cannot be personally served on him, It is therefore on motion of the complainants' counsel, Ordered, That notice be given to the said Daniel JONES, by advertisement, in the Edenton Gazette, for the space of two months; that unless he appears at or before the next term of the said Court, and be made a party defendant to the said cause, the said bill will be taken pro confesso against him; and the cause set for hearing on the said bill and answer. By Order, John B. BLOUNT, C. M. E. C. C.

(494) State of North-Carolina, Bertie County,) Superior Court, Oct. Term, '08. Whereas, William SLADE sued out an original attachment against the estate of George M'KENZIE, late of Edenton, returnable to this Court, in the term of April last; and it being represented to the said Court, that he is not an inhabitant of this state, It is therefore Ordered, That public notice be given to the said George M'KENZIE, by advertisement, in the Edenton Gazette, for two months, that unless he appears at the next Court, to be holden at the Court-House in Windsor, on the seventh Monday after the first Monday in March next, replevy his property and plead to the said action, that judgment final will be entered up against him. By Order, Simon TURNER, Cl'k.

(495) Notice. The subscribers have removed their Stock of Goods to their new Store House on the long wharf next door to the Post-Office, and are desirous of

13 January 1809

(495) (Cont.) disposing of the same on low terms for Cash. In consequence of the late law passed by the Legislature of this State prohibiting the collection of debts, they are under the necessity of informing all persons indebted to them, that they are resolved to close their accounts as speedily as possible by obtaining payment, or such security as the law allows. LITTLEJOHN & BOND. January 10, 1809.

(496) Taken up And committed to gaol in this County, on the 5th inst. a Negro Man of a yellowish complexion, who calls himself QUACKO, and says he is the property of a Mr. James BLOUNT, in Washington County, N. C. near Plymouth. He is 5 feet six and three quarter inches high, very stout made, and appears to be about 35 years of age. He says he left his master in April, 1807: But as no dependance can be put in him, perhaps some other person is his master. The owner can have him by applying to the subscriber, proving his property, and paying all expences. John C. BAKER. Brunswick County, N. C. December 8, 1808.)

Vol. III. Friday, January 20, 1809. Num. 152.

(497) The Gazette. Friday. Edenton, January 20, 1809. Our readers will please correct an error in Col. SPRUILL's last piece addressed to Henry FLURY, Esq. In the second column, 16th line from the top, for December 1807, read December 1801.

(498) Lorenzo DOW.--A report of the death of _his celebrated methodist apostle, in the Missi_ippi Territory, being in circulation in the papers, it may gratify his friends to be in_ormed that he has preached in Hudson se_eral times since he is stated to have died. Hudson Bee.

(499) The Altering & Repairing the Jail of Chowan County will be publickly offered by the Commissioners at said Jail on the 11th of next month, between the hours of 11 and 12 o'clock, and given to the lowest bidder--The alteration and repairs to be made.--Terms of payment, &c. may be known by applying to John LITTLE, one of the Commissioners. January 17, 1809.

(500) Notice is hereby given that the subscriber qualified at the December term of Washington county court, as administratrix to the estate of Daniel DAVENPORT, Esq. dec. All persons indebted..are requested to make immediate payment; and those having claims..are hereby notified to exhibit them properly authenticated, within the time limited by law. Lucretia DAVENPORT, Adm'x. Washington, Dec. 26, 1808.

(501) If Within Four Weeks, Ten Dollars reward will be given for apprehending, and delivering to the subscriber in Edenton, a negro man named HARRY, belonging to the estate of Richard BENBURY, dec'd. He is of middle stature, black, rather of an abject countenance and slow in speech--pretends to be a carpenter, and is extremely indolent--was thinly clad when he absconded. It is presumed he is either in Edenton where his wife resides, or its vicinity where his father and mother belong, or in some of the lower counties, where, in his master's life time, he attempted to seek a lurking place. ... Jos. B. SKINNER. Edenton, Jan. 16, 1809.

Vol. III. Friday, January 27, 1809. Num. 153.

(502) The Gazette. Friday. Edenton, January 27, 1809. .. State of North-Carolina, Chowan County.) Whereas application has been this 17th day of January, 1809, made to me Henry FLURY, one of the Justices of the Peace for the County

(502) (Cont.) aforesaid, on oath, by George SMALL, of the County aforesaid, that Alexander CUNNINGHAM of the State of Virginia, is justly indebted to him in the sum of twenty one pounds eight and six pence; and the said George SMALL having given security according to the Act of the General Assembly..and having filed his affidavit as to the justice of this debt; I have granted an attachment against the estate of the said Alexander CUNNINGHAM, which has been returned "Attached the schooner Delight, of Norfolk, Vir." at present lying and being along side of Mr. John SKINNER's wharf, in Edenton;--after which being returned. I have given judgment for the sum due him the said SMALL; and according to the directions of the law I now give public notice, that unless the said CUNNINGHAM, his agent or factor, comes forward at the expiration of thirty days and replevies his property, final judgment will be entered up against him, and the property so attached, will be sold by the Sheriff. Henry FLURY, J. P.

Vol. III. Friday, February 3, 1809. Num. 154.

(503) New-York, January 14. At a meeting of many thousands of such Citizens of the City of New-York, as disapprove of the recent measures of the Administration, particularly of the "Act making further provision for enforcing the Embargo," at Mechanic Hall, on Friday, the 13th of January, 1809. On motion of Judge PENDLETON, the Hon. Egbert BENSON, Esq. was chosen Chairman, and Edward DUNSCOMB, Esq. Secretary. .. Resolved, That the acts of Congress laying a permanent Embargo, are repugnant to the habits, and injurious to the welfare of the people, not to be justified by the state of public affairs, and inconsistent with the spirit of the constitution. Resolved, That this and other ruinous measures of the administration, have paralized every branch of industry, reduced the value of property, distressed all classes of our fellow-citizens, extinguished commerce, discouraged agriculture, nearly annihilated the public revenue, and must eventually load the people with heavy and oppressive taxes. .. Resolved, That whilst we cannot forbear to express a want of confidence in the wisdom and the impartiality of our present rulers; yet in a period of so much difficulty & danger, we feel it our duty, solemnly to call upon our fellow citizens, however aggrieved, to act with the utmost caution and moderation, and to abstain from every thing that might endanger the peace and safety of the country, or put the union of the states in jeopardy. ... Egbert BENSON, Chairman. Edward DUNSCOMB, Sec'y.

(504) The Gazette. Friday. Edenton, February 3, 1809. Federal Jack Affair. The schooner Federal Jack, laden with naval stores and said to be bound to Boston, where she is owned, has been detained, in this port, some months, owing to a difficulty in obtaining securities. At length, James JONES of Hertford and James HATHAWAY, Esq. of this place, consented to become securities, at the Custom-House, in very heavy bonds; but the latter objected to the master, who was engaged for the voyage, Presley HATHAWAY, and to two men by the names of TURNER and YOUNG, who appeared to be interested in the vessel and cargo, and were deemed suspicious. To remedy this difficulty, TURNER and YOUNG consented to relinquish their design of going on in the vessel; and Captain BROOKS a resident of this place was employed to proceed on to Boston, with powers to controul the Captain, who had been previously shipped. The Federal Jack cleared out the 2d ult. and sailed about the 13th, and arrived at the bar on the 21st. After she had sailed TURNER and YOUNG crossed Chowan river and proceeded by different routs to Washington, from whence they took passage for Occacock, and arrived a short time before the Federal Jack. As soon as she came to anchor, they came on board, when Captain BROOKS informed them they were not wanted on board, and directed them forthwith to depart.. The pilot who had been engaged to carry out the Federal Jack, was at this time engaged in carrying some other vessel over the bar. TURNER and YOUNG seeing this oppor-

(504) (Cont.) tunity, sent another pilot on board to whom they had, probably, given his cue. He informed the Captain that he was sent on board, by the pilot who had been engaged, who requested him to heave up and stand out to sea, when he would meet him. Captain BROOKS, at first, ordered him to desist, but afterwards, supposing his story correct, consented, and he accordingly got under way and stood out to sea. Capt. BROOKS retired below to write a line to his family; during which time, it appears that TURNER and YOUNG were received on board by Capt. HATHAWAY and concealed in the forecastle. Having gained some distance, so as to be out of reach of annoyance from the Revenue Cutter, they came from their place of concealment, and as Capt. BROOKS was stepping on deck, to his great astonishment he was met by TURNER, with YOUNG, close at his heels, who addressed him in a friendly manner and informed him they had no use for his services and did not wish for his company, and advised him to return to Edenton---that it was not their intention to mutiny or take the vessel from him, but that they intended to proceed on to Boston and did not need his assistance. They then, without further ceremony, put his trunk and baggage into the boat, and with the assistance of the crew, disposed of him in the same way, he being at the time so ill with intermittent fever, as to be incapable of helping himself. They presented him ten dollars to pay his expences, wished him a safe passage to Edenton and went their way: whether for Boston, or to make their escape from the clutches of "O grab me" time must determine.

Vol. III. Friday, February 10, 1809. Num. 155.

(505) The Gazette. Friday. Edenton, February 10, 1809. .. Union Canal and Road. The last Legislature of this State having passed an act, authorising the subscriber to sell out in shares the right of making a Canal and Road from the head of Little-River in Perquimans County through the Desart to intersect the main country Road near Pasquotank River Bridge. This is therefore to notify the public, that a scheme for that purpose is now opening in his hands for the disposal of the same, agreeable to the provisions of said act, which may be known by application to Thomas NICHOLSON. February 3d, 1809.

(506) New-York Republican Meeting. At a meeting of the Republican Citizens of the City and County of New York, for the purpose of expressing their sentiments on the measures of the general government; in the square in front of Mr. And?. MARTLING's, opposite the Park, on Wednesday, 18th Jan. 1809. Col. RUTGERS was chosen Chairman and Col. FEW, Secretary. The following resolutions were read, and carried unanimously. .. Resolve, That we continue to repose full confidence in the patriotism and talents of the President, Vice-President, and the republican majority in both houses of Congress of the United States. That viewing without partiality and with equal indignation the hostile acts of both the belligerent powers, we entirely approve of the Embargo and a rigid enforcement thereof.. Resolved, That in our opinion the conduct of the party opposing the measures of the present administration, is calculated to involve us in a war with the belligerent powers, inasmuch as it tends to exhibit us a people divided, even on questions involving our national independence.. .. Resolved, That the chair appoint nine of our republican fellow-citizens to be a corresponding committee to communicate with our republican friends in this and other of the United States on the interesting concerns of our country... The chairman in pursuance of the above powers has appointed the following persons.. Henry RUTGERS, William FEW, Tunis WORTMAN, Jonas HUMBERT, Samuel LAWRENCE, John HAFF, John BINGHAM, John MILLS, Abraham BLOODGOOD. ... Henry RUTGERS, Chairman, William FEW, Secretary.

17 February 1809.

THE EDENTON GAZETTE.
Friday, February 17, 1809. Edenton: Printed By James WILLS. Vol. III.-Num. 156.

(507) The Gazette. Friday. Edenton, February 17, 1809. .. A boat, with three men on board, which sailed from Salem harbor last summer, with fish for Martinique, (without papers) was taken and burnt by a French letter of marque, and the men carried into Bayonne as prisoners. They had been sent to Bourdeaux.— Their names are, Capt. (blank) DAVIS, Herbert READING, and (blank) ROGERS. We understand that the boat and men belonged to Gloucester. Salem Reg.

(508) To the number of highly respectable gentlemen who have resigned their offices, rather than be instrumental in executing tyrannical and unconstitutional acts, we add with satisfaction, the name of Hodijok BAYLIES, Esq. Collector at Dighton. Bost. Gaz.

(509) Fire.—On the 21st ult. the house occupied by John LYLE, at Carlisle, Pennsylvania, was destroyed by fire—both LYLE and his wife perished in the flames. It is said they had quarrelled the preceding evening and both went to bed intoxicated. An old woman made her escape, but was considerably burnt.

(510) Fresh Garden Seed, received from Norfolk, for Sale at the store of Henry A. DONALDSON. Edenton, Feb. 14, 1809.

(511) Notice. On Tuesday the 14th day of March next, will be Sold, before the Court-House in the Town of Edenton, that valuable Tract o_ Land, lying in Bear Swamp, containing 800 Acres, belonging to the estate of Mrs. Lydia BENNETT, dec'd. A credit of one, two, and three years will be given, the purchaser giving bond and approved security to the Executor. February 13th, 1809.

(512) From the New-Jersey Journal. Mr. KOLLOCK, I was much invested with Weevils in my barn, &c. and did not know how to get rid of them, till I found Tobacco was an effectual remedy. They are fond of it, eat it, go off and die. I deal in tobacco, and receiving two hogsheads (for which I had not room in my cellar at the time) I put them into the barn. On removing them I found thousands of dead Weevils on the barn floor, which cleared it entirely of this destructive animal. I then took two or three boxes, containing about six pounds of tobacco in each, and placed them in my granary, where I kept wheat, &c. This was soon cleared also, and I have not had any since. The boxes ought to be open enough to let the Weevils have free passage into them. If you think this will be of any use to your readers, it is at your service. I am yours, &c. Galvin SCOTT. Elizabeth-Town, Dec. 28, 1808.

Friday, February 24, 1809. Vol. IV.-Num. 157.

(513) Congress. House of Representatives. Saturday, Feb. 4. .. Mr. HOLMES from the committee of claims, reported a bill for the relief of John M. STOUT, of Kentucky. Referred to the committee of the whole on Monday. .. Wednesday, Feb. 8. .. The President of the Senate began to open the packets from the several electoral colleges, commencing at N. Hampshire and proceeding southward. .. The tellers after having counted the returns..reported to the President, who announced the same to the two Houses as follows: "From a report of the tellers for counting the votes given in for President and Vice-President of the United States they appear as follow:" .. The whole number of votes being 175, 88 of which are a majority. For President..James MADISON, of Virginia, has 122 votes, which being a majority of all the votes of the respective states, I therefore declare that the

(513) (Cont.) said James MADISON Is Elected President Of The United States for four years, commencing on the fourth of March next. And that George CLINTON, of New-York, having 113 votes,..I therefore declare that..George CLINTON Is Elected Vice-President Of The United States for four years, commencing on the fourth day of March next." ...

(514) Friday. Edenton, February 24, 1809. Mr. James WILLS, Office of the Edenton Gazette. Sir—After the publication in your paper of yesterday, tending to destroy the reputation of my brother, in which I can neither discover "justice propriety or impartiality," I presume you neither wish or affect a continuance of my patronage; I must therefore request you to discontinue my paper. I am your obedient servant, M. E. SAWYER. Feb. 18th, 1809.

Though the Editor of this paper has no inclination to humble himself before the author of the above angry note, yet he feels a sincere regret, at the idea of inflicting pain on the other, very respectable friends and connections, of the gentleman, supposed to be alluded to in the production signed "Jingle"—It came inclosed to the Editor, in the Western mail, accompanied by a small sum to pay for its insertion. Viewing it as a harmless production, incapable of injuring any mans reputation, he was, perhaps, inadvertently, lead to give it a place. Your paper, Doctor, is discontinued.

(515) Wilmington, Feb. 7. Yesterday the Federal Court began its session, his Honor Henry POTTER, Judge, Rob't. H. JONES, attorney for the United States, and Carlton WALKER, Clerk. The following causes were called and adjudged. The United States vs. Elias WILLIAMS, a prosecution for bringing negroes into this state contrary to law, verdict $1000 against defendant, and the lugger Fair-Trader, in which they were alledged to be brought, condemned. United States vs. Captain RIPLEY, for a violation of the Revenue act, in resisting, preventing and impeding the officers of the United States in the execution of their duty, verdict $25 against the defendant, and the schooner Throda, of which he was master, condemned for a violation of the Embargo act.

(516) Newbern, Feb. 16. The District Court of the United States, for the district of Pamptico, was holden at the court-house in this town on Friday last—Although there were several cases of seizure and penalties under the Embargo laws—only those relating to the brig Venus, John KER master, were tried. This vessel, being a foreign bottom, was condemned on one of the counts in the libel, stating "that she had proceeded from one of the ports in the U. States to another—viz. from..Baltimore, to the port of Ocracoke:" .. A penalty of $1000 was recovered against the master. .. The brig America, A. SHAW master, from Plymouth, in this state, is detained by the Collector of Ocracoke, her clearance manifest having no signature. Seized the schooner Abigail, whereof Josiah BACON was master, from Cape-Francois; it appears she was blown off the coast, and driven into the Cape, there sold, and purchased by Mr. Jas. SUTTON of Chowan, a small cargo of sugar and coffee on board, and several passengers who had unfortunately been blown off. .. We understand that the brig which ran away from Ocracoke, after having her sails unbent, is the brig Josephine, John AINSLEY master, belonging to a Mr. TUCKER of Norfolk, by the papers reetained in the Collector's office; but it is understood perfectly well who is the owner. Herald.

(517) Norfolk, February 15. .. February 17. .. Collector's Office, District Ocracoke, Feb. 4, 1809. Sir—The brig Josephine, Jno. AINSLY master, escaped from this port on Sunday evening, the 28th ult.—I had directed the officer of the Revenue Boat here to unbend her sails two days before, and otherwise to completely dismantle her.—The former part was observed, but I have to lament the other was

(517) (Cont.) not. It now appears that he brought a suit of sails from Norfolk with him, and availed himself of a moon-light night to get over our bar. .. I wish him published in every paper—I shall place him in the Newbern Herald. I am, very respectfully, Your obedient servant, James TAYLOR, Collector. Larkin SMITH, Esq. Collector, Norfolk.

(518) Rice JONES, Esq. a member of the House of Representatives of the Indiana Territory, was deliberately murdered in the streets of Kaskaskias, on the 7th of December, by Dr. James DUNLAP. Five hundred dollars are offered for the apprehending of DUNLAP.—ib.

(519) The 22d instant, being the birth day of the immortal WASHINGTON, was cele-brated in this place by the Edenton Volunteer Company, with that decent festivity, suited to the important day. At their request, an Oration was delivered, at the Episcopal Church, by Dr. Jonathan Otis FREEMAN.. In the evening a Ball was given, at the hall in the Court-House, attended by a numerous and brilliant assembly of ladies.

(520) The Subscriber offers his Medical services to the inhabitants of Edenton and country adjacent. Edm'd. B. HARVEY, No. 2, Cheap-Side.

(521) Public Meeting. Of the City and County of Philadelphia, Jan. 31. A numerous body of the citizens of the city and county of Philadelphia assembling in the State House yard in consequence of the call upon them to express their disapprobation of the Embargo and of the "enforcing act." Commodore Thomas TRUXTON, was unanimously called to the chair, and George CLYMER, Esq. appointed Secretary. The following resolutions were proposed to the meeting and adopted. .. Resolved, That we deem a longer continuance of the laws imposing the Embargo as unjust, oppressive, and impolitic. .. Resolved, That we consider the late act of Congress commonly called "the enforcing law" to be a direct invasion of the es-tablished principles of civil liberty, and of the express provisions of the constitution.. .. Resolved, That a committee be appointed to draft a memorial to Congress in conformity with the foregoing resolutions, to obtain the signature of our fellow citizens hereto, & to transmit the same to Congress. The following gentlemen were appointed..: Thomas TRUXTON, Thomas FITZSIMONS, George CLYMER, Timothy PAXSON, Joshua HUMPHREYS, Robert WAIN, Benjamin R. MORGAN, James MILNOR, and Charles W. HARE. Signed, Thomas TRUXTON, Chairman. George CLYMER, Sec'ry.

Friday, March 3, 1809. Vol. IV.-Num. 158.

(522) The Gazette. Friday. Edenton, March 3, 1809. .. Will Be Sold, At public Sale, on Saturday the 11th inst. at my late residence, in Green-Hall, about 100 Barrels of Corn. ... Baker HOSKINS. March 2d, 1809.

(523) Strayed or Stolen, from Gates Court-House, on Monday the 20th ult. a pretty likely Dark Bay Horse.. An exact description is not in my power to give, having been in possession of him only a few days, and having but an imperfect knowledge of the horse species—I will give a reward of Ten Dollars if delivered to me in Edenton, or Five Dollars if delivered to Capt. MITCHELL, in Gates County. Esther BENNETT. Edenton, March 1, 1809.

Friday, March 10, 1809. Vol. IV.-Num. 159.

(524) The Gazette. Friday. Edenton, March 10, 1809. .. On Tuesday night the 21st ult. at a tavern in Halifax, in N. C. a dispute arose between a Mr. ALSTON

(524) (Cont.) and a Mr. Tarlton JOHNSTON, in consequence of which Mr. A. took up a large carving knife to stab Mr. J, but failed in the attempt; they were separated, but Mr. A. soon afterwards returned and insulted Mr. J. again, which roused him to give Mr. A. a violent push, when he left the room in search of pistols, which he procured, and declared publicly he would put Mr. J. to death; but not being able to find him that evening, he next day repeated his search, and discovered through a window Mr. J. in a room with some gentlemen, who prevented his horrid intention from being put in execution. Mr. J. then applied to the civil authority to have A. arrested, but could not procure assistance to effect it. Mr. J. in order to guard against the threats of A. purchased a musket to defend himself, as he was then going out of town. Mr. A. followed him with a determination to take his life, and Mr. J. repeatedly turned round, desiring him to desist; but Mr. A. would not, and while Mr. J. was descending a hill, he Mr. A. snapped his pistol two or three times. Mr. J. then immediately after crossing a creek, finding Mr. A. determined to pursue, turned round, fired, and killed him on the spot. Mr. A. had just time before he expired, to request a gentleman that was near him to see him decently buried.—Mr. JOHNSTON returned to town, and gave himself up to the Court, when he was immediately let to bail. N. Her.

(525)   Col. Thomas COLES is appointed Collector of Providence, vice Col. OLNEY, resigned.

(526)   Baltimore, February 24. The Cotton Seed. When we first stated in this paper that Mr. JEFFERSON had written to a mercantile house in this city, requesting them to send two tierces of cotton seed, now on board a vessel in the river, to New-York, with intent that the same be shipped to France in the Mentor, the democratic papers pronounced the report to be false. .. We are now enabled to state, that Mr. John HOLLINS, a merchant of this city, and a connection of Gen. SMITH, has received a letter from Mr. JEFFERSON, in which his Excellency acknowledges, that he had obtained the cotton seed from a planter in Georgia, for the purpose of sending it to the Agricultural Society in Paris, and endeavours to justify his conduct; but as a clamour had been raised in consequence, he makes Mr. HOLLINS a present of the cotton seed, and authorizes him to dispose of the same as should be most agreeable to him. ...

(527)   Serious And Important. Extract of a letter from Lancaster, dated Feb. 27th, 1809. "Enclosed, you will find a message presented to the House of Representatives, this day, from the Governor. .. You will see by the message, that the Governor is making arrangements to call out a portion of the militia of this state to oppose at least, the Judiciary of the U. States."
    Governor's Message. "To the Senate and House of Representatives of the Commonwealth of Pennsylvania. Gentlemen, I have received information, that the supreme court of the United States, hath ordered a peremptory mandamus to be issued in the suit of Gideon OLMSTEAD and others, vs. Elizabeth SERGENT and Esther WATERS, executrixes of the late Mr. RITTENHOUSE, and that immediate application will be made to Richard PETERS, Judge of the district court of Pennsylvania for an execution against the persons and effects of the said Elizabeth SERGENT and Esther WATERS; or rather, as it is an admiralty proceeding, an attachment against their persons will be the compulsory process adopted on the occasion. By the act of the 2d of April, 1803, Mrs. SERGENT and Mrs. WATERS are directed to pay a sum of money arising out of the sale of the British brig active, captured during the late revolutionary war, into the state treasury; with the requisition of that law the said executrixes have complied. It now becomes my duty, agreeably to the provisions of that act, to protect the property and persons of the executrixes against such process. Painful as this duty is, I am compelled, and am now making arrangements, to

10 March 1809

(527) (Cont.) call out a portion of the militia for that service, that being the only means in the power of the executive. As the execution of this law may produce serious difficulties as it respects the relation of the state government with that of the United States, I have thought proper to make this communication, on which the Legislature can act as in their wisdom they shall think expedient. Simon SNYDER. Lancaster, Feb. 27, 1809."

Friday, March 17, 1809. Vol. IV.-Num. 160.

(528) The Gazette. Friday. Edenton, March 17, 1809. .. A New-York paper of March 3, has the following:—We yesterday received a letter from Mr. D. JOY, of New-Bedford.—This letter contains the following deaths, with common sickness, during the short period of 10 months and 24 days. The Deaths.—Died, at Nantucket, 12th March, 1808, Miss Mary JOY, aged 15 months—March 25, Miss Winifred JOY, aged 4 years—December 31, Franklin JOY, aged 10 months—January 26, 1809, Mrs. Kezia JOY, aged 33—and February 5, Miss Eliza JOY, aged 7 years.—The wife and children of Captain David JOY. ...

(529) The Cabinet. Robert SMITH, (Md.) Secretary of State. Albert GALLATIN, (Penn.)—the Treasury. Paul HAMILTON, (S. C.)—the Navy. William EUSTIS. (Mass.)—at War. C. A. RODNEY, (Del.) Attorney-General. It is stated in the morning papers, that the following appointments have been made by President MADISON: John Q. ADAMS, Minister to Russia. Thomas SUMPTER, (S. C.) Minister to Rio Janeiro, Brazils (sic). Henry HILL, Consul, ditto. David HOLMES, Governor Mississippi Territory. John BOYLE, Governor Illinois Territory. Nathaniel POPE, Secretary of ditto.

(530) Died—on Wednesday morning last, Mrs. Catharine BELL, wife of Capt. Daniel BELL, of this town.

(531) From the Bridgeport Advertiser. Mr. RIPLEY, Among the many who near the time of the end, according to the prophet Daniel, should run to and fro and by whom knowledge should be increased, Captain James ALLEN, of this borough, appears to be one. He has lately returned to his family and friends after an absence of about two and half years, traversing different seas and visiting different countries. At the port of Gargente, in the island of Sicily, in the Mediterranean, he spent considerable time. Among many things gratifying to the curious to hear, he lately described to me some enormous Human skeletons seen by him on that island. ... Joseph BACKUS.
    Bridgeport, Dec. 21, 1808. Joseph BACKUS, Esq. Sir, In compliance with your request, and in answer to your different enquiries, be pleased to accept the following statement. In the spring of the year 1807, I was master of the ship Jupiter, of Philadelphia, on a voyage up the Mediterranean; and in the month of May in that year, lay a considerable time in the port of Gargente, in the island of Sicily.. While lying there, I was informed that some human skeletons of vast size, had been lately dug from the ground, about three miles from Gargente. .. On arriving at the place I was shown two skeletons, the one much broken, the other entire, except a small piece of one of the leg bones being wanting. The bones of the entire skeleton were promiscuously laid in a box, but measured, when laid in a natural position 11 feet and 4 inches, Italian measure, in length 10 of which inches equal to 9 English, or very nearly; making the skeleton about 10 feet and a half English. I measured one of the thigh bones, which was 26 Italian inches long, and of a proportionate size—its diameter..being about 4 inches English. The head, including the skull and jaws, were about the dimensions of a common two gallon pail or bucket, and the rest of the bones were in suitable proportion to

(531) (Cont.) those described.. The discovery of the bones was made..about a year be-fore I was there. Some of the neighbouring people having pitched upon the place from whence they were dug (a vale by the side of a mountain) for the purpose of digging of sulphur..opened the ground, and by degrees descended to the depth of 170 feet, when they came to a marble wall, erected by art, and ornamented with heiroglyphical representations. While attempting to remove a part of it, the wall fell, when within was discovered a hollow place, in which were the bones described, and which appeared to have been enclosed in marble coffins or cases, also adorned with hieroglyphicks. The parts of the supposed cases were so broken by the falling of the wall, that their proper shape and design was not ascertained. One of the skeletons was also much broken at the same time; the other was however entire, as before stated.

The falling of the wall so deranged the parts of the vault, that it could not be determined whether it was in fact a sepulchre or some other building; nor was it ascertained whether those were skeletons deposited there by design, or were those of persons killed by the sinking of a city, and buried in its ruins at the time of some awful catastrophe, but that at some period of the world the place where the bones were found had been the site of some opulent city, adorned with the arts, and which had, by some great convulsion of nature, been sunk and overwhelmed by the sea, there can be no doubt: the marble blocks and slabs taken from the wall, part of which had not been removed, all engraved in the most curious manner, with various devices, and which I carefully viewed, having descended into the aperture to its bottom for that purpose, satisfied me of the fact. Besides, the earth through which the workmen descended was all made earth, appearing to be composed of sea-mud filled with oyster, scollop and other sea-shells of uncommon size. There was however no tradition among the inhabitants, as I could learn, of such a city, or of any such great convulsion as must have destroyed it. .. I am willing to make oath to the truth of my statement, when convenient for you to attend for that pupose. I am Sir, Your most obedient servant, James ALLEN.

State of Connecticut, ss. Bridgeport, Dec. 23, 1808.) Before me, Joseph BACKUS, Notary Public for the State of Connecticut, residing at said Bridgeport, peasonally appeared Captain James ALLEN, signer of the foregoing letter, and being duly sworn, made solemn oath to the truth of the statement therein contained. Joseph BACKUS, Not. Pub.

(532) From the Providence Gazette. Col. OLNEY's Resignation. .. Custom House, District of Providence, the 10th of Jan. 1809. Respected Sir, Having been honored with the confidence of the late father of his country, President WASHINGTON, and having received from him, so long ago as June 1790, the appointment and commission as Collector of the Customs for the district of Providence, state of Rhode Island, in which office I have since, by the indulgence of succeeding Presidents, continued—and after rendering long, faithful and impartial military and civil services to my country, for the course of twenty-seven, out of the last thirty four years of my life—I have..formed a resolution to resign my said commission (which is enclosed) and office, as Collector of the Customs, immediately, or so soon as you can select a person more willing than myself to execute the fatal Embargo act of the 9th January 1809, to succeed me in said office... Jeremiah OLNEY, Collector. Hon. Thomas JEFFERSON, President of the U. States.)

Friday, March 24, 1809. Vol. IV.-Num. 161.

(533) The Gazette. Friday. Edenton, March 24, 1809. We are under the painful necessity of publishing on a half sheet, until our paper, which has been some time sent for, shall arrive. The last Embargo act, which required bonds for six times

(533) (Cont.) the amount of vessel and cargo, has been the only cause of our disappointment in receiving paper in due time. This difficulty is now, we presume, finally removed. [Note: This issue contains only two pages.]

(534) Appointments, Made by President MADISON, by and with the advice of the Senate. Francis Xavier MARTIN, of North-Carolina, to fill the vacancy produced by the resignation of Peter Bryan BRUIN, a Judge of the Missisippi Territory. Obadiah JONES of Georgia, Jesse B. THOMAS of Illinois territory, and Alexander STUART, of Virginia, to be Judges of the Illinois territory. Thomas NELSON, Collector and Inspector of York, in Virginia, to be Commissioner of Loans for the state of Virginia.
    Navy Agents. Samuel STORER, Portland, Maine. Henry S. LANGDON, Portsmouth, N. H. Francis JOHONNET, Boston, Mass. Joseph HULL, Middletown, Con. John BULLUS, New-York. George HARRISON, Philadelphia. John STRICKER, Baltimore. Theo. ARMISTEAD, Norfolk. Nat. INGRAHAM & Son, Charleston. James MORRISON, Lexington, K. Keith SPENCE, New-Orleans. Archibald S. BULLOCK, Savannah, Geo. (sic) Daniel CARMICK, now a Captain of Marines, to be Major of Marines. James THOMPSON, Edward HALL, and Michael REYNOLDS, now First Lieutenants of Marines, to be Captains of Marines. Samuel C. MILLER, now a Second Lieut. of Marines, to be First Lieut. of Marines. Jasper HAND, of Pennsylvania, to be a Surgeon in the Navy of the U. States. Samuel BLAIR, and Samuel HORSELY, of Virginia, to be Surgeons Mates in the Navy of the U. States.
    Military Appointments, Made previous to the 4th of March last. Brigadier Generals. Wade HAMPTON. Peter GANSEVOORT. Regiment of Light Artillery. Lieut. Colonel--Vacant. Major--John SAUNDERS. Light Dragoons. Colonel--Wade HAMPTON, (promoted as above.) Lieut. Col.--Leonard COVINGTON. Major--Electus BACKUS. Riflemen, Colonel--Alexander SMYTH. Lieut. Colonel--William DUANE. Major--John FULLER. Third Regiment of Infantry. Colonel--Edward PASTEUR. Lieut. Col.--John SMITHE. Major--Homer V. MILTON. Fourth Regiment of Infantry. Colonel--John P. BOYD. Lieut. Colonel--John WHITING. Major--James MILLER. Fifth Regiment of Infantry. Colonel--Alexander PARKER. Lieut. Colonel--Wm. D. BEALL. Major--Tuily ROBINSON. Sixth Regiment of Infantry. Colonel--Jonas SIMONDS. Lieut. Colonel--Joseph CONSTANT. Major--Zebulon M. PIKE. Seventh Regiment of Infantry. Colonel--William RUSSEL. Lieut. Colonel--Robert PURDY. Major--Elijah STRONG.

(535) List Of Acts, Passed at the Second Session of the Tenth Congress. .. 4. An act for the relief of Andrew Joseph VILLIARD. .. 6. An act for the relief of Augustine SERRY. .. 10. An act for the relief of Edmund BEEMONT. .. 21. An act for the disposal of certain tracts of land in the Missisippi Territory, claimed under Spanish grants, reported by the land commissioners as ante-dated; and to confirm the claims of Abraham ELLIS and Daniel HAREGAL. .. 29. An act to extend to Amos WHITTEMORE and William WHITTEMORE, jun. the patent right to a machine for manufacturing cotton and wool cards. ...

(536) I Have For Sale, On a liberal credit, or cash at a handsome discount, a number of Likely Negroes, consisting of Men, Women, Boys and Girls. Joseph B. SKINNER. Edenton, March 23, 1808.

(537) Notice. The Subscriber has determined to discontinue the Ferry from his house i_ Washington County after the first day o_ April next, and gives this information, in order that no person may apply after that day. James SUTTON. March 23, 1809.

Friday, March 31, 1809--No. 162.

(538) The Gazette. Friday. Edenton, March 31, 1809. .. Extract from a letter written in Philadelphia. "Presuming it may be useful to you, we are induced to state, that David PARRISH, Esq. has, for a premium of 50 per cent. in_ured to the amount of 10,000 dollars, that vessels will be allowed to clear out from the United States to Great-Britain and her dependencies, on or before the 16th of April next." ... Balt. paper.

(539) Communicated. Married—on Tuesday the 21st instant, in Bertie County, Mr. Moses G. SPIVEY, to Miss Sally FREEMAN, daughter of Mr. Jeremiah FREEMAN, all of that County.

(540) Bank of Newbern. Edenton-Office, March 24, 1809. After the 6th day of April, all Bills, Bonds and Notes offered for discount at this Office, must be delivered to the Agent (under cover, mentioning the name of the offerer) every Thursday instead of Monday as heretofore. The discounts will be declared on Friday morning, and the money paid immediately. John B. BLOUNT, Agent.

(541) For Sale, Freight or Charter, The fast sailing brig Susanna, Benj. BISSEL, master, burthen 158 Tons. For terms (which will be reasonable) apply to Nath. C. BISSEL.

(542) Common Prayer Books, For Sale, by Simeon NYE.

(543) 25 Dollars Reward. Run-Away from the subscriber, living in Martin County, 3 miles above Hamilton, on the 3d inst. a negro man named POLIDORE. He is of a yellow complexion, about 20 years of age, 5 feet 5 or 6 inches high, and has a very notable scar on one of his ears in the form of a crescent or half moon. .. The above reward will be paid to any person on delivering said negro to me, if taken out of the limits of this County; or half that sum if taken within it. Joshua TAYLOR. Martin County, March 8, 1809.

Friday, April 7, 1809. Vol. IV.-Num. 163.

(544) The Gazette. Friday. Edenton, April 7, 1809. .. Rebellion! Pennsylvania Legislature. Thursday, March 2. A letter addressed to the Speaker accompanied with documents, from the Secretary of the commonwealth, were read as follow, viz. Sir—In compliance with a resolve of the House of Representatives of yesterday, I transmit to you a copy of a letter to the Adjutant-General; also a copy of the Governor's orders to Gen. Michael BRIGHT. .. N. B. BOILEAU, Sec'ry. Secretary's Office, March 2, 1809. Jas. ENGLE, Esq. Speaker of the House of Representatives.
    Secretary's-Office, Lancaster. Sir—I am directed by the Governor to inclose to you certain orders to Gen. Michael BRIGHT, the purport of which..requires that they should be immediately delivered. .. N. B. BOILEAU, Secretary. To Thomas M'KEAN, Junior, Adjutant General, P. M. Sir—By an act of the General Assembly of this commonwealth, passed the 2d day of April, 1808, Elizabeth SERGEANT and Esther WATERS, surviving executrixes of David RITTENHOUSE, deceased, were required to pay into the treasury of this commonwealth a sum of money arising out of the sale of the British sloop Active, captured in the late revolutionary war (which money had been paid to the said deceased in his life time, as the treasurer of this common-wealth, in pursuance of a decree of George ROSS, Esq. Judge of the admiralty court of Pennsylvania,) which requisition..has been complied with by the said executrix-es, contrary to a decree of Richard PETERS, Esq. one of the United States' Judges of the district court of Pennsylvania. .. And the Governor..is required by the said recited act.."to protect the just rights of the state, in respect of the

(544) (Cont.) premises, by any further means and measures that he may deem necessary for the purpose, & also to protect the persons and properties of the said Elizabeth SERGEANT and Esther WATERS, from any process whatever issued out of any federal court in consequence of their obedience to the requisition aforesaid." Having been informed that a peremptory mandamus has been issued from the supreme court of the U. States, commanding the said Richard PETERS to issue process against the said Elizabeth SERGEANT and Esther WATERS, it becomes my duty.. I, Simon SNYDER, governor of the said commonwealth, reposing special trust and confidence in you, Michael BRIGHT, commander of the first brigade of the first division of the Pennsylvania militia, do hereby authorise and require you immediately to have in readiness such a portion of the militia under your command, as shall be sufficient..to employ them to protect and defend the persons and property of the said Elizabeth SERGEANT and Esther WATERS, from and against any process founded on the decree of the said Richard PETERS.. In the execution of these orders..it is my express orders that you injure no person or persons, attempting to serve, or execute such process..unless the most imperious necessity compels you to do it .. Simon SNYDER. Lancaster, February 27th, 1809. To General Michael BRIGHT.

(545) Richmond, March 28. Fire. Yesterday a fire broke out in a house belonging to a Mr. MARKS of this city, situated upon the main street above the Bell-Tavern, which together with many adjacent thereto was soon reduced to ashes.—This building was contigious to the vendue store of Mr. James BROWN Jr. whose losses independent of his buildings, must, we presume, be infinitely greater than those of any other individual. ...

(546) Thomas PAINE died near New-York on the 24th ult.

(547) Letters remaining in the Post-Office at Edenton, April 1, 1809. Charles ARMOUR, Samuel BURGES, Jeremiah BRITE, Henry P. BENNETT, Benjamin BROWN, Samuel CHESSON, Mich'l CAPEHART, Joseph P. CAMM, John DREW, Robert DICKEY, Wm. EATEN, John FOSTER, Jas. GORDON and Co. Richard HOWETT, Edmund HOSKINS, Hannah SAUNDERS, Amelia HARRIS, Wm. HAUGHTON, Silvanus HOWETT, Arthur JONES, Andrew KNOX, King LUTON, Reuben MORGAN, Wm. MONTGOMERY, Matt. MECOM, Exum NEWBY, Elizabeth PEMBRUN, Silas PIPOON, Margaret PARISH, Sarah PARISH, Etheridge RICHARDSON, Zedekiah STONE, Wm. SLADE, Elizabeth SATTERFIELD, John SMITH, Peter WINSOR, Thomas VAIL. Hend. STANDIN, P. M.

Friday, April 14, 1809. Vol. IV.-Num. 164.

(548) The Gazette. Friday. Edenton, April 14, 1809. .. Appointments Made by the late President of the United States, in the recess of the Senate, in 1808, and which have since been submitted to and approved by them. James Charles JEWETT, of Massachusetts, Surveyor of the district of Portland and Falmouth, and Inspector of the revenue for the several ports within the same. Isaiah WESTON, Collector of the district, and Inspector of the port of New-Bedford, (already published.) John STEELE, of Pennsylvania, Collector for the district of Philadelphia. John ENNALS, of Maryland, Collector for the district, and Inspector of the revenue for the port of Vienna. Athanasius FENWICK, of Maryland, Collector for the district of St. Mary's. William JACKSON, of Maryland, Surveyor and Inspector of the revenue for the port of Nanjemoy. Eugene SULLIVAN, of Virginia, Surveyor and Inspector of the revenue for the port of West-Point. Robert H. JONES, of North-Carolina, Attorney of the United States for the district of North-Carolina. Levi BLOUNT, of North-Carolina, Collector for the district, and Inspector of the revenue for the port of Plymouth, in North-Carolina. John POOLER, of Georgia, Commissioner of Loans in the state of Georgia. Richard WALL, of Georgia, Collector for the district of

14 April 1809

(548) (Cont.) Savannah. Peter WILSON, of Ohio, Receiver of Public Monies for lands of the United States, at Steubenville. Charles MINIFIE, a Justice of Peace for the county of Washington, in the district of Columbia. Richard S. BRISCOE, a Justice of Peace for the same county. William ORR, of North-Carolina, Collector for the district, and Inspector of the revenue for the port of Washington, in North-Carolina.

(549) A premature account has been published, announcing the death of Thomas PAINE.--By the last advices from New-York, we are informed, that he has experienced a severe illness, but is at present in a convalescent state. N. Herald.

(550) Communicated. Died--on the 10th inst. near this place, after a lingering illness which she bore with christian fortitude, trusting in her blessed Redeemer, Mrs. Mary COTTON, wife of Mr. Lemuel COTTON, in the 49th year of her age.

(551) United States of America, Albemarle District,)ss. Whereas Robert H. JONES, Esq. Attorney of the said U. States, for the District of North-Carolina, hath exhibited a libel before the Honorable Henry POTTER, Esq. Judge of the District Court aforesaid, suggesting that Levi BLOUNT, Esq. Collector of the Customs..at the port of Plymouth, in the District aforesaid, on the 30th day of July..one thousand eight hundred and eight, at and within the District and port aforesaid, then and there..did seize and arrest..to the United States, a certain schooner called the Sally of Skewarky, together with her boat, tackle, furniture and apparel, the property of a certain Edward YELLOWLEY, a citizen of the said United States, resident within the District aforesaid, for this cause, to wit, that the said schooner..did, between the twenty-second day of December..one thousand eight hundred and seven, and the said day of seizure, depart from a port or place within the limits and jurisdiction of the said United States, without a clearance or permit, to a foreign port or place, to wit, from the port and District of Brunswick, in the Georgia District..to the Island of Jamaica.. Whereupon it is Ordered..That publication be made..that unless cause be shown to the contrary, at the Court to be held at the Court-House in the Town of Edenton, on the first Tuesday following the Friday next after the first Monday in June next, for Albemarle District, the said schooner..will, for the causes aforesaid, be adjudged forfeited to the said United States. Test, John W. LITTLEJOHN, Cl'k.

(552) Notice. The subscriber begs leave, respectfully to inform the public, that in addition to his usual business of repairing Clocks and Watches, making gold and silver work, &c. he has furnished himself with every thing necessary for Repairing and Touching the Mariner's Compass.--He returns his thanks to a generous public for past favors and solicits their continuance. Martin NOXON. Edenton, April 13, 1809.

(553) State of North-Carolina, Chowan County Court,) March term, '09. Whereas Henry GARDNER, hath sued out an original attachment against the estate of Alexander CUNNINGHAM, late of Norfolk, returnable before the County Court of Pleas and Quarter-Sessions for the County aforesaid--It is Ordered, That public notice be given to the said Alexander CUNNINGHAM, by advertisement in the Edenton Gazette for three months; that unless he appears at the next term of the said Court..at Edenton, on the second Monday in June next, and plead to his action, final judgment will be entered up against him. By Order, Elisha NORFLEET, Clerk.

Friday, April 21, 1809. Vol. IV.--Num. 165.

(554) The Gazette. Friday. Edenton, April 21, 1809. .. Married (after all)--

(554) (Cont.) on Thursday night last, Mr. William LONG, of Perquimans County, to Miss Polly HASSEL, daughter of Mr. Jesse HASSEL, of this county. In Raleigh, on the 30th ult. Mr. William W. SEATON, Printer, to the accomplished Miss Sarah Weston GALES, daughter of Mr. Joseph GALES, principal proprietor of the Raleigh Register.

Died--on the 12th inst. In Bertie County, Captain William ASHBURN, an old and repectable inhabitant of that County.

(555) For Sale, At a reduced price for Cash, A quantity of white oak pipe and hhd. and red oak hhd. Staves, on Yoppim river. For terms apply to Edm'd. HOSKINS. April 20th, 1809.

(556) The Subscriber Has for Sale some improved Wheat Fans. Thomas TROTTER. Washington county, April 11, 1809.

Friday, April 28, 1809. Vol. IV.-Num. 166.

(557) The Gazette. Friday. Edenton, April 28, 1800. .. Philadelphia, April 11. We understand that the Marshal of the district contrived to find admission into the house of Mrs. SERGEANT, one of the heirs o_ David RITTENHOUSE: the centinel placed on the Arch-street front of the house, not knowing the person of the Marshal, continued his usual walk in front of his post, and during the time after he had passed the door, the Marshal entered. One of Mrs. SERGEANT's daughters seeing the Marshal enter, shrieked, and this gave an alarm; Mrs. SERGEANT retired to the house of Mrs. WATERS, her sister, both houses communicating by the garden in the rear; the alarm being given, the centinel posted in the rear, entered, and the Marshal was compelled to decamp at the point of the bayonet.--The Marshal made a similar attempt to enter at Mrs. WATERS door in Seventh-street, but was repulsed. ..

April 17. The war, which has kept a part of the city agitated for these two or three weeks past, seems now near its close. The Marshal of this district, who was opposed vi et armis, by order of Governor SNYDER, in his attempt to serve process..found means by disguising himself..and entered the house of Mrs. SERGEANT, between 6 and 7 o'clock on Saturday morning, when he served his process on that lady. .. In consequence of his success the Marshall immediately published the following: It is with extreme satisfaction I announce..the execution of the process in the case of OLMSTEAD..thereby rendering it unnecessary for the citizens, summoned by me, to attend, as the power of the district, at the state house on the 18th inst. and their services are hereby dispensed with. John SMITH, Marshal Philadelphia, April 15th, 1809.

(558) Prosperous Times Coming. By the President of the United States.. A Proclamation. Whereas it is provided by the 11th section of the Act of Congress, entitled, "An Act to interdict the commercial intercourse between the United States and Great-Britain and France, and their dependencies; and for other purposes"--that "in case either France or Great-Britain shall so revoke or modify her edicts, as that they shall cease to violate the neutral commerce of the United States," the President is authorized to declare the same by proclamation.. And whereas the Honorable David Montague ERSKINE, his Britannic Majesty's Envoy Extraordinary and Minister Plenipotentiary, has..declared to this Government, that the British Orders in Council of January and November, 1807, will have been withdrawn as respects the United States, on the 10th day of June next. Now therefore I James MADISON, President of the United States, do hereby proclaim that the Orders in Council aforesaid will have been withdrawn on the said 10th day of June next; after which day the trade of the United States with Great-Britain, as sus-

(558) (Cont.) pended by the Act of Congress above mentioned, and an Act laying an Embargo on all ships and vessels in the ports and harbors of the United States, and the several acts supplementary thereto may be renewed. Given under my hand and the Seal of the United States, at Washington, the nineteenth day of April..one thousand eight hundred and nine, and of the Independence of the United States, the thirty-third. James MADISON. By the President, R. SMITH, Sec'ry. of State.

(559) An account of a dead body found under the porch of Christ Church, in Boston, in a high state of preservation. A circumstance occurred a short time since while the workmen were repairing Christ Church, in this town, and erecting some new tombs under it, that deserves to be recorded in the Anthology. The ground under the porch at the entrance of the Church was directed to be dug up, this spot having been given for the erection of two tombs. At the distance of six feet from the surface, a grave was discovered, in which was found a coffin of hard pitch pine, commonly called the Norway pine, very little decayed, which on being opened, contained another of the same wood, very handsomely made, and not at all injured; the lid of this being lifted, showed a body wrapped in tarred sheets, that on being removed from the face, presented the countenance of a man that appeared quite recently to have died; his face, was fresh and florid as though just shaved; the flesh hard to the touch, and every appearance of a new corps (sic), from a short and not painful illness; two or three sprigs of myrtle or box green as just from the stalk were also laying on the outside of the tarred sheets--Both coffins had on their lids, in brass nails, the letters J. T. and a grave stone, at the head of the grave, declared the person interred there, to be Mr. John THOMAS, of the Island of Barbadoes, aged 45 years, who died 25th June. A. D. 1726, more than 82 years ago--The number of persons who came to see this curious fact, from the firmness of the preservation, and the manner of it induced the wardens to direct the coffin to be closed again and buried, which it is, at the N. E. corner of the Church. The soil under the porch was a yellow clay, mixed with small stones and some gravel. ...

Friday, May 5, 1809. Vol. IV.-Num. 167.

(560) The Gazette. Friday. Edenton, May 5, 1809. The Editor informs his Patrons and the public that No. 170. which will be issued on the 2d of June, will complete three years of his establishment: After which period, owing to the increased price of every article essential to his business, he is, by imperious necessity, compelled to raise the terms of this publication to Three Dollars per annum, to be paid in advance. ...

(561) Thomas NEWTON, Esq. is re-elected in the Norfolk District, by a majority of 352 votes over Robert TAYLOR, the federal candidate.

(562) John RANDOLPH, Esq. is re-elected in Cumberland District, by a majority of 753 votes over his opponent Jeremiah BAKER, Esq.

(563) Notice. That on the first day of June next, will be exposed to public sale, in DURANTS' Neck, in the County of Perquimans, a valuable Tract or Parcel of Land and Plantation, the property of the subscribers, on easy terms. The quantity is One Hundred and Sixty Eight Acres.. Nearly One Hundred Acres cleared on the Plantation. Levin CATOR, Anna CATOR. May 4th, 1809.

(564) 20 Dollars Reward. In the night of the 26th inst. the Store of the Subscriber was broken open, and the following Notes, &c. stolen therefrom, viz. Ambrose SMITH's Note, dated 10th June, 1806, payable to Jackson S. HOYLE, for $103

(564) (Cont.) 69 Cents. James W. LANGLEY's acceptance, dated 2d July, 1807, drawn by William E. BEASTALL, in favor of do. for $7 80 Cents. Nathaniel WILLARD's Note, dated 27th July, 1807, for $2 65 Cents. Martin NOXON's due bill, dated 8th August, 1807, for $1 34 Cents. Woolsey HATHAWAY's Note, dated 16th May, 1808, payable to Jackson S. HOYLE, for $34 22 1-2 Cents. Jonathan O. FREEMAN's Note, dated 25th May, 1808, payable to do. for $188 with two endorsements. William MANNING's do. same date, payable to do. for $23 75 Cents. William SLADE's conditional Note, dated 11th June, 1808, payable to do. for $64 83 Cents. William RIGHTON's Note, dated 24th June, 1808, payable to do. for $48 25 Cents. William CLARK's do. dated 12th July, 1808, payable to do. for $215 73 Cents, with one endorsement. Thomas BRITT's do. dated 8th October, 1808 payable to do. for $94 40 Cents. Townsend ELLIOTT's do. dated the latter end of March or beginning of April, 1809, payable to do. for $15 18 Cents, or thereabouts. Willis WILDER's do. dated 16th April, 1808, payable to William TAYLOR, endorsed by him to Benj. COFFIELD, and by COFFIELD to John BATEMAN, for $16 50 Cents. Ten Dollars reward will be given for the recovery of the above described papers, and Ten Dollars for the detection of the perpetrators of this act of wanton villany--And all persons are forwarned not to buy or trade for any of the Notes abovementioned. Jackson S. HOYLE. Edenton, April 28, 1809.

Friday, May 12, 1809. Vol. IV.-Num. 168.

(565) From the American Citizen. Equal Rights! General Meeting. At a respectable meeting, consisting of about five hundred Adopted Republican Citizens of the city of New-York, held at LYON's Hotel, Mott-street, on Friday evening, the 4th inst. Mr. Archibald TAYLOR being unanimously called to the chair, and Dr. Stephen DEMPSEY appointed Secretary. The subjoined address and resolutions were unanimously adopted. Address To the Adopted Republican Citizens of the City of New-York. Fellow-Citizens, A long train of disagreeable circumstances have called us together and induced us to address you upon a subject, which for years, we have acutely felt and deeply deplored. Some of you groaning under oppression in your native land, have voluntarily emigrated from it, whilst others..find yourselves in..involuntary exile.--All, however, have chosen as a resting place in a journey through life, this "asylum for the oppressed of all nations." Here..we pleasingly anticipated..exemption from that religious persecution and civil tyranny, whose iron and inexorable reign has forced us from our native country. Alas! How greatly were we mistaken! .. We are denominated Foreigners, and treated as Slaves. .. Upon the illustrious names of MONTGOMERY, GATES, and MERCER, we reflect with proud satisfaction. Irishmen!
    Resolutions. .. Resolved unanimously, That repelling with just indignation a distinction made between republican citizens of the same state we will not support a ticket, in the formation of which we have been excluded from any participation. Resolved unanimously, That 500 copies of the above Address and Resolution be printed in handbills, for the benefit of our fellow republican adopted citizens. ... Archibald TAYLOR, Chairman. S. DEMPSEY, Secretary.

(566) The Gazette. Friday. Edenton, May 12, 1809. .. Raleigh, April 27. Morst horrid Murder!--We have to record the most daring and outrageous murder ever committed in this or any other country. On Friday night, a little before 11 o'clock, Mr. Patrick CONWAY, of this city, merchant, was found lying behind his counter, in the most shocking condition--He was first discovered, from his groans, by two young men John OWEN and Turner DAUTRY, who alarmed some neighboring gentlemen. Medical aid was procured, but to no effect--the decd had as many as 8 wounds about his head and face; his scull was fractured in some places, in others mashed, and his jaw and cheek bones broken--he spoke but twice and then only one or two

(566) (Cont.) words, and died in about half an hour. .. Among the blood, and about the body, were several fractured pieces of a green pine stick and bark which had apparently been knocked off the stick by the violence of the blows. It appears the murder was committed, in order to rob the store of the deceased, as the money drawer was found open; the money taken out and some dropped on the floor: Though it is believed that the perpetrator did not get much, as the bulk of the cash was kept in another place.

John OWEN, a cabinet-maker, one of the young men who first gave information of the situation of the deceased, has been suspected. He was taken up next day, and after a lengthy examination by the magistracy, and after hearing testimony, was committed to the jail of this city, to wait his trial the first Monday in October next. .. The but end of a pine stick has been found in the store of the deceased, not far from where he lay; it is bloody. A witness has proven that OWEN cut a pine stick in his presence, the afternoon before the murder; and on comparing the stick with the stump, they very exactly fit. Mr. CONWAY was an Irishman by birth, and had resided among us nearly two years, during which time he has sustained a worthy reputation. He was remarkable for a lively disposition, and desire to please. His death is therefore a considerable loss to our society. Minerva.

(567) Attention! The Edenton Volunteers are ordered to attend a general muster on Wednesday next, at 10 o'clock precisely, at the usual parade ground, properly equipped. By order of the Captain, James MOFFATT, Lieut.

Friday, May 19, 1809. Vol. IV.-Num. 169.

(568) Philadelphia, May 2. The jury in the case of the United States, against Michael BRIGHT, brought in a special verdict yesterday afternoon. The verdict states, the defendants to be guilty of knowingly and wilfully obstructing, resisting and opposing the Marshal, in his attempt to serve and execute the judicial writ of arrest mentioned in the indictment, but that the defendants acted under the order of the constituted authorities of Pennsylvania.. May 3. .. The sentences of the court, are that you Michael BRIGHT, be imprisoned for the term of three months and pay a fine of two hundred dollars, to the United States, and that you James ATKINSON, Wm. COLE, Abraham OGDEN, Daniel PHYLE, Charles HONG and John KNIPE, be severally imprisoned for the term of one month, and severally pay a fine of fifty dollars, to the United States, and stand committed till these sentences are complied with. ...

(569) The Gazette. Friday. Edenton, May 19, 1809. The Printer being obliged from home next week on business of the utmost importance to him, humbly begs the indulgence of his Patrons for that space of time.

(570) On the 20th ult. sixty Young Gentlemen received the degree of Doctor of Medicine, at the Medical Commencement in Philadelphia; amongst them were three from this State, viz. Tho's H. HOLLAND, Joseph W. HAWKINS and Hardy HOSKINS. The latter of this town.

(571) Died--In Tennessee, on the 6th ult. after a short illness, Col. Hardy MURFREE, late of Murfreesborough in this state, a veteran Officer of the Revolution. On the 10th inst. Mrs. Martha BEASLY, an old and respectable inhabitant of this County.

(572) State of North-Carolina, Perquimans County Court,) May Term, 1809. Whereas, Joseph SUTTON, Esq hath sued out an original attachment against the

(572) (Cont.) estate of Mrs. Cloah REED, the widow and relict of William REED, jun. Esq. dec'd. late of the County aforesaid, returnable to this Court, at this term—It is ordered, That public notice be given to the said Cloah REED, by advertisement in the Edenton Gazette, for six weeks; that unless she appears at the next term of the said Court, to be held at Hertford, on the second Monday in August next, replevy her estate and plead to said action, final judgment will be entered up against her. By Order, John WOOD, Clerk.

(573) State of North-Carolina, Perquimans County Court,} May Term, 1809. Whereas, Lemuel WHEDBEE hath sued out an original attachment against the estate of Mrs. Cloah REED, the widow and relict of William REED, jun. Esq. dec'd. late of the County aforesaid, returnable to this Court, at this term—It is ordered, That public notice be given to the said Cloah REED, by advertisement in the Edenton Gazette, for six weeks; that unless she appears at the next term of the said Court, to be held at Hertford, on the second Monday in August next, replevy her estate and plead to said action, final judgment will be entered up against her. By Order, John WOOD, Clerk.

(574) State of North-Carolina, Perquimans County,} In Equity, of March Term, 1809. Isaac WHITE, Complainant, vs. John CHOATE and John Q. WILLIAMS, Defend'ts.} Bill to Foreclose. In this cause the defendants having failed to appear and answer to the bill of the complainant; and the Court having understood that they are inhabitants of another government—It is Ordered, That unless they the said defendants appear and answer to the bill of the complainant within the three first days of the next term, the bill will be taken pro confesso, and a decree of foreclosure passed against them. And it is further Ordered, That notice of this rule be given to the said defendants, by publication in the Edenton Gazette for the space of six weeks. Zac. COPELAND, C. & M. E. P. C.

(575) Asa CHAMBERLAIN Returns his grateful thanks to a generous public for their past favors; and solicits a continuance of their patronage in his absence, to Mr. Nathan K. STRONG, who conducts his business; and who is duly authorized and empowered to settle his affairs and grant discharges. Edenton, May 17th, 1809.

(576) 25 Dollars Reward. Whereas, Wm. DAVENPORT was committed to the common jail of Washington County by me, Thomas WALKER, Sheriff of said County, by virtue of a capias issued by the Clerk of Washington Superior Court, in consequence of an indictment being found against him for murder, at the Superior Court held for said County, at May term, 1809; and the said DAVENPORT has broken jail and escaped therefrom. The aforesaid criminal is about five feet six inches high, head of a red complexion, sharp visage, takes snuff, is very forward, and is apt to swear hard at times. The above reward (if taken out of the county,) will be paid to any person who will deliver said DAVENPORT to me in Washington County, or Ten Dollars if taken within. Thomas WALKER, Sh'ff. May 10, 1809.

riday, June 2, 1809. Vol. IV.-Num. 170.

(577) Indian War In Louisiana. St. Louis, (U. L.) April 12. General Orders. Head-Quarters, St. Louis, April 6, 1809. The Commander in Chief, directs all the volunteer companies of cavalry, riflemen, and infantry, within the territory of Louisiana to hold themselves in readiness to march at a moment's warning. These together with the corps, which are already held in a state of requisition under the general orders of the 28th of November last, will form a body of reserve to act as their contiguity to the point of attack, or other circumstances, may render their services necessary for the defence of the Territory. .. Major William

2 June 1809

(577) (Cont.) CHRISTY is appointed to command the "Louisiana Spies" and is to be obeyed and respected accordingly. Major CHRISTY, under the directions and instructions of Brigadier-General CLARK, will muster and inspect the Spies.. The Commander in Chief directs, that the inhabitants of the frontier district of Saint Charles, extending from the Missisippi to the Missouri, do immediately erect such stockade-works, defended by block houses, as may by the field officers of that district, be deemed necessary to defend and secure the inhabitants of the same, and as far as circumstantes will permit, against the threatened invasion of the savages; Colonel Timothy KIBBY, Majors Daniel M. BOONE, and James MORRISON, or any two of them, are hereby constituted a Board of Vigilance, with both powers to determine on the necessary number of, and scites for the fortifications.. .. All persons who, from their exposed situations on the frontier would in the opinion of the Board of Vigilance seek protection for themselves and families in these fortifications are required, without exception, under the direction of the Board, to contribute their due proportions of labor in erecting the same. Meriwether LEWIS.

(578) Washington-City, May 22. Eleventh Congress. List of Members of the Senate of the United States. New-Hampshire.--Nahum PARKER, Nicholas GILMAN. Massachusetts.--Timothy PICKERING, Jas. LLOYD. Rhode-Island.--Francis MALBONE, Elisha MATTHEWSON. Connecticut.--James HILLHOUSE, Chauncey GOODRICH. Vermont.--Stephen R. BRADLEY, Jonathan ROBINSON. New-York.--John SMITH, Obadiah GERMAN. New-Jersey--John CONDIT, John LAMBERT. Pennsylvania.--Andrew GREGG, Michael LIEB. Delaware.--Saml. WHITE, James A. BAYARD. Maryland.--Saml. SMITH, Philip REED. Virginia.--William B. GILES, Richard BRENT. Kentucky.--Buckner THRUSTON, John POPE. North-Carolina.--James TURNER, Jesse FRANKLIN. Tennessee.--Jos. ANDERSON, Jenkin WHITESIDE. South-Carolina.--Th. SUMTER, John GAILLARD. Georgia.--John MILLEDGE, Wm. H. CRAWFORD. Ohio.--R. J. MEIGS. One vacant.
List of Members of the House of Representatives, according to states. New-Hampshire. Daniel BLAISDELL, John C. CHAMBERLAM, William HALE, Nathaniel A. HAVEN, James WILSON. Massachusetts. Ezekiel BACON, Orchard COOK, Richard COTTS, William ELY, Gideon GARDNER, Barzillai GANNETT, Edward St. Loe LIVERMORE, Benjamin PICKMAN, Josiah QUINCEY, Ebenezer SEAVER, William STEDMAN, Samuel TAGGART, William BAILLIES, Jabez UPHAM, Joseph B. VARNUM, Laban WHEATON, Ezekiel WHITMAN. Rhode-Island. Richard JACKSON, Elisha R. POTTER. Connecticut. Epaphroditus CHAMPION, Samuel W. DANA, John DAVENPORT, Jonathan O. MOSELY, Timothy PITKIN, jun. Lewis B. STURGES, Benjamin TALLMADGE. Vermont. William CHAMBERLAIN, Martin CHITTENDEN, Jonathan H. HUBBARD, Samuel SHAW. New-York. William DENNING, James EMOTT, Jonathan FISK, Barent GARDENIER, Thomas R. GOLD, Herman KNICKERBACKER, Robert Le Roy LIVINGSTON, Vincent MATTHEWS, Gurdon S. MUMFORD, John NICHOLSON, Peter B. PORTER, Erastus ROOT, Thomas SAMMONS, Ebenezer SAGE, John THOMPSON, Uri TRACY, Killian K. VAN RENSELLAER. New-Jersey. Adam BOYD, James COX, William HELMS, Jacob HUFTY, Thomas NEWBOLD, Henry SOUTHARD. Pennsylvania. William ANDERSON, David BARD, Robert BROWN, William CRAWFORD, William FINDLEY, Daniel HEISTER, Robert JENKINS, Aaron LYSLE, William MILNOR, John PORTER, John REA, Mathias RICHARDS, John ROSS, Benjamin SAY, John SMILIE, George SMITH, Samuel SMITH, Robert WHITEHILL. Delaware. Nicholas VAN DYKE. Maryland. (blank) BROWN, John CAMPBELL, Charles GOLDSBOROUGH, Philip B. KEY, Alexander M'KIM, John MONTGOMERY, Nicholas R. MOORE, Roger NELSON, Archibald VAN HORN. Virginia. Burwell BASSETT, Wm. A. BURWELL, Matthew CLAY, John CLOPTON, John DAWSON, John W. EPPES, Daniel SHEFFEY, Thomas GHOLSON, jun. Peterson GOODWYN, Edwin GRAY, Michael SWOOPE, John G. JACKSON, Walter JONES, Joseph LEWIS, jun. John LOVE, J. STEPHENSON, Thomas NEWTON, Wilson C. NICHOLAS, John RANDOLPH, John SMITH, J. T. ROANE, James BRECKENRIDGE. Kentucky. Henry CHRIST, Joseph DESHA, Benjamin HOWARD, Richard M. JOHNSON, Matthew LYON, Samuel M'KEE. North-Carolina. Willis ALSTON, jun. James COCHRAN, Meshack FRANKLIN, James HOLLAND, Thomas KENAN, William KENNEDY, Nathaniel MACON, Archibald

2 June 1809

(578) (Cont.) M'BRIDE, Joseph PEARSON, Lemuel, SAWYER, Richard STANFORD, John STANLEY, Tennessee. Pleasant M. MILLER, John RHEA. One not certain. South-Carolina. Lemuel J. ALSTON, William BUTLER, Robert CALHOUN, Robert MARION, Thomas MOORE, John TAYLOR, Richard WINN, Robert WITHERSPOON. Georgia. Wm. W. BIBB, Howell COBB, Dennis SMELT, George M. TROUP. Ohio. Jeremiah MORROW.

Delegates From The Missisippi Territory, George POINDEXTER. Indiana Territory, vacant. Orleans Territory, J. POYDRAS.

May 23. .. Gen. VARNUM is appointed Speaker of the House of Representatives--Mr. MAGRUDER, Clerk--Thomas DUNN, Sergeant at arm_ and Thomas CLAXTON, Door-Keeper.

(579) The Gazette. Friday. Edenton, June 2, 1809. Lewis WALTERS, Esq. is elected Sheriff of Hertford County, in the room of Thomas DEANS, Esq. resigned.

(580) Married--on Sunday evening last, in Tyrrel County, John HAUGHTON, Esq. of this County, to Miss Mary HOOKER, of the former place.

(581) Arrived since 18th. Schr's. Regulator, DOUGH, Petersburg, 19th.. Sloops. Vermont, GODFREY, New-York.* .. *On board of this vessel came a Spanish Merino Ram, the first we believe, ever imported into this state, belonging to Mr. John DEVEREALX, of Newbern, and cost, we understand, $150. He is on his way to Mr. DEVEREALX's plantation on Roanoke.

(582) Attention! The Edenton Volunteers are ordered to attend at the usual parade ground, properly equipped, on Saturday the 10th inst. at 10 o'clock precisely. Duncan M'DONALD, Captain.

(583) Fresh Goods. The Subscribers have just received from N. York, a few Fancy & Summer Goods, which they offer for Sale on reasonable terms for Cash... M'COTTOR & MUIL. June 1st, 1809.

(584) For Sale, On Perquimans River by the Subscriber, 150 M. redoak hhd. Staves, 50 white ditto ditto, 30 feet pine Scantling, 350 22 inch Shingles, 100 bbls. Indian Corn, A few bbls. whole Herrings, and some Bacon, on low terms for cash.. Samuel NIXON. Float-Bridge, May 26, 1809.

(585) For Sale. Good green Coffee, at 25 cents per bag or bags in cash, or 27 cents 60 days credit. Also, Sugar by the barrel at $11 per hundred, cash, or $12 50 cents per bbl... Apply to Mr. Henry A. DONALDSON in Edenton, or to Lemuel CREECY, at his own house. May 30th, 1809.

(586) Notice is hereby given to all whom it may concern, that David R. SUMNER, of Hertford County, is dead, and that the subscriber qualified as administrator to his estate, (with the will annexed) at last May term of Hertford County Court. All persons indebted to the estate of said dec'd are desired to make immediate payment; and those having claims..to exhibit them properly attested... William JONES, Adm. June 1st, 1809.

(587) Brick Makers. New Invention.--Asa FROST, Cas?enovia, has obtained letters patent under the seal of the United States for a machine called a Brick Machine. The advantages to brick makers to be derived from the use of this machine are numerous. ...

Friday. June 9, 1809. Vol. IV.-Num. 171.

9 June 1809

(588)   From the South-Carolina State Gazette. Eloquent And Impressive.   At the
Court of General Sessions of the Peace, holden at Union Court-House, in March Term
last, before the Honorable Judge WILDS, John TOLLISON was tried & found guilty of
the wilful murder of John MATHIS--and when the unhappy criminal was brought to the
Bar, to receive the sentence of the law, the following eloquent and impressive
Address, was delivered by the Judge.. John TOLLISON, The duty which yet remains
to be performed towards you, of all others to me the most awful and distressing,
it is my misfortune to be obliged to perform alone. The laws of our common
country have commissioned me to announce to you your doom; I hold your death warrant in my hand. .. You have, but my heart sickens at the thought, a wife who
tenderly loves you--you are the father of children, who look to you for bread; for
them at least you ought to have lived.--Cruel, thoughtless man, what have you
done! .. The Sentence of the Court is, that you be now carried from hence to the
place from whence you came, and that on the last Friday in May next, between the
hours of eleven in the forenoon and two in the afternoon, you be carried to the
place of public execution, in the District of Union, and there to be hanged by the
neck until your body be dead, and may the Almighty God have mercy on your soul.

(589) The Gazette. Friday. Edenton, June 9, 1809. .. Frankfort, (K.) May 4.
Extract of a letter from Dr. GAITHER, of Washington County, (K.) to the Editor of
the Western World, dated Springfield, April 26, 1809. Believing it the duty of
professional men, and particularly of the healing art, to lay before the public
such occurrences in their practice, as from their singularity, may either awaken
useful enquiry, or promote substantially the happiness of man, by increasing the
catalogue of facts whence a knowledge of the animal economy is derived, I, who am
a young and diffident practitioner in the science of medicine, beg leave to submit
to the public a fact of that description. .. On the 7th April, in the county of
Washington, I was called to visit a female child, the daughter of John MILBOURN,
jun. The child was two years and nine months old, and was supposed to be affected
with the ascites or dropsy of the belly. She died about 3 hours after my arrival.
Her parents gave me a detailed account of her case, and its various symptoms.   I
was by no means satisfied that it was a real dropsy, tho' there was great
tumefaction and tenseness of the abdomen, and fluctuations evidently felt when
prest by the hand. .. I prevailed on her parents to permit an instrumental
examination. The operation was performed in the usual way, by a longitudinal
incision, passing from below the sternum and reaching near the Pubis; and a
transverse one passing through the epigastric region sides. A cavity was opened
to about half the distance between the abdominal cavity and the exterior surface,
that discharged between three quarts and a gallon of yellow water, which smelt
like rotten eggs.--Within the cavity was found a monster, or imperfect child, and
also an animal substance of a whitish colour. The monster weighed one pound and
fourteen ounces--the substance weighed two ounces, was rather of an oval figure,
and was connected to the child from which it was taken, by a cord that had some
resemblance to the umbilical. .. The monster occupied part of the epigastric and
the umbilical regions.--It was not connected to the inner surface of its cavity by
a cord or any visible medium.. .. The position of the monster in its envelope
was awkward; its thighs drawn up to its abdomen, and attached to it in places. ..
From the knees to the shoulders there is considerable perfection of form. ...
Edward B. GAITHER.
    I certify, that I examined with anxiety and attention the monster above
described, and also the substance, and believe the description to be accurate.   I
also conversed with the young gentleman who was present and assisted at the opera-
tion--his statement were (sic) correspondent with the above narration of facts and
circumstances. ... John ROWAN. April 26, 1809.
    I, Thos. J. COCKE, do certify that I have examined the above described

(589) (Cont.) monster, and that it answers to the description given; and that I have the fullest belief of the whole of the facts as related. April 28, 1809.

I do certify that I have particularly examined the monster above described, and it corresponds with the above statement; and I have the fullest confidence that all the circumstances as stated are correct. John CALHOON. April 28, 1809.

(590) Died—on Monday last, after a long and painful illness, Mrs. Tamer HAUGHTON, wife of Mr. Charles HAUGHTON, deceased, of this County.

(591) Unanimity Lodge, No. 54. The Members of Unanimity Lodge, of this place, will celebrate the Festival of St. John the Baptist, on the 24th inst. An oration suited to the occasion will be delivered, at the Church, at 11 o'clock, A. M. at which place the Ladies and Gentlemen of Edenton and its vicinity are invited to attend. Those Brethren who are disposed to join in the celebration, may procure tickets of admittance at this Office. By Order, James WILLS, Sec'ry. Edenton, June 8th, A. L. 5609.

(592) Advertisement. Being still desirous of moving, I again offer the following valuable property for Sale, viz. my Farm in HARVEY's Neck, and a Tract of Land lying on the North-east side of Perquimans river, containing 106 acres..one other Tract containing 200 acres, lying on the south west side of said river, about 4 miles above the farm.. I will also sell the Farm on which I live; and to accommodate purchasers, I will sell all the Negroes, Stock of every kind, and the Farming Utensils that belong to the two farms. ... John SKINNER. MOSELEY's-Point, June 4, 1809.

Friday, June 16, 1809. Vol. IV.-Num. 172.

(593) The Gazette. Friday. Edenton, June 16, 1809. Edmond HOSKINS, Esq. is re-elected She___f of this County. Josiah TOWNSEND, Esq. is elected She___f of Per-quimans County, in the room of _homas HOSEA, Esq.

(594) Elder David BARROW, of Kentucky, and __der William BROWN, of Virg. will preach __ Elizabeth-City, on Monday the 19th inst...

(595) The large Golden Eagle is a bird now ___dom seen in this part of our country; and ___as therefore we note the following circum___nce:—Mr. William CHAMBERS, a respec___le farmer, near Jobstown, Burlington coun__ had several Lambs carried away by an __gle of this description.. Mr. __AMBERS watched..and with a good fowling-piece, ___l charged with buck-shot, brought him to ___ ground as he was soaring at a great height. He measured 7 feet 1 inch from the end of ___ wing to that of the other. Tren. True Am.

(596) Washington-City, June 6. Francis MALBONE, Esq. Senator from Rhode-Island, suddenly dropped down dead, on Sunday morning last, on his way to divine service, at the foot of Capitol Hill. .. The Senate have duly honored his memory. He was yesterday interred, notwithstanding the pouring of the rain, with legislative and national distinction.

(597) The following is an extract of a letter from Christopher GREENUP, Esq. late Governor of Kentucky, to a gentleman in this city, dated May 23. "I am happy to inform you that by letters lately received from Kaskaskias, we learn that the alarm of the Indian war has subsided."

(598) 20 Dollars Reward. Run away from the subscriber some time in February

(598) (Cont.) last, a likely negro woman named PRISS, about 36 or 7 years old, very tall and well made, of a yellowish complexion, with a very full mouth, her eye-teeth out, her right thumb is stiff in the second joint, and when she walks has a very nimble step. There is a very notable scar on one of her arms near the elbow, she has a very mild speech and look, talks long.. I expect she is in Perquimans or Pasquotank Counties among the free negroes.—Any person or persons that will deliver the said negro to me, or confine her so that I get her shall receive the above reward by applying to Joseph PARKER, near Gates Court-House. June 6th, 1809.

(599) Internal Improvement. Twenty Thousand Dollars, May be gained for two and an half Dollars!! In The Third Class Of the Lottery authorised by Law for removing obstructions in the River Lehigh. .. To draw 500 tickets each day, at the State House in Philadelphia, and the prizes to be paid by Thomas ALLIBONE, Esq. the Treasurer, in this city, 30 days after the conclusion of the drawing, subject to a deduction of 15 per cent. ... George TAYLOR, jun. No. 85, south second street. Philadelphia, Dec. 16, 1808. Those who may be disposed to adventure in the above Lottery, may obtain? tickets by applying to Henderson STANDIN, at the Post Office, Edenton Price $3 each.

(600) The following Droll advertisement is from a Massachusetts paper: "Ranaway from the Subscriber, on the 28th of September, 1808, Nathaniel GROVER, near six feet high, grey hair, one side curled and the other straight, pea-porridge colored eyes. Whoever will take up said runaway and fetch him back to Royalston and cause a guardian to be put over him, shall receive three dollars reward. Deborah GROVER.

(601) At the West precinct in Bridgewater in this state, (says the Boston Gazette) a Cow belonging to Mr. Thomas AMES of that place, calved Four Calves at one calving, three of them were alive and like (sic) to do well when our informant saw them.

Friday, June 23, 1809. Vol. IV.-Num. 173.

(602) From the Montreal Courant of May 22. Melancholy Circumstance. .. Elizabethtown, (Upper Canada) May 10, 1809. Mr. MOWER, A most cruel murder having been perpetrated in this place lately on the body of Isaac D. UNDERHILL, a resident here, I deem it my duty, through the channel of your paper, to lay before the public a statement of the affair; and must request you will as early as possible, insert the following circumstances and letters.
     On the 1st inst. an American vessel, said to be bound from Ogdensburgh in the state of New-York, to Oswego, anchored in a bay on the British shore of the St. Laurence, having on board a William P. BENNETT, of the 6th United States regiment of infantry, and some of his men. While laying in said bay, Captain BENNETT, who had received information of an American deserter being in our settlement teaching school, ordered his serjeant, by the name of John GRAVES, to pursue and take him: the serjeant and two of his men then went on shore, proceeded to the school-house, took the said UNDERHILL, tied his hands before him, and drove him some distance through the woods with their guns and bayonets, pricking him continually in a most cruel manner to make him run, till they came to the King's highway, when the said UNDERHILL looking towards a Mr. FULFORD's house, where he boarded, felt a wish to escape to it, & run; he had not proceeded more than 4 or 5 rods when he was fired at by the said serjeant and his men, on the second discharge of a gun he was mortally wounded, when the serjeant and his men run up to him and were going to blow his brains out, but he begged his life, saying he had received his death

(602) (Cont.) wound, and wanted a few moments to make his peace with his Maker; on which the soldiers left him, ran to the shore, went immediately on board the schooner, and from thence with their Captain BENNETT fled instantly to the American shore. UNDERHILL, with assistance, reached Mr. FULFORD's house, where he lay in excruciating torture, till Tuesday afternoon, when he expired. The Coroner's inquest sat on the body the next day, and bro't in a verdict of Wilful Murder, (after hearing the testimony of Davis & Robert HUGENON, two seamen belonging to the vessel mentioned in their deposition, also many other strong and convincing testimonies.) The following letter from Capt. BENNETT, with my answer, will further elucidate the matter. I am, Sir, Your humble servant, Henry ARNOLD.

(Copy.) At Anchor off Major FORD's, May 2, 1809. Sir, I have not the honor of an acquaintance with you, nor is it necessary to my purpose, as I am not personally interested in the communication, but induced to it from friendship to an innocent men, Captain HOLMES, who seems to be in difficulty from my act yesterday. Why, Sir, is Captain HOLMES implicated in this affair? Is it because my boat..happened to be along-side of his vessel? .. Or is it because your people are determined to grasp at the smallest opportunity of annoying the United States? I pledge my honor as a soldier and gentleman, that Captain HOLMES & his men were as ignorant of the affair as you. I am the responsible person: what was done was in obedience to my orders, and I am proud that my serjeant executed the orders with so much spirit and promptness. The man had not become a subject of Great-Britain, and why should your people be so anxious to protect a deserter, and fellon? What I did I considered my duty, and on like occasion would do again, and will at all times take my men where and when I can, if it can be accomplished without injury to the inhabitants of the country or place I take them from. ... (Signed) Wm. P. BENNETT, Capt. 6th U. S. Regt. Infantry. (Address to) Henry ARNOLD, Esq. Canada. ...

(603) The Gazette. Friday. Edenton, June 23, 1809. .. Died—on Friday morning last, Master William WILLIAMS, son of Mrs. E. HANKINS, of this town, in the 19th year of his age. On the 8th ult. after a tedious illness, Thomas PAINE, aged 74, author of the Age of Reason, &c. ... New-York Gazette.

(604) The Subscriber Has for Sale, 16,000 feet of pine Plank and Scantling, And 40,000 Cypress Shingles, which he will sell low for Cash.. The above Lumber will be delivered at Windsor Bridge, Bertie County. John BOZMAN. Windsor, June 20, 1809.

Friday, June 30, 1809. Vol. IV.-Num. 174.

(605) Congress. House of Representatives. Thursday, June 15. .. Friday, June 16. Mr. MACON from the committee to whom was referred the affair of Edward LIVINGSTON and the New-Orleans Bature, asked to be discharged from any further consideration of the subject. Granted. .. Mr. JOHNSON from the committee of claims, on the petition of Hannah FOSTER, reported unfavorable—The report was ordered to be laid on the table and be printed.

(606) Letter from Mr. Henry LATROBE, on repairs in the temporary Senate chamber. The Vice-President of the United States, President of the Senate of the United States. Capitol, Washington, June 12, 1809. Sir, I herewith have the honor to lay before you an account of the expenditures on the temporary Senate chamber, its galleries, committee rooms, and other conveniencies provided for the present session. As far as they were applicable, the old materials of the house have been used in the solid parts, of the work: for the rest I thought it best to make a single contract with Mr. George BRIDPORT, who has fitted up, canvassed, papered

30 June 1809

(606) (Cont.) and painted the apartments, and found all other materials of every kind. The very high price of canvas, of which 548 yards were required, has enhanced the amount of this contract beyond what it would have been twelve months ago, by a large sum. ... B. H. LATROBE, Surveyor of the Public Buildings of the U. States.

The Honorable Senate United States.　　　　　　　Dr. to Sundries.
To George BRIDPORT, for fitting up the temporary
　Senate chamber, labor and all materials except
　the framing and timber, per contract, Dolls. 950　00
Travelling expences and freight)　　　　　　70　00　　1,020　00
Lewis LABILLE, upholsterer, as per his account,　　　　131　30
Nov. 1808. John PETER, for carpeting and baize,
　for the chamber on the ground floor,　　　　　　　60　31
John COX, for　　do.　　　　　　　　　　　　90　15　1-2
To Henry INGLE's repair of furniture,　　　　　　33　37　1-2
Mrs. SWEENY, making and repairing carpets,　　　　35　00
Lewis DEBLOIS, 60 yards moreen, at 50 cents,　　　　30　00
　　　　　　　　　　　　　　　　　Dolls. 1,399　34

B. Henry LATROBE, Surveyor of
the Public Buildings United
States. June 12, 1809.

(607) The Gazette. Friday. Edenton, June 30, 1809. .. 40,000 Dollars Found!— Forty thousand Dollars in specie, were lately found in a hollow tree in Grayson county, in this state, by a man named PERKINS, a farmer. .. On this circumstance being mentioned here a few days ago, in the presence of an intelligent country gentleman, he immediately remarked that the dollars must be of "CHISELL's making." By this gentleman we are informed, that about 45 or 50 years ago, a man named CHISELL discovered, and commenced the working of the Lead Mines, on New-River, in Grayson county—that as usual, some silver was found among the ore, and that CHISELL had obtained a permit from the British King to coin as much money from time to time, as would pay off his workmen. True to the adage, he took the ell for the inch, and probably the discovery of PERKINS is the fruits of CHISELL's industry, which a premature death (foul play cannot prosper) prevented him from enjoying.—In this county, our informant adds, at the place now occupied by Capt. Robert HUNTER, on the main Richmond road, CHISELL quarrelled with, and stabbed to death, a man named RUTLEDGE. CHISELL was seized, carried to Williamsburg, tried, and condemned to the gallows. He was found dead in the jail on the morning of the day destined for his execution. (Lynchburg Star.)

(608) Died—very suddenly, a few days past, in Bertie County, Col. John FOLCH, an inhabitant of that County.

(609) 4th of July. On that day at 11 o'clock, an Oration, suitable for the occasion, will be delivered in the Church, by a gentleman of this Town. Those who are disposed to join in celebrating the day, can procure Tickets of admittance of James MOFFATT, John M'COTTOR, James NORFLEET,) Managers.

(610) Attention! The Edenton Volunteers, are ordered to attend parade, at sunrise, at the usual place, on the Fourth of July, properly equipped, with 24 rounds of blank cartridges, in order to celebrate the 34th anniversary of American Independence. Duncan M'DONALD, Captain.

(611) Joseph MANNING, Tailor, tenders his sincere thanks to his customers (particularly those who have been punctual in their payments) for their past favors in

(611) (Cont.) the line of his business, and earnestly solicits a continuance of them--He at the same time requests all those who are in arrears to him to make immediate payment..in order that he may be enabled to pay for such articles as his business and a large family, necessarily oblige him to run in debt for. .. Wanted immediately, Two or three good Journeymen... Edenton, June 29, 1809.

(612) Notice Is hereby given to all the creditors of the late Col. James LONG, of the County of Washington, that the subscriber qualified as executor to his last will and testament at December term 1808; and they make known their demands within the time limited by law, otherwise they will be barred of recovery. Those indebted to said estate are requested to make immediate payment. Martin R. BYRD, Ex'r. 4th june 1809.

Friday, July 7, 1809. Vol. IV.-Num. 175.

(613) The Gazette. Friday. Edenton, July 7, 1809. On Sunday the 9th instant, the Rev. Isaac HUNTER, of Gates County, is expected to preach in the Court-House at this place, at 11 o'clock.

(614) On Tuesday last, the 4th of July, the citizens of this Town celebrated the 34th Anniversary of American Independence with that joy and festive mirth which ought always to characterise the free born sons of Columbia. The morning was ushered in by the firing of cannon and small arms from the Volunteer and Artillery companies, commanded by Captains M'DONALD and BOZMAN. At half past 11 o'clock they repaired to the Church, where Dr. Jonathan Otis FREEMAN, the orator of the day, delivered a very handsome and appropriate Oration. At 2 o'clock the Volunteer company proceeded to the Court-House, when, after appointing Mr. H. STANDIN president, and Dr. James NORCOM vice-president, they sat down to a sumptuous Dinner, provided by Mrs. HORNIBLOW...

(615) Information Wanted. Whereas, a certain James TAYLOR left the County of Edgcombe in the State of North-Carolina, on a journey to Georgia, sometime in the month of December, 1807, and has not since been heard of. If any person can inform his disconsolate wife respecting the said James TAYLOR, such information will be thankfully received, if directed to Nancy TAYLOR residing in the County and State aforesaid.

(616) John R. CARY, Carpenter And House-Joiner, Wishes to engage in business with some one in the above line, and will contract with any person in this or any convenient place near Edenton. As he is a transient person he would rather engage for yearly employ: And, as he is acquainted with extensive business, having worked in large cities to the Northward, he flatters himself he is perfect in theory, and can execute well in the various branches of Architecture. ... July 6th, 1809.

(617) A List of Letters remaining in the Post-Office, Edenton, July 1, 1809. Samuel BRYANT, Micajah BUNCH, Thos. CABARRUS, Charles COLLINS, Job COMSTOCK, Thomas CREECY, Charlton MIERS, Moses E. CATOR, Abraham ELLIOTT, Wm. EATON, Miss Eliza FEREBEE, Joseph GREGORY, Wm. GOODWIN, James JORDAN & Co. James HATHAWAY, Bartlett HOLMES, Sheriff of Chowan, Arthur JONES, John LOCKWOOD, Ensign S. C. MABSON, William LANE, General Silas PIPOON, Abraham PIERCE, Thomas SMITH, John SKINNER, Hannah SAUNDERS, Eliza WILLIAMS, John WILLIAMS, James WALLACE, Miss Susan D. BENNETT, Joseph UNDERHILL. Henderson STANDIN, P. M.

Friday, July 14, 1809. Vol. IV.-Num. 176.

(618)   The Gazette. Friday. Edenton, July 14, 1809. On the first Saturday and
Sunday in August, the Rev. Mr. BUXTON, presiding elder, William P. HARDY, and some
others of the Methodist Church, expect to hold a two-days meeting in the Court-
House at this place. .. All persons having characters becoming the Gospel of
Christ of every denomination, are invited to commune with us.

(619) .The Inhabitants of the lower part of Chowan County celebrated the Fourth of
July at the common muster ground five miles below Edenton, when 17 rounds being
fired, and an Oration delivered by Leonard MARTIN, Esq. adapted to the occasion,
and a dinner being prepared, Capt. James SAUNDERS was chosen president, and James
SUTTON, Esq. vice-president.

(620)   Oration Delivered at Windsor, on the 4th of July, By James W. WARBURTON.
Whilst the old world is convulsed by war, desolation and carnage, permit me to
congratulate a portion of the new one, on having once more peaceably assembled to
celebrate the natal day of our Independence...

(621) State of N. Carolina, Bertie County,) Court of Pleas and Quarter Sessions,
May Term, '09. Joseph JORDAN, jun. vs. Ann B. POLLOK,} Petition to erect a Mill.
It being represented to the Court that the defendant Ann B. POLLOK, is an
inhabitant of the city of New-York, in the state of New-York, It is ordered, That
notice be given the said Ann by advertisement for three weeks successively in the
Edenton Gazette, that unless she put in her answer to the petition of the
petitioner at the next term of this Court, to be held at the Court-House in
Windsor, on the second Monday in August next. judgment will be taken against her
pro confesso, and set for hearing exparte. A copy from the minutes, Teste. Jos.
BLOUNT, D. C.

(622)   Ran away from the subscriber in March, 1808, a Negro Girl about 18 years
old, named RHODA, of rather a light complexion, high cheek bones, and a tolerable
long face, rather tall and slender than otherwise. She has lately been in
Plymouth, and passed there by the name of Rhoda JONES; and it is supposed by some
that her next aim will be for Edenton.—Twenty Dollars reward will be given by the
subscriber to any person who will deliver said Negro in Bertie County, or lodge
her in some jail so that he may get her again; and all reasonable expences shall
be paid. William PUGH. Bertie, July 1, 1809.

Friday, July 21, 1809. Vol. IV.-Num. 177.

(623)   The Gazette. Friday. Edenton, July 21, 1809. .. The following is as
accurate an account of what came under our observation on the 12th and 13th inst.
as we are capable of laying before the public. Being on a circuit of preaching we
arrived __ Washington, where our ears were saluted ___h the melancholy sound of
affliction, issu___ from the house of a widow, whose son ___ on the margin of the
grave. .. _f it were necessary we could say, that in __t of intellect, there are
few youth who ___sent a more flattering prospect of future ___fulness; this, connected with the idea of ___ being the only remaining pledge of a ten___ husband's
love, who was conducted to ___ solitary mansions of the dead about seven ___rs
before, filled the bosom of a tender af____ionate mother with all the anguish of
o___whelming distress. .. Thus departed Samuel COOK, of Washington, at a little
past 12 years old. ... Signed, William CREATH, William DOSSEY,} Anabaptist
Preachers.

(624)   Shocking.—It has never fallen to our lot to record a more tragical
occurrence than the following, which took place in Halifax county on the 5th inst.

(624) (Cont.) A young man in that county of the name of William PARKER, had for 2 or 3 years paid his addresses to a Miss Dolly GRIFFIN, and the marriage of the parties was expected; recently however Miss G. had discarded him. On the 5th, they, with some other company, dined at a Mrs. HARRIS's, where PARKER behaved towards Miss G. with some rudeness. His conduct and some expressions which fell from him, excited her suspicions that he meditated some serious mischief, and she invited two of her friends to accompany her home. When they had nearly reached her mother's, PARKER came out suddenly from an angle of the fence, and presenting a gun at Miss G. shot her through the arm, and lodged the contents in her side. She fell instantly, and on the horses rode by the other young ladies being frightened, they were also thrown. PARKER then began very deliberately to reload his gun; the young ladies bereft by their fears of the power either of flight or resistance, entreated him not to kill them. He told them he had no such intention, that he was then loading for himself, and asked one of them for a corner of her shawl for wadding, which he tore off. When he had finished loading, he placed the muzzle to his breast and sprung the trigger with his foot; it missed fire; he then pecked the flint, and on the second attempt the load entered his breast—he tottered to the fence, against which he leaned with much agony, & desired the young ladies to pray for him; he then walked towards the dying Miss GRIFFIN, and fell beside her. Both expired in a few minutes. Ral. Star.

(625) Masonic. Davie Lodge, No. 39. State of N. Carolina, Bertie County. Resolved, That William HODGES, be, and is hereby forever expelled from this Lodge, for conduct disgracing him as a man and as a Mason. Extract from the minutes. Teste, Lem'l. MURDAUGH, Sec. June 26, 1809.

Friday, July 28, 1809. Vol. IV.-Num. 178.

(626) The Gazette. Friday. Edenton, July 28, 1809. .. We are particularly requested by the Rev. Martin ROSS, to correct an error which appeared attached to the signatures of William CREATH and William DOSSEY in our last; for the words "Anabaptist Preachers," read Baptist Preachers.

(627) We understand a Duel was fought on the 12th inst. on the borders of North-Carolina, between Col. MEUSE, of Middlesex, and Mr. Caleb B. UPSHER, of Richmond county, in this State. At the first fire, the ball of Col. M. struck his antagonist on the right side, where its course was checked by two Spanish milled dollars, and a pen knife, that happened to be in the waistcoat pocket of Mr. UPSHER, and against which the force of the ball was spent!—but for this lucky hit, Mr. U. must inevitably have lost his life. The parties, with their seconds, arrived in this town on Friday last, and we learn the misunderstanding which gave rise to the duel between Mr. U. and Col. M. has been happily and satisfactorily adjusted. Pet. Intel.

(628) Notice is hereby given that James MARGRE, late of Bertie county, is dead, and that the subscriber qualified as Executor to his estate at last term of said County Court. All persons indebted..are requested to make immediate payment; and those having claims..to bring them forward... Benj. HARDY, Ex'r. Bertie county, July 24 1809.

(629) In pursuance of the last will and testament of James MARGRE, dec'd. will be Sold, on Saturday the 2d of September next, at public sale, on a credit of 6 and 12 months, on the premises, 3 or 400 Acres of Land, belonging to the estate of said deceased, lying about 7 miles from Colerain. ... Executor. Bertie county, July 24, 1809.

4 August 1809

Friday, August 4, 1809. Vol. IV.-Num. 179.

(630) From the Monthly Magazine. An Account of the Sufferings of the Crew of two Schooners, part of the Squadron of General MIRANDA, which were taken by two Spanish Guarda-Costas, in June 1806.--Written by one of the Sufferers who made his escape. [The world knows little of the extraordinary expedition of General MIR-ANDA to the Spanish Main, in 1806; but it will be remembered that he arrived in the Gulf of Mexico with an armed Brig and two Schooners, and that in a rencountre with two Guarda-Costas, the Schooners were both taken. We are now enabled to lay before our readers the particulars of the treatment their crews met with from the Spaniards. The trials tend also to throw some light on the Expedition itself.]

Towards the end of June, the Lieutenant-Governor of Caraccas, accompanied by four assistant officers or judges, together with an interpreter for each officer, arrived at Port Cavello, for the purpose of taking the examination of the prisoners. They assembled in the guard-house, within the walls of Castle St. Philip, in a large room fitted up for that purpose. .. The judges being ready to proceed, caused five of the prisoners to be brought up in the first place. They were informed of the charges exhibited against them, viz. piracy, rebellion, and murdering one of his Catholic Majesty's subjects. .. They continued to examine them for the space of four or five hours, when they were returned to the prison, and five others brought up in their places. In this manner the examination proceeded for the space of two weeks before it ended. The following were the general questions and answers, put to one of the prisoners, who has since regained his liberty. Q. How old are you? A. About 22 years. Q. Where was you born, and where do your parents reside? A. I was born in the State of Massachusetts; my parents reside in N. York. Q. Why did you leave New-York? A. To seek my for-tune. Q. Who engaged you to go on board the Leander? A. Col. ARMSTRONG. Q. Where was you engaged to go? A. to Jacmel, and from there to other places, not disclosed to me at the time of the engagement. .. Q. Did MIRANDA also engage you to go on board of the Leander? A. I did not know there was such a person until the Leander had left the port of N. York. Q. In what capacity did you enter on board of the Leander? A. As a printer. Q. How came you to change that capacity and accept of a military commission under MIRANDA? A. From motives of personal convenience. .. Q. Did you not come to the Main for the purpose of assisting MIRANDA in fighting against this government, and in revolutionizing the country? A. It was represented by MIRANDA, that no fighting would be necessary to effect the object, whatever it was, he had in view. .. Q. Did you understand that MIRANDA fitted out his expedition by the consent of your government? A. No. He kept his object and operation concealed from the public. It was a private undertaking of his own. ..

The following were questions put to another prisoner, who has also effected his return home. Q. What religion are you of? A. The presbyterian persuasion. Q. Where was you born and brought up? A. In New-York. Q. Who engaged you to embark in MIRANDA's expedition? A. One John FINK, of N. York, butcher. .. Q. Why did you not all rise and take command of the schooner, after you discovered her intention? A. We did attempt it once, but failed. .. On the 20th of July, about eleven o'clock in the morning, the prison doors were thrown open, which pre-sented to our view a large body of armed soldiers, drawn up round the prison door with muskets aimed towards us, loaded, cocked, and bayonets fixed. .. There was little danger of the prisoners escaping, being in irons, and so weak and emaciated as to just be able to walk.

Shortly appeared the interpreter, accompanied by one or two officers, and two or three Roman Catholic priests. The following persons being called: Francis FARQUARSON, Daniel KEMPER, Charles JOHNSON, John FERRIS, Miles L. HALL, James GARDNER, Thomas BILLOPP, Thomas DONAHUE, Gustavus A. BERGUD, Paul T. GEORGE. The

4 August 1809

(630) (Cont.) interpreter then read to them..the following sentence: "In the morning of to-morrow, at 6 o'clock, you and each of you are sentenced to be hung by the neck until dead; after which your heads are to be severed from your bodies and placed upon poles, and distributed in public parts of the country." The following persons were then called & sentenced to ten years imprisonment, at hard labour, in the castle of Omon?, near the Bay of Honduras, and after that time, to await the King's pleasure: John T. O'SULLIVAN, Henry INGERSOLL, Jeremiah POWELL, Thomas GILL, John H. SHERMAN, John EDSALL, David HECKLE and Son, John HAYS, John MOORE, Daniel M'KAY, John M. ELLIOTT, Bennett B. VEGUS, Robert SAUNDERS, Peter NAULTY.

The following persons were sentenced to the same punishment, for the same length of time, and at the castle of Porto Rico. Wm. W. LIPPINCOTT, Moses SMITH, John BURK, Matthew BUCHANAN, Alex. BUCHANAN, John PARSELLS, David WINTON, John SCOTT, Stephen BURTIS, Phineas RAYMOND, Joseph BONNETT, Eaton BURLINGHAM, Jas. GRANT, Frederick RIGGUS. And the following persons were sentenced to the same punishment, at the castle of Bocca Chica, in Carthagena, except their terms..were eight years instead of ten. William LONG, Benjamin DAVIS, Joseph L. HECKLE, Henry SPERRY, Robert STEAVISON, Benjamin NICHOLSON, Samuel PRICE, Elery KING, Hugh SMITH, Daniel NEWBURY, William CARTWRIGHT, Samuel TOUZIER, William BURNSIDE, Abraham HEAD, James HYATT, Wm. PRIDE, Pompey GRANT, George FERGUSON, Robert RAINS.

On the morning of the 21st of July, about 6 o'clock, the prisoners were alarmed by the noise of an assemblage of Spanish soldiers at the door of the prison.. The ten prisoners to be executed were then brought out, and with their hands lashed fast before, and with white robes on, that extended from the lower part of their necks to their heels, and white caps upon their heads, were placed in front. .. Mr. FARQUARSON being first selected to meet his fate, was led to the steps of the gallows, by a negro slave.. The rope being placed round his neck, he rose up on his feet and took a final farewell of his companions, wishing them a better fate. The negro then gave him a push from the top of the scaffold, and launched him into eternity. ...

Edenton Gazette Extra.
_riday, August 4, 1809.-No. 179.

[Note: This Extra appears to have been inserted in the middle of the regular issue of 4 August 1809.]

(631) The following, we are informed, is a copy verbatim of the orders given by the Brigadier General of 1st Brigade, for discharging from further service the quota of Militia raised pursuant to act of Congress of the 20th of March, 1808: Camden County, June 27, 180_ Sir Your are hereby Requested to inform the the (sic) officers & Soldiears Raised at the Requeste of the President of the U. States that are to be held in Readiness no Longer a? Coppey you have herein Closed—two muc_ praise Cannot be Given to those Gentlemen officiers & Soldiers who volunteered them Selves so freely to first meet their Enemy th_ thanks of the undersigned is Requested to b_ presented to the a bove mentioned Detach—I have the pleasure of high assurances and Respect with which I have Great Esteem __ Regard your humble Servent Jer. BRITE, BG 1st. Brigade. The Commanding Officer of (blank) County.

(632) The Gazette. Friday. Edenton, August 4, 1809. .. State of N. Carolina, Tyrrel County,) June Term, 1809. Whereas John WEST hath sued out an original attachment against the estate of Thomas CUSACK, late of said County, returnable before the County Court of Pleas and Quarter-Sessions for the County aforesaid, It is Ordered, That public notice be given to the said Thomas CUSACK, by

(632) (Cont.) advertisement in the Edenton Gazette for 60 days, that unless he appears at the next term of the said Court, to be holden for Tyrrel county, at the Court-House in Columbia, on the 4th Monday in September next, and plead to his action, final judgment will be entered up against him. By Order, Chas. SPRUILL, Cl'k.

(633) State of N. Carolina, Tyrrel County,) June Term, 1809. Whereas John MARINER hath sued out an original attachment against the estate of Thomas CUSACK, late of said County, returnable before the County Court of Pleas and Quarter-Sessions for the County aforesaid, It is Ordered, That public notice be given to the said Thomas CUSACK, by advertisement in the Edenton Gazette for 60 days, that unless he appears at the next term of the said Court, to be holden for Tyrrel county, at the Court-House in Columbia, on the 4th Monday in September next, and plead to his action, final judgment will be entered up against him. By Order, Chas. SPRUILL, Cl'k.

(634) 40 Dollars Reward. Ran away from the subscriber on the night of the 15th inst. a Negro man named DAVIE, between 22 and 23 years old, about 5 feet 6 or 7 inches high, yellow complexion, thick lips and very little beard, has been used to the sea, and walks like a sailor. .. The above reward will be given to any person who will secure the said Negro man DAVIE so that I get him again—and all owners and masters of vessels are forwarned from employing or carrying off the said Negro man, as the law will be rigidly enforced against those who may offend. John W. HOWSON. Halifax County, July 24, 1809.

Friday, August 11, 1809. Vol. IV.-Num. 180.

(635) The Gazette. Friday. Edenton, August 11, 1809. .. Under the Frederick-Town (Md.) head of July 27, we find the following:—On Friday last there came in the George-Town stage to Mr. COOKE's tavern in this town, a Mrs. JONES, and two gentlemen, one was Mr. J. HOWARD from the City of Washington; the other was Mr. Isaac SMITH of Alexandria; the woman left a trunk at Mr. COOKEs to be forwarded on to Winchester, (Va.) but before the Winchester stage arrived on Sunday, Mr. COOKE had to go in the room where the trunk was left, he found as soon as he entered the room there was a very disagreeable smell, which he mentioned to his wife, and wished her to search; she did so..they opened the trunk, and to their surprise found a dead infant wrapped up in women's apparel.—They immediately sent for a Coroner, who called a jury of inquest, but not understanding how it came by its death no verdict was given. It has since been reported that a Mr. JONES of Alexandria was married at HOLTZAM's tavern in George-Town on the 18th inst. to a woman who was in a very pregnant state, and she is supposed to be the same that left the trunk. She went on to Winchester on Saturday last.

(636) The Trustees of Edenton Academy, are requested to attend the annual examination of the Students, commencing on the 31st of August. Parents residing at a distance, who have children at the Academy, are informed that the vacation begins, on the 3d of September and will continue until the first Monday in October.—There will be public speaking by the Students, in the Court-House on Saturday the 2d of September. By resolve of a Board of Trustees. Jos. B. SKINNER, Sec'y. Aug. 10, 1809.

(637) SMITH's & Colerain Ferries. The public are respectfully informed that the Ferry Boats, kept at the aforesaid Ferries, on Chowan River, 12 miles from Edenton, are now in complete order for carrying Passengers, Horses and Chairs in the utmost safety. A new Boat having been built at Colerain, and the one at SMITH's

11 August 1809

(637) (Cont.) thoroughly repaired, the subscribers cherish a hope that they will meet with such encouragement as their attention and a desire to please may entitle them to. Good Entertainment for Man and Horse, is constantly kept at both Ferries. Stephen SMITH, George M'CLENNY. Chowan River, Aug. 9, 1809.

(638) Fryeburg, (Mass) July 6. Singular Occurrence—One night last week a young man by the name of Isaac CHANDLER, residing in Fryeburg, got up in his sleep, went about half a mile to a neighbor's barn, procured a cord and a bundle of hay and carried them into the woods at a considerable distance from the house. He then ascended a maple tree with the cord and hay. After reaching the height of 28 feet, he placed the hay in a crotch of the tree, ascended about 6 feet higher, tied the cord to a limb and then fastened it round his ancle, after which he swung off head foremost, so that his head touched the top of the hay. In this horrid situation he awoke, and with his cries roused the nearest neighbors, who directed their course to the place from whence the noise proceeded. It was about break of day when they arrived. They there to their astonishment found the young man in the situation described, suspended by the heels 34 feet in the air. A num-ber of attempts were made to climb the tree..but it being large, without many limbs near the bottom, and the bark smooth, they proved ineffectual, and he after becoming composed enough to relieve his situation, recovered his former posture on the limb from which he made his descent, loosened the cord, and came down very much to the satisfaction of himself and friends.. There are more than 20 who can attest to the foregoing relation as being strictly true. Portland Gazette.

Friday, August 18, 1809. Vol. IV—Num. 181.

(639) From the Boston Patriot. Captain FOLGER's Statement. This remarkable statement, which occupies three full columns in the N. York Evening Post, of June 20 (and which has been copied into most of the Anglo—American papers) is addressed to the Editor of that paper, dated Boston, 20th March, 1809, & signed S. FOLGER. .. Real Statement of Facts. Captain Laban FOLGER, the hero of the above political fiction, sailed from Boston, Feb. 1809, in the brig Acorn of 120 tons.. He was not part owner of the brig Acorn. On his return he sailed for Cherburg in France, with freight, and it is believed did not put into North Bergen. He arrived in safety at Cherburg, where he discharged his cargo, and had his freight paid him, took in another freight for a port in the North of Europe.. He then returned to France again, where he remained several months, spent the freight the vessel had earned, and run in debt upwards of 50,000 livres. He then took the brig's long-boat, fled his creditors, and left his mate in charge of the brig.— The government never took possession of the brig till after his escape, and proof of her intercourse with England. The mate, George THAXTER, of Hingham, a young man of good character, was committed to prison by the French government, where it is believed he still remains. Capt. WATERMAN, to whom it is said Gen. ARMSTRONG refused his aid, came from England with FOLGER; but we have heard nothing of his complaint of General ARMSTRONG's conduct. ...

(640) The Gazette. Friday. Edenton, August 18, 1809. Returns of Members of Assembly chosen at the late Election. Chowan—Frederick NORCOM, 128 Thomas BROWNRIGG, 90) Senate. Samuel M'GUIRE, 162 Myles WELCH, 91 Micajah BUNCH, 82 James SUTTON, 72 Richard HOSKINS, 69 Job LEARY, 62 John HAUGHTON, 46 Clement H. BLOUNT, 5 Town of Edenton—John BEASLEY, without opposition. Bertie—Joseph JORDAN, Senate. William CHERRY and Joseph H. BRYAN, Commons. Washington—Ebenezer PETTIGREW, Senate. Josiah FLOWERS and James FREEMAN, Com's. Perquimans--Willis RIDDICK, Senate. Isaac? BARBER and Johh CLARY, of infamous memory, Commons.—That men, who have been guilty of the basest seduction should be chosen to

(640) (Cont.) represent us, is a disgrace to all the moral civil and religious rights of our country. Pasquotank--William S. HINTON, Senate. William T. RELFE and James CARVER, Commons. Camden--Caleb PERKINS, Senate. Joseph DOZIER and Thomas BELL, Commons. Currituck--J. LINDSAY, Senate. (The Commons not heard from.) Gates--Joseph RIDDICK, Senate. Humphrey HUDGINS and Kedar BALLARD, Commons. Tyrrel--Jesse ALEXANDER, Senate. Moses E. CATOR and Thomas GARRETT, Commons. Martin--Jeremiah SLADE, Senate. Henry WILLIAMS and Joel CHERRY, Commons.

(641) Mr. WILLS, The annals of human nature afford a humiliating proof, that scarcely any crime however enormous has escaped its depravity. In the black catalogue of crimes which have stained the human character, no one, we should suppose would excite in a mind of any common degree of purity, more horror and detestation, than that of a husband's seducing the young and unsuspecting daughter of his wife, reared under his own roof, and looking up to him for guidance and protection. .. Every man who has given his suffrage for John CLARY, has virtually declared his approbation of his conduct, has given his sanction to the crime, and though silently, yet emphatically has declared that, placed in similar situation, he could be guilty of the same unparalleled wickedness. ... Censor.

(642) Mr. WILLS, Sir--By giving the following advertisement a place in your paper, you will discharge a duty, inform the ignorant, shame the malicious, and much oblige yours, and the publick's most obedient servants, William CREATH, William DOSSEY. To the Editor of the Edenton Gazette. In a paper which issued from your press some time in July inst. the public is presented with the remarkable circumstances attendant upon the death of Samuel COOK, late of Washington, N. C. the names Wm. CREATH and William DOSSEY attached to the narrative we acknowledge; but the additional epithets of Anabaptist Preachers, we, before the world disclaim. ... When we prepared the piece above mentioned, modestly withheld from the world the office which we held in the Church of Christ. But to instruct the ignorant, and silence the reproachful, we at present subscribe William CREATH, William DOSSEY,} Elders of the Baptist Church. July 29, 1809.

(643) On the second Saturday and Sunday in September, the Rev. Isaac HUNTER, of Gates County, the Rev. Thomas SHANDS and Wm. P. HARDY, of Bertie circuit, in company of others, are expected to hold a two-days meeting in the Town of Edenton. On Saturday preaching will begin at 11 o'clock. On the Sabbath about 9 o'clock we expect to have love feast. We are authorised to say, that without some accident we may at that time occupy our Chapel.

(644) From a Rutland, Vermont paper--July 1. The Dove.--On a Sunday in August last, while the Rev. Isaac BEAL was preaching in the Baptist meeting-house at Pawlet, a Dove flew into the house, and after lighting upon the head of the preacher, and also upon his bible, went out at a window. The Dove was an uncommonly tame one, and belonged to a farmer in the neighborhood. It would frequently perch upon the head of persons as they passed by, and the aforesaid preacher had often sported with it at the house of the farmer. This trifling incident, which was little if at all known beyond the precincts of the parish where it happened..has been published in most parts of the United States--and by a concealment of the principal facts, and the addition of a few new traits of embellishment, has been made to assume one of those marvellous appearances so eagerly sought after by the credulous of all ages. ...

(645) By the President of the United States of America. A Proclamation. Whereas in consequence of a communication from his Brittanic Majesty's Envoy..declaring that the British Orders in Council of January and November, 1807, would have been

(645) (Cont.) withdrawn on the 10th day of June last..I, James MADISON, President..did issue my proclamation..on the 19th of April last, declaring that the Orders in Council aforesaid would have been so withdrawn on the said 10th day of June, after which the trade suspended by certain acts of Congress might be renewed; and whereas it is now officially made known to me that the said Orders..have not been withdrawn..I do hereby proclaim the same, and consequently that the trade renewable on the event of the said orders being withdrawn, is to be considered as under the operation of the several acts by which such trade was suspended. Given under my hand and the seal of the United States at the City of Washington the ninth day of August in the year of our Lord one thousand eight hundred and nine, and of the Independence of the said United States the thirty-fourth. (Signed) James MADISON. By the President, R. SMITH, Secretary of State.

(646) Remarkable Trial--The Gaz. published at Bedford, Pennsylvania, states "that the following is an authentic account of a remarkable trial held in Queen Ann's county, state of Maryland--from attested notes taken in court at the time by one of the counsel." Queen Ann's County Court. State of Maryland, use of James, Fanny, Robert and Thomas HARRIS, devisees of Thomas HARRIS, versus Mary HARRIS, administratrix of James HARRIS.} Action of Debt on administration Bond. .. The facts in the above cause were as follows: There were two brothsrs, Thomas HARRIS and James HARRIS. Thomas the elder held a piece of land in fee as he supposed.-- He had the four children abovenamed, and for whose use this action was brought; those children were illegitimate. Thomas made his will, directed his land to be sold, but did not thereby appoint any person to make sale of it.--He devised that the proceeds that should arise from the sale of his land, together with all his other estate should be divided amongst his four abovenamed illegitimate children, and appointed his brother, Jas. HARRIS, executor of his will, who after the death of his brother Thomas, caused the said will to be proved, and took out letters testamentary thereon. James HARRIS, executor returned an inventory of the personal estate of his brother, Thomas HARRIS, and made sale of the land abovementioned, believing that his said brother had been seized in fee, and that he was authorized under the said will to make sale thereof. When the purchase money was paid to James HARRIS, and counsel was applied to draw the conveyance, it was then for the first time discovered to James HARRIS that his elder brother (T. H.) was not seized in fee, but in tail, of the land and that of course he had no right to devise it, nor could it descend to his children, because of the illegitimacy, but that he James HARRIS, was the heir in tail, and entitled to the land in his own right, and without any title derived under his brother's will. He then conveyed his right to the purchaser, and claimed the purchase money to himself.

About two years after, James HARRIS died intestate; his widdow Mary HARRIS, the present defendent, administered on his estate: this suit was brought on her administration bond, to recover the estate of Thomas HARRIS for the use of his illegitimate children, to whom he had devised all his estate. The only point of the dispute was, whether the proceeds of the sale of land in question were to be considered as the estate of Thomas HARRIS. Before the trial of the cause, this case had made much noise, it having been said that the ghost of Thomas HARRIS had in the life time of his brother James HARRIS, frequently appeared to a man by the name of BRIGGS, and the reason..was to compel James HARRIS his younger brother, to return the proceeds of the sale of the land to the orphan's court: to make himself responsible for it as a part of the estate of Thomas HARRIS. The fact was that such was the communication of BRIGGS to James HARRIS, relative to his brother's ghost having appeared to him, that he, James HARRIS, did go to the orphan's court, returned himself debtor to the estate of his brother, to the amount of the purchase money of the land.--James was soon after taken sick and died. ..
..BRIGGS was known to be a man of character, of firm, undaunted spirits; had been

(646) (Cont.) a soldier in the revolutionary war, and perfectly disinterested between, and unconnected with the parties. This cause was tried in 1798 or 1799.

After the nature of the action the ground of controversy had been stated with great solemnity, by the counsel on both sides, and the very extraordinary reports that had been in circulation, relative to the appearance of the ghost..William BRIGGS the witness was produced and sworn, and his relation was as follows. Wm. BRIGGS said he was forty three years of age; that Thomas HARRIS died in September, in the year 1790--In the March following he was riding near the place where Thomas HARRIS was buried, on a horse which formerly had belonged to Thomas HARRIS:--after crossing a small branch, his horse began to walk on very fast--it was between the hours of 8 and 9 o'clock in the morning; he was alone; it was a clear day; he entered a lane adjoining to the field where Thomas HARRIS was buried; his horse suddenly wheeled in a pannel of the fence, looked over the fence into the field..towards the grave yard and neighed very loud; witness then saw Thomas HARRIS coming towards him in the same apparel as he had last seen him in his lifetime; he had on a sky blue coat; just before he came to the fence, he veered to the right and vanished; his horse immediately took the road.--Thomas HARRIS came within two pannels of the fence to him--he did not see his features, nor speak to him. He was acquainted with Thomas HARRIS when a boy and there had always been a great intimacy between them.--He thinks the horse knew Thomas HARRIS, because of his neighing, pricking up his ears and looking over the fence.

About the 1st of June following he was ploughing in his own field, about three miles from where Thomas HARRIS was buried;--about dusk, Thomas HARRIS came along side of him and walked with him about two hundred yards; he was dressed as when first seen; he made a halt about two steps from him; John BAILEY, who was ploughing with him, came driving up and he lost sight of the ghost--he was much alarmed; not a word was spoken; the young man, BAILEY, did not see him..it preyed upon his mind so as to affect his health. He was with Thomas HARRIS when he died, but had no particular conversation with him.--Sometime after he was laying in bed, about eleven or twelve o'clock at night, he heard Thomas HARRIS groan; it was like the groan he gave a few minutes before he expired.. Sometime after, when in bed, and a great fire light in the room, he saw a shadow on the wall, at the same time he felt a great weight upon him. Sometime after, when in bed and asleep, he felt a stroke between his eyes which blackened them both; his wife was in bed with him and two young men were in the room; the blow awakened him and all in the room were asleep; is certain no person in the room struck him; the blow swelled his nose. About the middle of August he was alone, coming from Dickey COLLIN's, after dark, about one hour in the night, Thomas HARRIS appeared, dressed as he had seen him when he was going down the meeting-house branch, three miles and a half from the grave yard of Thomas HARRIS. It was star-light; he extended his arms over his shoulders; does not know how long he remained in this situation; he was much alarmed; Thomas HARRIS disappeared; nothing was said; he felt no weight on his shoulders; he went back to Col. LINSI, and got a young man to go home with him; after he got home he mentioned it to the young man; he before this time told James HARRIS that he had seen his brother's ghost.

In October, about twilight in the morning, he saw Thomas HARRIS about one hundred yards from the house of the witness..he had no conception why Thomas HARRIS appeared to him--On the same day, about 8 o'clock in the morning, he was handing up blades to John BAILEY, who was stacking them; he saw Thomas HARRIS coming along the garden fence..he vanished, and always to the east; was within 15 feet of him; BAILEY did not see him; about one hour and a half afterwards, in same place, he again appeared..came up to the fence, leaned upon it within ten feet of the witness..witness advanced towards Thomas HARRIS; one or the other spoke as witness got over the fence, on the same pannel that Thomas HARRIS was leaning on. They walked off together about five hundred yards; a conversation took place as they

(646) (Cont.) walked on; he has not the conversation on his memory; he could not understand Thomas HARRIS, his voice was so low; he asked Thomas HARRIS a question, and he forbid him; witness then asked why not go to your brother instead of me? Thomas HARRIS said, ask me no questions; witness told him his will was doubted; Thos. HARRIS told him to ask his brother if he did not remember the conversation which passed between them on the east side of the wheat stacks, the day he was taken with his death sickness; that he then declared that he wished all his property should be kept together by James HARRIS until his children arrived at age, then the whole should be sold and divided among the children, and should not be immediately sold as expressed in his will; that he thought the property would be most wanting to his children when minors, therefore he had changed his will, and said that witness should see him again; he then told witness to turn, and disappeared.. Witness then went to James HARRIS, and told him he had seen his brother three times that day, and related the conversation he had with him; asked Jas. HARRIS if he remembered the conversation between him and his brother at the wheat stacks; he said he did, and told him what had passed: said he would fulful his brother's will; he was satisfied that witness had seen his brother, for that no other person knew that conversation. On the same evening, returning home about an hour before sun-set, Thomas HARRIS appeared to him, came along side of him; witness told him that his brother said he would fulfil his will; no more conversation on this subject..he has never related to any person the last conversation, and never would. ... Hon. Robert TILGHMAN, Judge. Hon. Robert WRIGHT, the late Governor of Maryland, and the Hon. Joseph H. NICHOLSON, were the council for the plaintiffs. The Hon. Richard T. EARLE, and John SCOTT, Esq. were council for the defendant.

Friday, August 25, 1809. Vol. IV.-Num. 182.

(647) The Gazette. Friday. Edenton, August 25, 1809. Further Election Returns. Craven—William BRYAN, Senate. Wm. BLACKLEDGE and John S. NELSON, Commons. Town of Newbern—William GASTON. Halifax—M. C. WHITAKER, Senate. W. _. WEBB and Joseph BRYAN, Commons. Town of Halifax—William DREW. Northampton—William EDMUNDS, Senate. Green TURNER and Andrew JONES, Commons. Nash—William ARRINGTON, Senate. Exum PHILLIPS and Michael COLLINS, Commons. Granville—Thomas TAYLOR, Senate. William HAWKINS and Henry YANCY, Commons. Currituck—Brickhouse BELL and Jesse BARNARD, Commons.

(648) On the 7th instant, departed this life, at his seat at Lebanon, His Excellency Jonathan TRUMBULL, Esq. Governor of the State of Connecticut, aged 69.

(649) Norfolk, August 18. Fire!!!—On Wednesday night, between the hours of eleven and twelve o'clock, a Fire broke out in an untenanted Ware-House situate on SOUTHGATE and DICKSON's Wharf. .. But what commanded our admiration..was the Ware-House of Mr. Thomas DICKSON, adjoining the houses that were on fire. For nearly three hours did the flames beat with unabated fury against it, without producing visible effect—It stands an imperishable monument of the policy and interest of erecting fire-proof houses; as, had it not been for this happy circumstance, Norfolk would this day present as gloomy an aspect as it did in the winter of 1804. .. Five Ware-Houses..were consumed.. Messrs. SOUTHGATE and DICKSON have sustained a heavy loss..and Messrs. John PROUDFIT and N. HERON have lost the contents of their stores, with all their books and papers. ...

(650) Married—on the 17th inst. Capt. Daniel BELL, to Miss Mary WALTON, both of this town. Died-at New-Orleans, on the 19th ult. Lieut. Edward MASON, of the 3d regiment of United States Infantry.

25 August 1809

(651) One or Two Negro Boys Will be taken as Apprentices to the Carpenters business. Apply to William NICHOLS. August 24th, 1809.

(652) State of N. Carolina, Currituck County Court,) May Term, 1809. Whereas
Abner Nash VAIL, Esq. hath sued out an original attachment against the real estate
of John STANDLEY, late of the County aforesaid, returnable to this Court at this
term, It is ordered, That public notice be given to the said John STANDLEY, by
advertisement in the Edenton Gazette, for six weeks, that unless he appears at the
next term of the said Court, to be held at Currituck, on the last Monday in August
next, replevy his estate and plead to said action, final judgment will be entered
up against him. By Order, T. BAXTER, C. C. C.

(653) Notice. On Thursday the 5th day of October next, will be Sold, to the
highest bidder, at the house of Willis GALLOP, Esq. on the North Banks, in Currituck County, the Lands belonging to the estate of Willis SAWYER, dec. of Bertie
County, lying on and near MARTIN's Point; the boundaries and quantity will be
ascertained previous to the day of sale. Indisputable titles will be given. ...
Sarah SAWYER, Ex'rx. By her Agent, Henry BAKER. August 17, 1809.

Friday, September 1, 1809. Vol. IV.-Num. 183.

(654) The Gazette. Friday. Edenton, September 1, 1809. The Editor having been
informed that a paragraph attached to the account of the election of BARBER and
CLARY of Perquimans, has been supposed to allude to the former, takes this method
to declare, that no part of the observation was supposed to be applicable to, or
was intended, in any way, to apply to Mr. BARBER.
    Further Election Returns. Robeson--Benjamin LEE, Senate. Hugh BROWN and Wil-
liam STERLING, Commons. Chatham--Roderick COTTON, Senate. John MEBANE and
Charles CANNON, Commons. Columbus--Bun WHITE, Senate. Benjamin FRANKS and Wil-
liam NANCE, Commons. Duplin--Joseph RHODES, Senate. David WRIGHT and Daniel
GLISSON, Commons. Guilford--Jonathan PARKER, Senate. Robert HANNER and John
HARWELL, Commons. Moore--Col. Benj. WILLIAMS, Senate. Archibald M'NEIL and
Edward WADE, Comm's. Montgomery--Edmund DEBERRY, Senate. Joseph PARSON and Wm.
CRITONTON, Comm's. New-Hanover--Timothy BLOODWORTH, jun'r. Senate. David JONES
and Hinton JAMES, Com. Randolph--Michael HARVEY, Senate. Jno. BROWER and Solomon
GOODMAN, Commons. Rockingham--Nathaniel SCALES, Senate. Mark HARDEN and T.
WORTHAM, Commons. Sampson--Joab BLACKMAN, Senate. Wm. R. KING and James MAT-
THEWS, Commons. Wayne--James RHODES, Senate. William SMITH and (blank) DEAN,
Commons. Town of Wilmington--Wm. W. JONES. Town of Fayetteville--Gen. Thos.
DAVIS. Wake--Wm. HINTON, Senate. N. JONES, (W. P.) and Kimbro' JONES, Commons.
Warren--Henry FITTS, Senate. W. R. JOHNSON and John H. HAWKINS, Commons. Frank-
lin--Jeremiah BRICKELL, Senate. Jas. J. HILL and Thomas LANIER, Commons. Orange-
-James MEBANE, Senate. John THOMPSON and David MEBANE, Commons. Town of Hills-
borough--Catlett CAMPBELL. Johnston--J. WILLIAMS, Senate. J. RICHARDSON and S.
NARSWORTHY, Commons. Pitt--Robert WILLIAMS, Senate. John MORING and Benjamin
MAY, Commons. Lenoir--Simon BRUTON, Senate. Lazarus PEARCE and John WOOTEN, Com-
mons. Cumberland--William LORD, Senate. Jas. CAMPBELL and John RAY, Commons.
Bladen--Samuel ANDRESS, Senate. James OWEN and Thomas BROWN, jun. Commons. Rich-
mond--Duncan M'FARLAND, Senate. John SMITH and Thorogood PATE, Commons. Greene--
Wm. D. SPEIGHT, Senate. Henry J. G. RUFFIN and Jonas WILLIAMS, Comm's. Carteret-
-Belcher FULLER, Senate. John ROBERTS and Jacob HENRY, Commons. Beaufort--
Frederick GRIST, Senate. Jas. WILLIAMS and Thomas BOYD, Commons. Onslow--Christ-
opher DUDLEY, Senate. W. JONES and Edward WILLIAMS, Commons. Jones--Durant
HATCH, jun. Senate. James C. BRYAN and L. SIMMONS, Commons. Edgecomb--Henry I.
TOOLE, Senate. Hardy FLOWERS and Wm. BALFOUR, Commons.

1 September 1809

(655)   Notice Is hereby given that on the 31st day of December next, the Copartnership of SAWYER and NORCOM will be dissolved. The Subscribers, therefore, earnestly request that all persons indebted to them will call and close their accounts.   .. Attendance for the above purpose will be given every day, from 9
o'clock in the morning until 3 in the afternoon, at the shop of SAWYER & NORCOM.
Edenton, Aug. 29, 1809.

Friday, September 8, 1809. Vol. IV.-Num. 184.

(656)   The Gazette. Friday. Edenton, September 8, 1809. Further Election Returns. Caswell--Azariah GRAVES, Senate. Isaac RAINEY and Nathan WILLIAMS, Commons. Rockingham--Nathaniel SCALES, Senate. Mark HARDEN and Hugh MILLS, (sic)
Commons. Stokes--Henry B. DOBSON, Senate. Jonathan DALTON and Chas. BANNER, Commons. Surry--Gideon EDWARDS, Senate. Nicholas HORN and Wm. DOOLING, Commons.
Rowan--Jacob FISHER, Senate. Jesse A. PEARSON and (blank) WELBORN, Commons. Town
of Salisbury--Archibald HENDERSON. Mecklenburg--Gen. Geo. GRAHAM, Senate. Thomas
HENDERSON and H. G. BURTON, Commons.

(657)   To the Lovers of Plain Dealing. Whereas certain characters, unfortunately
men of some little influence through the medium of property, have maliciously
insinuated (no doubt with a view to injure his practice) that Dr. James USHER is
the author of a publication signed "A Student," which appeared in the Edenton
Gazette on the 25th ult. and that I, his student, am used as an instrument to
probe the wounded sensibility of those unfortunate practitioners who apply their
means at random. As I am unwilling any man should suffer a false accusation on my
account, I conceive it a duty I owe the cause of truth and justice to declare..my-
self the author: And am able to prove that Dr. USHER knew not there was such a
piece for several days after it was written. .. I write for my own amusement and
the cause I have espoused, viz. the study of Physic and Surgery: But when such
glaring mistakes are made by a practitioner as an attempt to trepan a sound scull,
although a Student, I feel alarmed for the situation of my fellow creatures, and
the honor of the profession; especially when men of influence incorrigibly persist
in persecuting the man who has firmness and skill to detect such intended operation. John CRITTENDEN. Gates C. House, Sept. 1, 1809.

(658)   Newbern Academy. The Trustees of this Institution are desirous to engage a
person to superintend it, who possesses the requisite qualifications, with respect
to morals, learning, and assiduity. The building, which will probably be completed and fit for the reception of scholars by the end of October, is furnished
with spacious apartments for the separate accommodation of pupils of both sexes:
it is situated in the centre of three acres of ground, in a dry, airy, and healthy
part of the town, and near to wells of excellent water. .. Letters addressed to
the Board at Newbern, the postage being paid, will be promptly attended to; or application may be made individually to the subscribers. John Louis TAYLOR, President. Spyres SINGLETON, Edward PASTEUR, William BLACKLEDGE, William SHEPARD, William GASTON, John S. WEST, Francis HAWKS. Newbern, N. Carolina, 27th August,
1809)

(659)   Notice. On Tuesday the second day of the next Superior Court, to be held
for the County of Bertie, before the Court-House door in the Town of Windsor, and
between the hours of 12 and 4 o'clock, will be offered for one or more years, as
may best suit the person or persons wishing to rent the same, the noted Fishery
belonging to the estates of Mr. John STEWART and Robert ARMISTEAD, decd. situated
on the Broad Creek, near the River Roanoke, furnished with large and strong Fish-
Houses, a good Salt-House, and a Cook-House with two rooms sufficiently large to

8 September 1809

(659) (Cont.) accommodate the hands employed in fishing and a sufficient quantity of Stands Troughs and Flats for the fishery, by the Adm'x & Administrato_. Plymouth, Sept. 4, 1809.

(660) Anti-Duelling Association. New-York, August 8, 1809. Agreeably to public notice, a large number of respectable citizens met at the North Dutch Church, this day, to receive the report of a committee appointed at a former meeting, relative to the adoption of measures for the suppression of duelling. Hon. John BROOME, Esq. in the Chair. Col. Lebbeus LOOMIS, Secretary.
    The following plan was reported..and unanimously adopted, viz. "We, whose names are hereunto subscribed, viewing with alarm the increase of Duelling; desirous of opposing to its further prevalence the strongest lawful resistance; and persuaded that a proper use of the Right of Suffrage, will have a powerful effect in discountenancing and banishing it; do hereby unite ourselves in an Association, to be called the Anti-Duelling Association Of New-York: And do, by our signatures hereunto annexed, solemnly pledge ourselves to each other, not to vote at any election for any man, whom, from current fame, or our own private conviction, we shall believe to have sent, accepted, or carried a challenge to fight a Duel, or acted, as a Second or Surgeon therein, after the date hereof. ... By Order of the Meeting, John BROOME, Chairman. Lebbeus LOOMIS, Sec'y.

Friday, September 15, 1809. Vol. IV.-Num. 185.

(661) The Gazette. Friday. Edenton, September 15, 1809. Further Election Returns. Hertford—Gen. Thomas WYNNS, Senate. Abner PERRY and Boon FELTON, Commons. Anson—Thos. THREADGILL, Senate. Wm. PICKET and Lawrence MOORE, Commons. Burke—Israel PICKENS, Senate. Isaac T. AVERY and Charles M'DOWELL, Commons. Iredell—James HART, Senate. G. L. DAVIDSON and Samuel KING, Commons.

(662) New-York, August 30. Counterfeiters Detected.—Yesterday afternoon, Seneca PAGE, belonging to Vermont, and Harris COVERT, of Cayuga, attempted to pass a counterfeit Three Dollar Manhattan bank note, on Samuel BEACH, Esq. post-master at the city of Jersey, who immediately discovered the bill was a forgery; and Mr. BEACH being a Judge of the County, immediately arrested and examined the above named counterfeiters, and found on them from 20 to 30,000 dollars of forged notes on the different banks in the United States. After which they were committed to Hackensack gaol. ...

(663) Married—on the 5th inst. in Bertie County, Mr. Henry PETERSON, to Miss Elizabeth FREEMAN, daughter of Mr. Charles FREEMAN, all of that County. On Tuesday last, in Perquimans County, Mr. William WILSON, of Pasquotank County, to Miss Elizabeth SKINNER, daughter of Joshua SKINNER, Esq. of the former County. On Thursday evening, at the house of Wm. ROBERTS, Esq. dec'd. Mr. John DICKINSON, of this town, to the amiable Miss Eliza MAIR, youngest daughter of John MAIR, Esq. dec'd. of this place.

(664) Taken up, And committed to the Jail of Currituck County, Four Negroes, who when first taken up said they were free and had passes; but after examination said they were slaves and run-aways, to wit, JACK, a black man about 24 years of age, 5 feet 10 inches high, says he belongs to Mr. Edward HARRIS, of Newbern. ROSE, a girl of a yellowish complexion, about 25 or 26 years of age, 5 feet high, and says she belongs to the aforesaid HARRIS. SAM, about 25 or 26 years of age, 5 feet 6 inches high, says he belongs to Dr. H. JONES, of Mattamuskeet. PHEBE, about 25 or 30 years of age, 5 feet 2 inches high, black complexioned, and says she belongs to the estate of Timothy MURRY, of Mattamuskeet. The owners of the above slaves are

(664) (Cont.) requested to come forward, prove their property, pay all charges, and take them away; otherwise they will be dealt with as the law directs. C. ETHERIDGE, Sheriff of Currituck. September 6, 1809.

Friday, September 22, 1809. Vol. IV.-Num. 186.

(665) Auburn, (N. Y.) August 23. Tragical Event.--We have the disagreeable task to record a most cruel murder of an infant of nine months old, in the town of Reading, Steuben county.--Our informant..relates to us the following circumstances:--A young man, son of a Mr. Isaac BALDWIN, of Litchfield, (Con.) being deranged in his mind in consequence of disappointed love, was sent to Mr. Elisha WARD, of Reading, (a friend of his father) in hopes that a change of situation would conduce to restore him to his senses. .. He lately insisted upon going home to his friends, and made several attempts to escape, but on Mr. WARD's stopping him..he got into a passion, and threatened revenge if not permitted. On Wednesday last he accomplished his threat; he took Mr. WARD's child from the arms of a young woman, went out of the house, took up an axe, and laying the child's head on a stump, which was before the door, deliberately cut it off! .. This unfortunate young man appeared greatly affected after he had committed the fatal deed. He confessed the murder..and said he did it with an intention, whilst the family was in confusion, to make his escape to Connecticut. Coroner's inquest-- Wilful Murder.

(666) The Gazette. Friday. Edenton, September 22, 1809. .. From the Balt. Ev. Post. Case of the men arrested as deserters from the frigate L'Africaine, by John HUNTER, Esq. Sheriff of Baltimore--at the request of Wm. WOOD, Esq. British Consul for the port of Baltimore. An Habeas Corpus was applied for to Judge SCOTT, late on Thursday evening on behalf of 7 men arrested, and held in custody by the Sheriff, at the request, and on the statement of the British Consul that they were deserters, by their council. The Habeas Corpus was issued..returnable the next morning at 9 o'clock--Accordingly this morning the men were brought up..and the Sheriff made return that he had arrested and detained the men in custody in virtue of the following authority from the British Consul:--British Consul's Office, Baltimore, September 6th, 1809. John HUNTER, Esq. Sir--Having received information that 13 seamen having deserted from L'Africaine frigate, and are now in this city- -I have to request that you will be pleased to secure them till they can be sent on board. I am, &c. Wm. WOOD. By virtue of this authority, I have arrested and put in prison the following persons--to wit: John NOWLAND, William WHOKES, Dennis MURPHY, Richard HEWES, John EARL, John BURWELL, Jacob LAMB. .. In the course of a few minutes Mr. WOOD came into Court, and the counsel for the prisoners, Messrs. GLENN and J. L. DONALDSON, moved..that the men be discharged, sufficient cause for their detention not appearing, on the return. Mr. WOOD's counsel, Mr. Walter DORSEY, requested to be allowed time to enquire into the law, and said that they would be ready to prove that these men were deserters from his Britannic Majesty's ship. The counsel for the prisoners objected to the delay; and the Judge declaring that the arrest had been unlawful..ordered them to be discharged, which took place amid the plaudits and heartfelt rejoicings of a numerous concourse of people.
    The above released British seamen inform, that the following persons, American citizens, have been impressed, and are now detained on board L'Africaine: Edward SWAINE, John FERGUSON, George WILSON, John BUTLER, John WILLIAMS, Ambrose CRUSE. The 3 last are black men.

(667) Died--at Nixonton, on the 10th inst. Mr. J. LOCKWOOD, principal teacher in the Academy at that place. Died--on Monday the 18th instant, at the house of

22 September 1809

(667) (Cont.) Major William JONES, in Hertford County, very much lamented by his relatives and a large cricle of acquaintance, William CHERRY, Esq. Attorney at Law, of Windsor.

Friday, September 29, 1809. Vol. IV.-Num. 187.

(668) The Gazette. Friday. Edenton, September 29, 1809. .. Died at Elizabeth-City on the 22d instant, Mr. James T. STUART, Merchant of New-York in the 31st year of his age.--His amiable disposition and social manners had endeared him to all his acquaintance. He bore a painful illness with the most exemplary fortitude and met the approach of death with the magnanimity of a Christian Hero.
     Died in Washington County on the 19th inst. Mrs. Ann SWAIN. She became a member of the Methodist Episcopal Church many years ago, and continued so until her decease. ...

(669) Elizabeth WILLIAMS. Has just removed from Bertie to this place, and has opened School in the house lately occupied by Mr. Benjamin HASSEL, where she teaches, Reading, Writing, and Needle-Work, on moderate terms. She will also accommodate a few girls as boarders. Her terms are, Boarding and Schooling, per quarter, $18 Schooling, 4 ...

(670) William MANNING, Cabinet Maker, Informs..that he has just returned from New-York, with a full supply of Materials for carrying on his business. ... Edenton, Sept. 18, 1809.

(671) 40 Dollars Reward. Ran away from the subscriber on the 17th instant, a dark Mulatto Man, named QUACKO, he is about thirty-seven years of age, five feet seven inches high, and very stout made, he is very artful, and professes to be a Cooper and Job-Carpenter. I expect he will have a pass, as he can write. He formerly belonged to Mr. James BLOUNT, of Washington County, and came to this County as a freeman, calling himself John BROWN; and when he was apprehended produced several papers to prove his freedom, which was written by himself, and he had signed the names of several Justices of the Peace to said papers. ... John C. BAKER. Brunswick County, Sept. 18, 1809.)

(672) Interesting To Mariners. Wm. THOMPSON, of Brooklyn, (N. Y.) publishes, that he has tried the following experiment, and doubts not that it would be the means of preserving the lives of such of our sea-faring people as should be so unfortunate as to abandon their vessel and trust their lives to the boat. A fourteen-feet (sic) boat, with an empty puncheon lashed to the rising of the boat on the inside, will float with four men in it when full of water, and in that case may be bailed out. .. In the above case a boat may live in the sea, without danger of turning bottom up.

Friday, October 6, 1809. Vol. IV.-Num. 188.

(673) Arrestation for Murder. [By the following account taken from the Saratoga Independent American, it appears that a man who calls his name Abijah STERNS, and who in two letters, which he has written since his commitment to Stephen JACOBS and Elijah PAIN, Esquires, of Vermont, styles himself "Chief Judge of the Supreme Court" of that state, was last week apprehended in the county of Washington, and committed to the jail in Saratoga county, New-York, charged with being the perpetrator of a murder committed at a place called Newtown, in the town of Half-moon, about 14 years ago.--No account is given..of the causes which have..led to the apprehension of this man--neither who the person was that was murdered.]

6 October 1809

(673) (Cont.) Ballston Spa, September 5, 1809. .. Ballston Jail, Aug. 21, 1809.
To Judge Stephen JACOBS, of Windsor. Sir, I take this opportunity to inform you,
that I have been on business to Albany, and on my return to Waterton, have been
apprehended on suspicion of murdering a man in Halfmoon 14 years ago, the same
that was murdered by WILLIAMS and ADAMS, who was convicted before you and Judge
PAINE, and WHITE and WILSON, on the 23d of January, 1809. .. I was wounded and
my life almost exhausted by reason of bleeding. I went to Lansingburg and paid
the money for advertising the murderers.. I have left a warrant with Mr. WARD,
High Sheriff in the Susbury, in the county of Worcester, and State of Massachusetts; and another in Boston, to commit them to prison—but have been neglected.
.. I desire you to come and bring other witnesses of their confession. .. Abijah STERNS, Chief Judge of the Supreme Court.
    To Elijah PAIN, Judge of the Circuit Court of the United States. Honored Sir,
I take this opportunity to acquaint you with my unhappy situation. I have been on
business to Albany, and on my return home, have been apprehended in Greenwich, on
suspicion of having committed murder in Halfmoon. Sir, I was travelling from Albany to Arguyle about 14 years ago, and came in sight of two men who committed
murder, namely, Ebenezar Heredall WILLIAMS and Belton ADAMS. On the twenty-third
January, one thousand eight hundred and seven, they came into Windsor, Vermont,
where I saw them and accused them of committing the murder, and the Judges of the
Supreme Court called a special Court, and they were both convicted of committing
the murder in Halfmoon, before Judge Stephen JACOBS and Judge WHITE, and Judge
WILSON and your honor, and one of the Judges of Windsor county, and Judge HUNTER
and a number of the Justices of the Peace and myself. It was also proved upon the
trial of ADAMS by the oath of WILLIAMS and Polly FOX, that ADAMS had committed
murder in Looningburgh, and that both of them had confessed the justness of the
sentence, and they were committed to JOHN, to PAGE and another, to commit to
prison, and made their escape. I am now suffering in prison, for the crime committed by WILLIAMS and ADAMS. Sir, I earnestly entreat you to have mercy on an
innocent man, and come immediately and see me and set me at liberty. ... Abijah
STERNS, Chief Judge of the Supreme Court. Ballston Jail, Aug. 31, 1809.

(674) The Gazette. Friday. Edenton, October 6, 1809. .. Arrived at Plymouth
the sch'r. Anthony, BRITT, from Martinique—Sept. 22, in lat. 33, 13, N. long. 78,
00, spoke the brig Cyrus, of and for Baltimore, out 13 days from St. Bartholomews,
Capt. Shepley SMITH, master, who had on board Capt. John KITTS and part of the
crew of the sch'r. Matchless, from Philadelphia, bound for Curracoa, which vessel
upset in a hurricane in lat. 24, 30, N. long. 65.

(675) Royal Edwin Lodge. The Brethren of Royal Edwin Lodge of this place, are
requested to attend the funeral of our dec'd Brother William CHERRY, at the house
of Mr. Solomon CHERRY, sen. on Sunday the 29th instant, at 10 o'clock—The Members
of the different Lodges are invited to attend. Ant. COPELAND, Sec. P. Tem. Windsor, Oct. 5, 1809—A. L. 5809.

(676) State of N. Carolina, Currituck County.} Aug. Term, 1809. Elizabeth BAL-
LANCE, per Guar. vs. Moses BALLANCE,} Pet. to acc'nt. In this case it appearing
that the defendant is a resident of the State of Virginia, & on motion of the complainant by his counsel, it is ordered, That public notice be given the defendant
in the Edenton Gazette for six weeks..that unless he appears at the next term for
said County, on the last Monday in November next, and answer the petitioner's petition, &c. on oath, that judgment will be taken pro confesso, and the cause set
for hearing at the next November term ex parte. Attest, T. BAXTER, C. C. C.

(677) List of Letters remaining in the Post-Office at Edenton, Oct. 1, 1809.

6 October 1809

(677) (Cont.) Thomas BATEMAN, Lemuel COTTON, Robert DICKEY, James C. DUNBIBEN, Caleb ELLIOTT, Abraham ELLIOTT, Perrygrine ELLIOTT, James GREGORY, Stephen GODFREY, William GOODWIN, Capt. Benjamin HUBBELL, Mrs. Mary H. HAUGHTON, Richard HAUGHTON, jr. Andrew KNOX, Capt. Elias LAW, Jno. LOCKWOOD, Philip MILLER, John MUSE, Abraham PIERCE, Thomas SATTERFIELD, James WALLACE, John WESKETT, Ann WARRING. Hend. STANDIN, P. M.

(678) To The Public. This may certify, that my wife Sarah DRAPER, has quit my bed and board without any cause, and I do hereby forwarn any person or persons from trading with her upon my account, as I am determined not to pay any debt that she may contract from this date. Joseph DRAPER. Perquimans, Sept. 26, 1809.

Friday, October 13, 1809. Vol. IV.-Num. 189.

(679) Law Case, Decided by Judge TAYLOR at last Perquimans Superior Court; and published at the request of the citizens present. This indictment comes before me upon the submission of the defendants, six in number, whom it charges with a riot, attended with circumstances of peculiar, and uncommon outrage against the person of John CLARY, the prosecutor. The evidence..discloses these facts;--that the defendants, armed with offensive and deadly weapons, proceeded from the town of Hertford, at a late hour of the night, to CLARY's dwelling house, whence they forcibly dragged him, in spite of the entreaties, struggles, and _hrieks of his wife, who from their menacing appearance, and violent behaviour, had eve_y reason to fear that their design was upon his life. Some of the party threw him down; _nd, from his half stifled shrieks, the witness supposed, they endeavored to strangle him; but..this was..prevented. .. Having secured their prey, they conveyed him upwards of a mile from his own house _o a spot, which they had previously agreed _n, as the scene of the final indignity they meant to offer him: here they proposed to _trip him, but again the request of one of the party prevented it, and they contented themselves with covering him with tar and feathers, and in this condition left him to reach _ome as he could. ..
    John CLARY, the prosecutor, a man in moderate circumstances, intermarried with a widow lady, of respectable connexions, of irreproachable character, and affluent fortune. By her former husbands, she had several children, the youngest of whom was a female of seven or eight years of age.. .. But alas! in the bloom of beauty, and the dawn of womanhood, beloved by her friends, and sought for in marriage, by worthy men..it was the cruel fate of this tender, and confiding, female to find in her father--a seducer!.. Thus bereft of reputation and peace, she is exposed to the unpitying scorn of a society, which had her father possessed a common sense of duty..she might have been qualified to adorn. To complete her wretchedness, she is compelled, prematurely, to discharge the duties of a mother, with a heavy heart, and a wounded spirit..
    It further appears in evidence that one of the defendants every way worthy of this young lady had paid honorable addresses to her, that some of the others were related to her, and that soon after the crime of the prosecutor had become notorious, at a moment when their indignation was raised to the highest pitch they resolved to fix upon him this mark of ignominy. .. Upon a view of all the case the Court adjudges that five of the defendants pay to the State a fine of one hundred dollars each, and the other a fine of forty dollars.

(680) The Gazette. Friday. Edenton, October 13, 1809. .. Married--on the 3d inst. in Hertford county, Mr. Matthew MEACOM, of Gates county, Minister of the Methodist persuasion, to Miss Rebecca GALE, of the former place.

(681) On the first Saturday and Sunday in November there is to be a quarterly

13 October 1809

(681) (Cont.) meeting held in this Town; attended by the Rev. John BUXTON, and several other Preachers belonging to the Methodist Episcopal Church. .. As we have now a convenient house for divine worship, we shall be happy to see those who may find it convenient to attend from the country. Edenton, Oct. 12, 1809.

(682) Attention!! The Edenton Volunteers are ordered to attend a General Muster at the usual parade ground, on Friday next, at 9 o'clock, in summer uniform, properly equipped, with 24 rounds of blank cartridges. Absentees will be fined agreeable to the strict letter of the law. Duncan M'DONALD, Capt. October 13.

Friday, October 20, 1809. Vol. IV.-Num. 190.

(683) The Gazette. Friday. Edenton, October 20, 1809. .. Murder!! On Saturday the 23d inst. on board the brig Intercourse of Washington, Capt. GALLAGHER, between 2 and 3 o'clock, a most horrid Murder was committed on the body of Moses DAVIS, a seaman of the said brig, by a certain Archibald DAVIDSON, who is understood, to be part owner and supercargo of said vessel. .. DAVIDSON then attempted to shoot himself, but did not succeed—he then..made his escape to a point of land near the inlet. .. About half after 8 o'clock at night, I received a note from the Captain, of which the following is a copy. "Brig Intercourse, Sept. 23, 1809. Sir—An accident having happened today about 3 P. M. whereby one of my seamen, by the name of DAVIS, has unfortunately met with death, I must request of you to have a jury of inquest summoned as soon as possible.. John GALLAGHER." John MAYO, Esq. Portsmouth." Newbern Herald. [Here follows the Hue and Cry of J. MAYO, Esq. which we deem unnecessary to publish: having been credibly informed that the said Archibald DAVIDSON died at Washington a few days past by taking a large quantity of laudanum.]

(684) Married—on Sunday evening last, Mr. Nathaniel BOND, merchant, to Miss Penelope DICKINSON, youngest daughter of the late Dr. DICKINSON, all of this town. Died—on Wednesday evening last, Mrs. Mary COFFIELD, consort of Mr. Benjamin COFFIELD, of this County.

(685) To Contractors. On the 1st day of November next, in the Town of Murfreesborough, Will Be Let, To the lowest undertaker, the building of the Hertford Academy, at Murfreesborough. .. Particulars and a minute description cannot now with convenience be given—It may, however, be well to say, that the building is to be of Brick, in the form of an L. to front 40 feet two ways, by 20. More particular information may be had by applying to William P. MORGAN, at the P. Office, Murfreesborough. October 9, 1809.

(686) Stop A Villain!! 25 Dollars Reward Will be given to any person or persons within the United States, that will apprehend and convey to Warren, (R. Island) a certain Daniel SALISBURY, master and part owner of the Sloop Lydia, of Warren, who left this place on the 13th instant, taking with him upwards of 500 dollars in gold and silver, belonging to the subscribers. .. The said SALISBURY is about 5 feet 8 or 9 inches high, tolerably well set, stoops in his shoulders very much, red face, drinks pretty freely at times, has a scar on one of his cheeks, occasioned by a wound from a splinter, and is about 30 years of age. ... Joseph ALGER, James SALISBURY, Noble HOOD,} Part Owners. Edenton, Oct. 19, 1809.

Friday, October 27, 1809. Vol. IV.-um. 191.

(687) The Gazette. Friday. Edenton, October 27, 1809. .. Five Dollars Reward. Run away from the subscriber on Saturday the 14th instant, without any

(687) (Cont.) provocation, an indented Apprentice named George GRUNDY, about 18 years of age, low in stature, well made, down look, and chews tobacco. ... Wm. BIDDLE, Tailor. Norfolk, Oct. 18, 1809. [The above mentioned lad, we are requested to say by a worthy Knight of the Thimble, was in Edenton in July last, at work with him, and passed for a while, under the name of John SHARPS; but afterwards confessed he was an apprentice to Wm. BIDDLE, of Norfolk, and that he had run away; who, after some persuasion, consented to return.]

Friday, November 3, 1809. Vol. IV.-Num. 192.

(688) New-Orleans, Sept. 11. .. "Garrison Orders, New-Orleans, Sept. 4, 1809. No citizen is to pass into the garrison by any route, unless passed in by an officer---and it is expected that no gentleman will introduce a stranger or a man, who from the tenor of his general line of conduct, may be deemed hostile to the government of the United States. No citizen, unless holding a commission, civil or military under the government, is permitted to enter Fort St. Charles, under any pretext whatsover. Z. M. PIKE, Major Commandant." ...

(689) The Gazette. Friday. Edenton, November 3, 1809. .. Married---on the evening of the 26th ult. near this Town, Mr. John TAYLOR, aged 57 years, to Mrs. Elizabeth LILES, aged 68. .. On the 31st ult. in Bertie County, the Rev. (blank) DORSEY, to Miss Mary OUTLAW, daughter of George OUTLAW, Esq. of that County. On the same evening in Camden County, Jethro D. GOODMAN, Esq. attorney at law, of Pasquotank, to Miss Elizabeth BURGES, daughter of Col. Dempsey BURGES, of the aforesaid County. And on the same evening in Currituck, Mr. C. ETHERIDGE, to Miss Hulda FEREBEE, daughter of Colonel Samuel FEREBEE, all of that County.

(690) 20 Dollars Reward. Run away from the subscriber upwards of a year past, a likely Negro Fellow, named FRANK, commonly known by the name of Frank MUTTON. He is about 5 feet 9 or 10 inches high, thick set, and pretty black, has some of his fore-teeth out, and somewhat ball-headed, has a smiling artful countenance when spoken to, and is a very desperate blood-thirsty fellow. .. I will give the above reward to any person that will confine him in Perquimans jail so that I get him again. Elizabeth P. DICKINSON. Edenton, Oct. 12, 1809.

Friday, November 10, 1809. Vol. IV.-Num. 193.

(691) Piracy. A pirate of the name of Priam PEASE was cruising out of the port of St. Martins in an open boat, of about three tons and capturing every vessel he could fall in with. An American ship and schooner were lately taken by him, sent into St. Martins, plundered and condemned, and their cargoes sold. He is a native of Martha's Vineyard, should he ever return to America it is hoped he will meet the reward he merits.

(692) The Gazette. Friday. _denton, November 10, 1809. The Federal District Court for the District __ Pamptico, was opened in Newbern by the _on. Judge POTTER, on the 20th ult. when the _h'r. Favourite, owned by John SHAW, Esq. __ Nixonton, was condemned at her apprai__d value, under a charge of proceeding to _ foreign port, from Nixonton, in violation __ the Embargo Law, and its first supplement...

(693) Curiosity---Mr. Seth HALL, Fairfield, (C.) __ys he has now in his possession a single ___lk of Indian Corn, which grew in his field ___s season, with 51 ears upon it, which will __ shown to any one who may doubt it.

(694) Fort Wayne, Oct. 3. A treaty was concluded at this place, on ___ 30th ult. by his Excellency William Hen__ HARRISON, Governor of the Indiana Ter__tory, and Commissioner on the part of the _nited States, with the Miammies, Potawa__mies, and Eel River tribes of Indians; by _hich they have ceded to the United States a __act of Land on both sides of the Wabash __ver, extending from the land heretofore _wned by the United States around Vincennes, _p to within 12 miles of the mouth of Ver_illion river. They also ceded..a tract of 12 miles wide, extending __ong the former boundary line, established _y the treaty of Greenville, as high up as _ort Recovery. The foregoing cessions are computed at 600,000 acres, and contain some of the finest land in the United States. ... John JOHNSTON, Indian Agent.

(695) Capt Wm. P. BENNETT, of the 6th regt. of United States Infantry, has had his sword re__ored to him by the decision of a General _ourt Martial at Fort Columbus, and has _eceived the command of his company. Her.

(696) Departed this life, on the 26th ult. in the 26th year of his age, at the residence of his brother, in Columbia, Tyrrel County, Doctor Hardy HOSKINS, late of this town--a young gentleman of amiable deportment, and benevolence of disposition, whose entire conviction of the extreme importance of a virtuous and moral conduct, was exemplified in the performance of every personal and social duty. .. Intended for the practice of physic, after assiduously devoting himself to the preliminary cause of study here..he repaired to Philadelphia, for the purpose of compleating his medical education, just meriting and receiving with reputation and "eclat," the honors of that University, by having the Doctor's Degree conferred upon him. ...

(697) On Tuesday the 12th of December next Will Be Sold, To the highest bidder, the following Property, belonging to the estate of Alexander MILLEN, dec'd. Lot No. 9, on Water St't. with the water Lot opposite to it--on the former is a new Dwelling-House, and all necessary out-houses. Lots H. I. on King Street, formerly the property of Capt. Thomas COX, dec'd. on which there is a good Dwelling-House, Kitchen, &c. A Negro Man about 28 y's of age, who is a good bricklayer. A Negro Woman about 25 years of age. A Negro Girl about 14 y's of age. ... Josiah COLLINS, jr. John LITTLE, Henry KING,} Ex'rs. At the same time will be Sold..A Wharf with a good Warehouse thereon; and A Tract of Land, near this place, containing 360 Acres, both formerly the property of Mr. King LUTON. ... Edenton. Nov. 9, 1809.

(698) Richmond, October 24. Tribute Of Public Respect. Mr. JEFFERSON, the late President of the United States, having visited this city on some law concerns, a meeting of the citizens was called to testify their respect by a public address. .. On Friday last the citizens of Richmond having been informed in the morning, that Thomas JEFFERSON, our late illustrious President, had arrived in town the preceding evening, a meeting was held at the Capitol: Dr. William FOUSHEE, Sen'r. President. William MUMFORD, Secretary. .. Resolved, That this meeting are penetrated with the highest respect and admiration for the exalted character, as well as the sincerest gratitude for the distinguished services of Thomas JEFFERSON, late President of the United States. Resolved, That a committee be appointed to prepare and forthwith to report to this meeting an address to Mr. JEFFERSON..expressive of the sentiments contained in the foregoing resolution. Philip Norborne NICHOLAS, William WIRT, Andrew STEVENSON, Thomas RITCHIE, William ROBERTSON, Peyton RANDOLPH, and William B. HARE, were appointed a committee for that purpose...

17 November 1809

(699) The Gazette. Friday. Edenton, November 17, 1809. .. On the night of the 22d October, 4 Negro Men went to the house of Mr. John ELY (who keeps a public house on the post-road in the County of Harford, state of Maryland) and knocked at the door, saying they were travellers wanting refreshment; Mr. ELY first refused to get up, but being much importu_ed, put on his clothes. When he opened the door two of them went in. Mr. E. went _ut to get cyder from an out-house, when one __ the negroes out of doors struck at him and _roke his left arm..Mr. E. ran from the house _rying murder! the negro followed, and with the next blow struck him down, and left him __r dead.--In the mean time the negroes in __e house fell upon Mrs. E. her son, about 12 _ears of age, and a poor sailor..these they beat and cut in a most __ocking manner, particularly the sailor.. The negroes then compelled Mr. _LY's son to shew them where the money was, _hich they took, about 15 dollars and some __her trifling things.
    It is with satisfaction the public are inform__ that the perpetrators..are secured; three of the negroes are __e property of Capt. Edward HOWARD, the other belongs to Jeremiah FORD, Esq. two of these have made a full confession and all are safely lodged in gaol. .. Mess. HOWARD and FORD cheerfully assisted in securing them.

(700) Died at Wilmington, (D.) Samuel WHITE, Esq. formerly a Senator in the Congress of the United States, from that State.

(701) Asa CHAMBERLIN, Boot and Shoe Manufacturer, begs leave to inform..that he has lately returned from the Northward, with a large assortment of Shoes.. He returns his thanks to his customers for the liberal encouragement he has received, and solicits a continuance of their favors. Edenton, Nov. 15, 1809.

(702) The Gazette. Friday. Edenton, November 24, 1809. We are under the pain- ful necessity of publishing on a half-sheet, until our usual supply of paper arrives from New-York, which is momently expected.

(703) We learn, that on a representation made to him in favor of the Six persons lately convicted at the Superior Court of Perquimans County, of committing an outrage on the person of John CLARY, his Excellency the Governor has remitted the fines to the State which were severally adjuged against them. Raleigh Register.

(704) Died--on Monday the 20th inst. Mr. Samuel R. CLARKSON, late of Windsor, __ Tuesday his remains were committed to th_ grave, followed by most of his Masonic B__thren in this place. His funeral obsequ___ will be attended on Sunday following, in Unanimity Lodge.. The brethren of Unanimity Lodge ar_ hereby di- rected to meet at the Lodge on Su_day next at 10 o'clock, A. M. in order to make suitable arrangements. .. By order of the Worshipful Master, James WILLS, Sec.

(705) Notice. The Subscriber, expecting to leave the State in a few days, has left his Business under the direction of Col. Henry A. DONALDSON, who is authorised to act for him in his absence. Persons wanting Pumps, Blocks, &c. by sending their orders to him, may depend on having them made immediately, and on the same terms as they have been heretofore done by Henry FLURY. Edenton, Nov. 23, 1809.

(706) 75 Dollars Reward. Runaway from the Subscriber the following Negroes.

(706) (Cont.) STEPHEN, RUTH & PETER. STEPHEN went off about the first of April, a dark Mulatto about 36 years of age, has a bald place on the top of his head, and has generally a grim countenance. .. RUTH went off the 12th of June, a bright Mulatto Girl about 18 years of age, has a very handsome face, is very round shouldered, and an excellent house servant. .. PETER went off soon after RUTH, a black fellow about 26 years of age, low and spare made. .. Any person that will apprehend and secure the said Negroes..shall receive the above reward; or any person that will apprehend and secure any one of them shall receive 25 Dollars. Charles E. JOHNSON. Nov. 20, 1809.

Edenton, November 31, 1809.

(707) The Gazette. Friday. Edenton, December 1, 1809. (sic) Married—on the 23d ult. near this place, Mr. Lemuel COTTON, to Mrs. Parthena STANDIN, widow of Lemuel STANDIN, Esq. dec'd. On the same evening in Currituck, Abner N. VAIL, Esq. of this County, to Miss Mary MACKEY, of the aforesaid place.

Died—on the 17th ult. at Newbern, much regretted, Mr. John S. PASTEUR, Editor of the Federal Republican, of that place. His remains were committed to the grave by the members of St. John's Lodge, No. 3, of which he was long a member.

(708) Tavern. Having determined to remove to the country, the subscriber will rent for one or more years that well known Tavern which he at present occupies; or, should no person apply to rent it by private contract before the first of January next, he will on that day offer it at public auction..for one year. The person renting it, can be supplied with Servants and Furniture, if they choose. If that is not desired, the Furniture will be sold at the same time..and the Servants..hired out. ... Myles O'MALLEY. Edenton, Nov. 30th, 1809.

Friday, December 8, 1809. Vol. IV.-Num. 197.

(709) The Gazette. Friday. Edenton, December 8, 1809. .. From the Newbern Herald. Mr. Printer, I have lately read in the public prints, Mr. Nathaniel SPENCER's remarks and queries respecting the variation and progress of the Magnetic Needle, usually called the variation of the Compass. .. I shall therefore, very cheerfully communicate some occurrences which I have experienced in the course of my practice as a land surveyor, and whilst surveying the State of North-Carolina, jointly with Mr. John STROTHER, a Map of which we have lately published—and also whilst surveying the coast of North-Carolina, in the year 1806, from Cape-Hatteras to Cape-Fear, being one of the Commissioners, appointed by Congress on this survey.

In the year 1796, being then on the survey of..North-Carolina, we made observations with an excellent Azimuth Compass, and other proper instruments, at different places, in order to find the variation of the Compass, especially at the town of Newbern, where we found it to be..2 degrees 40 minutes Easterly.. .. And I think it may not be amiss to mention, that we found the variation to increase easterly, as we proceeded along the coast to the southern extremity of the state.. and I have been informed..that at the Bar of Charleston, the variation was about 4 degrees, or upwards, easterly, although Mr. Edmund M. BLOUNT, in the draught of that harbor, in his American Coast Pilot, published in October, 1806, lays it down 5 degrees westerly. ... Jonathan PRICE. Newbern, Nov. 8, 1809.

(710) CLARY Expelled. We congratulate the virtuous and respectable part of the citizens of Perquimans county on their success, in expelling from the Legislature of the State, that monster of iniquity, John CLARY. ...

(711)   Notice Is hereby given to the creditors of George D. REED, Esq. of Bertie
County, North-Carolina, that he is dead, and that Jonathan JACOCKS of said State
and County acts as Executor to his will, and unless they make known their demands
as the law directs, this will be plead in bar thereof; his debtors are also
desired to make payment. Bertie County, Nov. 21, 1809.

(712)   Will Be Sold, At the former dwelling house of George D. REED, Esq. in
DURANT's Neck, Perquimans County, on the 18th December next, the Stock of Sheep,
Horses, Cattle, Hogs, Corn, Wheat, &c. at 6 months credit:--same time will be of-
fered for Sale, two Tracts of Land, in said County, belonging to the said estate..
Also, at his late dwelling house in Bertie County, on the 20th December, will be
Sold, the residue of his Perishable Estate, at 6 months credit.--Bonds and ap-
proved securities will be required by the acting Executor. November 21, 1809.

(713)   Will Be Sold, To the highest bidder, on Tuesday the 12th of December next,
before Mrs. E. HORNIBLOW's Tavern, in Edenton..the following property: Lot No.
187, on Water-Street.   Three comfortable Houses for small families, late the
property of Francis VALETTE, deceased, situated on John SKINNER's wharf.   One
commodious Store-House and a Shop, now occupied by Henry FLURY, Esq. situated on
James W. LANGLEY's wharf. Six Negro Men.. One Negro Boy.. Two Negro Women..
Bonds with approved security will be required by the subscriber, who is Agent and
authorised to receive them. Joseph B. SKINNER. Nov. 10th, 1809.

denton, December 15, 1809.

(714)   The Gazette. Friday. Edenton, December 15, 1809. This day the election
closes in Perquiman_ county. We are credibly informed that John CLARY, who has
the unparalleled effrontery __ offer again, will, without doubt, be elected by a
large majority.   Will our virtuous Legi_lature again expel him from the House?
They undoubtedly must and will.
     Mr. George I?. RYAN is elected to the Legislature from Bertie County, to
supply the vacancy occasioned by the death of William CHERRY, Esq.

(715)   General Assembly. House Of Commons--November 23. The Legislature met in
Raleigh on the 20th..proceeded to ballot for Speaker; when Gen. Thos. DAVIS was
elected in opposition to Mr. GASTON.--Gen. Joseph RIDDICK is elected Speaker of
the Senate. .. Saturday, Nov. 25. Mr. HILL moved that the House do enter into
the following resolution.--Whereas, John CLARY, a member of this Hosue from the
county of Perquimans, has been legally convicted of cohabiting with the daughter
of his wife; and whereas, this crime, detestable in itself, was committed under
such circumstances of aggravation and enormity as manifested an utter depravity of
heart, and destitution of moral principle. And whereas it is due to the honor of
the House of Commons of the State of N. Carolina to free itself from the contamin-
ation of grossly impure and unworthy characters. Resolved, That the said John
CLARY be, and he is hereby expelled from this House, and his seat therein declared
vacant. Ordered to lie for consideration till Monday next.
     Monday, Nov. 27. Mr. M'GUIRE presented the petition of Malachi HALSEY,
praying to be remunerated for services performed during the revolutionary war...

(716)   Thomas F. ADAMS, Watch And Clock Maker, Informs..that he has taken a shop
on Main-Street, where he will repair Clocks and Watches of every description on
the shortest notice.--He flatters himself from the experience he has had in the
line of his profession, to give entire satisfaction to his employers. Edenton,
Dec. 14, 1809.

15 December 1809.

(717)   Notice is hereby given to all the creditors of Edward B. REED, of Bertie County, that the said REED is dead, and that the subscriber qualified as Administrator to his estate. All those indebted..are requested to make immediate payment; and those having claims to present them properly attested, within the time limited by law... Starkey S. HARRELL, Adm. December 6th, 1809.

(718)   Twenty Dollars Reward. Ran away from the Subscriber on the 15th November last, a Negro Boy named DICK, formerly the property of the late James GRANBERRY, Esq. of this town. He is about eighteen years old, of a very dark complexion, slim, and five feet seven or eight inches high. His upper lip is remarkably thick, and has a double appearance when he laughs. He was raised in HARVEY's Neck, in Perquimans County, where it is probable he at present lurks. The above reward will be given to any person who will deliver him to the Subscriber, or to Mr. TREDWELL in Edenton, or fifteen dollars, if lodged in the jail of Perquimans County. Augustus CABARRUS. Edenton, December 11, 1809.

__enton, December 22, 1809.

(719)   The Gazette. Friday. Edenton, December 22, 1809. .. We have at length received a supply of paper from the Northward. Our paper will next week resume its usual size.

(720)   Flour. Fresh ground superfine and fine Flour, Ship-Stuff and Bran, constantly on hand and for Sale, by the subscriber, for ready money only. M. E. SAWYER. Edenton, Dec. 21, 1809.

(721)   Will Be Rented out to the highest bidder, on the first of January next, before Mrs. HORNIBLOWs tavern in Edenton, my House and Lot on Church Street, now in tolerable good order to receive a family. Also, on the 10th of January, at James JACKSON's, 10 miles above Edenton, A Negro Man DICK; and two thirds of the Plantation formerly belonging to Exum ELLIOTT, deceased. Terms made known on the day of hiring. Thomas BROWNRIGG. December 19, 1809.

(722)   20 Dollars Reward. Runaway from the subscriber on the 7th inst. a likely mulatto Negro Man named CHARLES, late the property of John COBB, dec. of Bertie. He is about 5 feet 10 inches high, stout made, and about 34 years of age. He carried off with him sundry articles of homespun clothing; and somewhere about 70 dollars in hard and paper money, his own property. He has, I understand, a free pass, wrote in a handsome hand by a widow woman of this County, who, as a compensation, received 10 dollars. I will give the above reward to any person who will deliver him to me, or secure him so that I get him again. All masters of vessels are hereby cautioned against carrying him off at their peril. David GASKINS. Bertie, Dec. 21, 1809.

Friday, December 29, 1809.   Vol. IV.-Num. 200.

(723)   Congress. In Senate.--December 14. Mr. LEIB submitted the following motion, for consideration--Resolved, That the President of the United States be requested to cause to be laid before the Senate a copy of the correspondence between him and the Governor of Pennsylvania in the case of Gideon OLMSTEAD. ...

(724)   The Gazette. Friday. Edenton, December 29, 1809. .. General Assembly. House Of Commons--December 6. Mr. George L. RYAN, representative from Bertie, appeared and took his seat. .. Saturday, Dec. 9. .. The committee of emancipation recommended the passage of a bill to emancipate DAVID, the property

(724) (Cont.) of Thomas TROTTER of Washington county, and a bill to emancipate BEN, a man of color of Hertford county. Monday, Dec. 11. Mr. BARBER presented a bill to appoint commissioners to establish the boundaries between the counties of Perquimans, Chowan & Gates.

Wednesday, Dec. 19. John CLARY appeared again from Perquimans, re-elected; but he had not long occupied his seat, before a resolution for expelling him was carried, 68 to 28. [We understand that Captain Jesse COPELAND, son of Mrs. CLARY, and one of the ring-leaders of the tar and feather mob, who had sworn fidelity to each other on the Holy Evangelists, when in the act, turned traitor, accompanied his virtuous friend to Raleigh, for the express purpose of compelling the Legislature to accept of his services. The member who could introduce CLARY to the House as re-elected, must possess sentiments little inferior to the culprit himself.

(725) Died--on the 25th instant at Thos. BROWNRIGG's, Esq. after a few moments notice, Mr. Angel VAUNIER, of this place, a gentleman of correct deportment and amiable manners.

(726) Notice. On Thursday the 4th day of January next will be hired out at the house of Mr. Caleb NASH, the Negroes belonging to the estate of Wm. ROBERTS. At the same time will be rented or leased, that valuable Plantation, now in good order, at the mouth of Rockahoc-Creek, belonging to the same estate, on which are two very good Fisheries. .. Executrix. 20th December 1809.

(727) Notice. All persons having claims against Robert HENDRY, dec'd. are informed, that the said HENDRY died in 1805, and that all demands brought in hereafter will not be paid... Jas. WILSON, surviving Executor. Bertie, Dec. 20, 1809.

(728) For Sale. On the 2d day of January ensuing will be disposed of at public sale, before Mrs. HORNIBLOWs, a Negro Woman belonging to the estate of Nathaniel ALLEN, dec'd. ... Executor. Edenton, Dec. 20, 1809.

(729) Notice. Two valuable Fisheries for shad and herrings on Chowan river, in Bertie County; and the Plantation, on which there is a large Dwelling-Hous, Barn and Stable, and other out-houses, where Joseph A. BROWN, dec'd. formerly lived, called Point Comfort, are offered for rent, for 1, 2 or 3 years. The above property will be rented altogether or separate as may be most agreeable to those inclined to rent. For terms apply to the subscriber in Edenton. Elisha NORFLEET. Dec. 20, 1809.

END OF VOLUME I

BLODGET (Cont.)
Charles 345
BLOIS
 74
BLOODGOOD
Abraham 505
BLOODWORTH
T. F. 378
Timothy, Jr.
654
BLOUNT
 35,295
Ann 224
Chas. C. 276
Clement H. 640
Edmund M. 709
Fanny (CONNOR)
189
Jacob 99
James 496,571
John B. 194,
215,282,283,336,
357,468,493,540
Jos. 621
Joseph 130,189
Levi 548,551
Sharpe 167
Thomas 122,371
Thos. 136
William 187,295
BLYTHE
Joseph 385
BOILEAU
N. B. 544
BOLLMAN
 248
BONAMY
As: 112,114
BONASSON
Ant. 331
BOND
 23,61,
166,495
John 278
John, Jr. 17
Lewis 141
Nathaniel 584
Penelope
(DICKINSON)
684
BONNER
Miles 461
Nancy 461
BONNETT
Joseph 630
BOON
Joseph, Jr. 378
BOONE
Daniel M. 577
BOOTH
 298
BOOTWRIGHT
James 75
BOUCHERIE
Anthony 291
BOUSH
Caleb 449
BOUTCHER
James A. 424
BOWDEN
 315
BOWLES
Jesse 75
BOYD
Adam 578
John C. 433
John P. 534
Thomas 654
BOYLE
John 529
BOZMAN
 614
John 604
Joseph 33
Levan 367
BRADFORD
 184,445
David 197
John 35
BRADLEY
 197

BRADLEY (Cont.)
S. R. 136
Stephen R. 201,
578
BRANDON
Matthew 486
BRANTON
William 378
BRECKENRIDGE
James 578
BRENT
Richard 438,578
BREVARD
Thomas 388
BRICKELL
Jeremiah 654
Wm. 457
BRICKHOUSE
William 365
William, Sr. 63
BRIDGES
 373
BRIDPORT
George 606
BRIGGS
William 646
BRIGHT
Michael 544,568
BRISCOE
Richard S. 548
BRITE
Jer. 631
Jeremiah 547
BRITT
 674
Thomas 564
BRITTON
John 337
BROCK
Samuel 157
BROOKS
 35,504
Asa 276
BROOM
 157
BROOME
John 660
BROTHERS
E. 15
BROUVARD
 330
BROWER
Jno. 654
BROWN
 413,578
Benjamin 547
Cotton 157
Hugh 378,654
James, Jr. 545
Jeremiah 444
John 35
Joseph 332
Joseph A. 91,
174,729
Martha 76
Montgomery 184
Robert 136,578
Thomas, Jr. 378,
654
William 86,594
Wm. 262
BROWNLOW
Robert 331
BROWNRIGG
Thomas 337,367,
640,721
Thos. 725
BRUCE
 152
Philip 79,373
Phillip 299
BRUIN
Peter Bryan 534
BRUTON
Simon 378,654
BRYAN
James C. 370,
654
Jos. H. 487
Joseph 213,647
Joseph H. 363,

BRYAN (Cont.)
Joseph H. (Cont.)
640
William 647
BRYANT
Samuel 617
BUCHANAN
Alex. 630
Matthew 630
BUCK
A. A. 239
BUFFINGTON
Samuel 15
BULFINCH
Charles 408
BULLITT
 35
BULLOCK
Archibald S.
534
Francis 378
John 31
BULLUS
John 534
BUNCH
Micajah 276,
617,640
BUNN
Bennett 457
Redmond 378
BURBECK
H. 344
Henry 199
BURCH
 125
BURGES
Dempsey 689
Elizabeth 689
Samuel 491,547
BURK
John 630
BURKITT
Lemuel 107,146,
470
BURLINGHAM
Eaton 630
BURN
John 22
BURNET
Jacob 197
BURNSIDE
William 630
BURR
 36,84,105,
109,114,117,248
A. 117
Aaron 36,51,75,
106,111,160,197
BURROUGHS
Stephen 74
BURROWS
 99
BURTIS
Stephen 630
BURTON
 411
H. G. 656
Jas. 394
BURWELL
John 666
Wm. A. 136,578
BUTLER
Samuel 56,155,
312
William 578
Wm. 136
BUXTON
 618
John 681
William 187
Wm. 99
BYNUM
Francis A. 370
BYRD
Martin R. 68,
612

—C—

CABARRUS
August 418

CABARRUS (Cont.)
Augustus 718
Stephen 206,
364,418
Thos. 617
CALDWELL
Andrew 388
Kincaid 35
CALHOON
John 589
CALHOUN (See also
COLHOUN)
Robert 578
CALL
Daniel 437
CALLENDER
John 99
CAMERON
D. 379
CAMM
Joseph P. 547
CAMP
J. 193
CAMPBELL
 8,241,245
Catlett 378,654
George 317
George W. 268
Hugh G. 292
J. 136
James 378
Jas. 654
John 122,578
Mary (SCOTT) 317
William 302
CAMPELL
G. W. 136
CANNON
Charles 654
Palmer 487
Richard 316,
321,325
CAPEHART
Mich'l 547
Michael 491
CARBERY
 197
CARLTON
Peter 136
CARMAN
Samuel 422
CARMICK
Daniel 534
CARONDOLET (See
also DE CARONDOLET)
 121
CARPENTER
Miriam 140,173
CARTER
David 394
Hill 438
CARTWRIGHT
William 630
CARVER
James 640
CARVINE
Jean Baptiste
331
CARY
John R. 616
CATHALAN
Stephen 218
CATO
 135
CATOR
Anna 563
Levin 563
Moses E. 367,
617,640
CHALMERS
 302
CHAMBERLAIN
Asa 142,337,
432,575
William 578
CHAMBERLAINE
John C. 396
CHAMBERLAM
John C. 578
CHAMBERLIN
Asa 701

CHAMBERS
 197
Henry 385
James 197
William 595
CHAMPION
E. 136
Epaphroditus
578
Wm. 15
CHAMPLAIN
Adam 345
CHANDLER
Isaac 638
John 136
CHAPMAN
Benjamin 15
CHASE
Joseph 291
Samuel 291
CHAUNCEY
 84
Isaac 92,145
CHAUNCY
 193
CHEETHAM
 135
James 134
CHERRY
Joel 640
Solomon, Sr. 675
William 640,
667,675,714
CHESSON
Elizabeth 108
John 76
Samuel 108,337,
547
CHESTER
John 130
CHILDRES
Joseph 67
CHISELL
 607
CHITTENDEN
Martin 136,578
CHIVERS
Larkin 15
CHOATE
John 574
CHRIST
Henry 578
CHRISTY
William 577
CLAIBORNE
 114,248
J. 136
William C. C.
144
Wm. C. C. 38
CLARK
 207,577
Daniel 136,198,
248
Isaac 74
James W. 411
Nathan 207
Rebecca 323
William 99,187,
276,337,564
CLARKE
 328
Daniel 37
CLARKSON
Samuel R. 704
CLARY
 654,724
John 640
John 641,679,
703,710,714,715,
724
Robert, Jr. 15
CLAXTON
Thomas 122,578
CLAY
Jos. 136
Matthew 136,578
CLEMENT
James 456
CLEVELAND
Robert 458

157

PRICE (Cont.)
Jonathan 709
Samuel 630
Wm. 111
PRIDE
Wm. 630
PROUDFIT
John 649
PRUNTY
John 438
PUGH
J. 136
William 622
PURDY
Robert 534

-Q-

QUINCEY
Josiah 136,578
QUINCY
____ 124

-R-

RAINEY
Isaac 656
James 458
RAINS
Robert 630
RALSTON
Robert 188
RAMCKE
Frederick 71
RAMSAY
Henry 167
RANDOLPH
____ 125,184
Beverly 200
J. 136
John 125,245,
562,578
Peyton 698
RATFORD
Jenkins 83
RAY
John 654
RAYMOND
____ 25
Phineas 630
RAYNER
____ 229
REA
John 136,578
READING
Herbert 507
REDDICK
Job 100
REED
Cloah 572,573
Edward 88
Edward E. 717
George 88
George L. 711,
712
Philip 136,578
William, Jr.
572,573
REILEY
Edward 131
REILLEY
Gregory 220
REILY
Edward 432
RELFE
William T. 640
RENFRO
____ 15
RENSHAW
James 401
REVERE
J. M. 124
Paul 124
REW
Sarah 425
REYNOLDS
Michael 534
RHEA (See also
RAY,REA)
John 136,578
RHODES

RHODES (Cont.)
J. T. 164
James 378,411,
654
Jas. 153
Joseph 654
Joseph T. 370,
378
RICHARDS
Jacob 136
Mathias 578
Matthias 136
RICHARDSON
Etheridge 491,
547
J. 654
Joseph 378
Stephen 208
Wm. 111
RICKETSON
Shadrack 96
RIDDICK (See also
REDDICK)
____ 147,457
Joseph 255,
367,434,442,458,
640,715
Willis 367,640
RIDGELY
Charles G. 337,
420
RIDGLEY
Charles G. 491
RIELY (See also
REILEY,REILLEY,
REILY)
Edward 276
RIGGS
Israel 15
RIGGUS
Frederick 630
RIGHTON
William 564
RIKER
Saml. 136
RIPLEY
____ 515,531
RITCHIE
Thomas 698
RITTENHOUSE
____ 527
David 544,557
ROANE
J. T. 578
ROBARDS
____ 465
William 367
ROBASON
Jesse 487
ROBERTS
____ 15,74
Ann 202
Charles 161
J. 370
John 654
Mary 215
Sally 179
William 88,
118,161,162,215
Wm. 76,99,663,
726
ROBERTSON
William 698
ROBINSON
Jonathan 136,
578
Josiah 214
Tuily 534
ROCKWELL
Chas. 272
RODGERS
John 292
RODNEY
C. A. 529
ROGERS
____ 507
Allen 376
ROMBOUGH
Elizabeth 172
William 172,
340,427

ROOT
Erastus 578
ROSS
George 544
John 578
Martin 491,626
ROWAN (See also
ROANE)
John 136,589
ROWLAND
Alexander 256,
378
ROYLE
J. 136
RUFFIN
Henry J. G.
654
Robert 295
RUSH
Richard 92
RUSS
Thos. 378
RUSSEL
____ 229
Jonathan 397
William 534
RUSSELL
J. 136
William R. 187
Wm. 276
RUTGERS
Henry 506
RUTHERFORD
John 176
RUTLEDGE
____ 607
RYAN
____ 381,462
Cornelius 335,
374,381,462
George 411
George I. 714
George L. 724

-S-

SAFFORD
____ 240
SAGE
Ebenezer 578
ST. MAURICE
____ 99
SALESBURY
John 337
SALISBURY
Daniel 686
James 686
SAMMONS
Thomas 578
SANDERS
William 337
SANSBURY
Elizabeth 191
Hillary 191
SANSOM
____ 184
SATTERFIELD
____ 276
Elizabeth 547
Elizabeth HARRIS
294
Thomas 276,382,
491,677
William 294
SATTERWHITE
Edwin 457
SAUNDERS
Hannah 547,617
James 62,403,
404,412,619
John 534
Robert 35,438,
630
SAUNDERSON
Samuel 491
SAWIS
____ 114
SAWYER
____ 287,367,
655
Enoch 223

SAWYER (Cont.)
Fred. B. 487
Harriot C. 223
Lemuel 136,201,
371,578
M. E. 514,720
Malachi 42,45
Matthias E. 32,
322,361
Sarah 318,392,
653
Willis 258,318,
319,392,653
SAY
____ 456
Benjamin 578
SCALES
Nathaniel 388,
654,656
SCHOLEFIELD
James 43
SCOFFIELD
Jesse 487
SCOTT
____ 666
Galvin 512
John 317,346,
630,646
Joshua 395
Marmaduke 370
Mary 317
Nancy 258
SCULL
Crissy 262
Elisha 262
SEARS
Henry E. 24
SEAT
John 159
SEATON
Sarah Weston
(GALES) 554
William W. 554
SEAVER
Ebenezer 136,
578
SEAWELL
Henry 472
SEBASTIAN
____ 35,198
Benjamin 200
SEDDON
John 451
SELBY
Henry 394
SELDEN
Miles 111
SELLMAN
John 197
SERGEANT
____ 557
Elizabeth 544
SERGENT
Elizabeth 527
SERRY
Augustine 535
SHAKELY
Peter 157
SHANDS
Thomas 643
SHARPS
John 687
SHARROCK
David 72
SHAW
A. 516
John 38,292,
692
Samuel 578
SHEFFEY
Daniel 578
SHEFFIELD
I. 219
Ichabod 207
Ishabed 218
SHEFFOY
Daniel 438
SHEPARD
William 658
SHERIFFS
DEANS

SHERIFFS (Cont.)
DEANS (Cont.)
Thomas 579
ETHERIDGE
C. 664
GREEN
William H.
431
HOSEA
_homas 593
HOSKINS
Edmond 162,
321,593
James 63,
365
HUNTER
John 666
M'IVER
Kenneth 487
ROBERTS
Charles 161
William 88,
161,162
TOWNSEND
Josiah 593
WALKER
Thomas 576
WALTERS
Lewis 579
WARD
____ 673
SHERMAN
John H. 630
SHOBER
G. 388
SHORT
Charles 77,163
Thos. 157
SIMMONS
Benj. 197
L. 654
Willis 370
SIMONDS
Jonas 534
SIMONS
Elizabeth 163
Joshua 154,
156,163
SIMPSON
Eleanor 343
James 207
John 343
John O. 343
SINGLETON
Spyres 658
SKINNER
____ 73,161
Charles 309
Elizabeth 663
Henry 179
John 26,50,
107,263,502,592,
617,713
Jos. B. 26,
501,636
Joseph B. 182,
366,536,713
Joshua 196,663
Mary (CREECY)
309
Sally (ROBERTS)
179
SLADE
Jeremiah 640
William 368,
494,564
Wm. 547
SLOANE
James 136
SLOCUM
Ezekial 378
SLONGER
____ 7
SMALL
____ 155,347
George 502
Reuben 141,187
SMELT
Dennis 136,578
SMILIE
____ 276

159

VAIL
    ---- 404
    Abner 99,187
    Abner N. 403,
707
    Abner Nash 403,
652
    Benners 99
    Elizabeth
    (HOSKINS) 409
    Mary 99,276
    Mary (MACKEY)
707
    Thomas 409,547
VALETTE
    Francis 713
VAN ALLEN
    Jas. J. 136
VAN AMBERCH
    Betsey 135
VAN CORTLAND
    P. 136
VANDERHORST
    R. W. 385
VAN DYKE
    Nicholas 578
VANDYKE
    Nicholas 136
VANHOOK
    Robert 394
VAN HORN
    Archibald 578
VAN HORNE
    Archibald 136
VAN NEAZ
    Jesse 276
VANPELT
    Daniel 156
VANRENSELLAER
    Killian K. 578
VAN RENSSELEAR
    Killian K. 136
VANZANDT
    Nicholas B.
122,125
VARNUM
    ---- 578
    Jos. B. 136
    Joseph E. 122,
201,578
VAUNIER (See also
WARNIER)
    Angel 725
VEAZEY
    Jesse 15
VEGUS
    Bennett B. 630
VERPLANCK
    ---- 450
VERPLANK
    Daniel C. 136
VILLARD
    Andrew Joseph
455
VILLIARD
    Andrew Joseph
535
VINZANT
    John 15

—W—

WADE
    Edward 554
    Seth 378
WADSWORTH
    D. 248
WAIN
    Robert 521
WALBACT
    ---- 111
WALKER
    Carlton 515
    John 183,222
    Thomas 576
WALL
    Richard 548
WALLACE
    ---- 35
    James 617,677
WALTERS

WALTERS (Cont.)
    Lewis 367,579
WALTON
    Leah 491
    Mary 650
WAMPLER
    Geo. 7
WARBURTON
    James W. 620
WARD
    ---- 315,673
    Elisha 665
    John 315
WARDEN
    Sarah 347
WARE
    William 83,152,
157
    Wm. 152
WARING
    George 385
WARNER
    W. 313
WARNIER (See also
VAUNIER)
    Angel 99,187
WARREN
    William 157
WARRING
    Ann 420,677
WARRINGTON
    Elijah 276
WASHINGTON
    ---- 252,367,
519,532
WATERMAN
    ---- 639
WATERS
    ---- 557
    Esther 527,544
WATKINS
    Thomas 438
WATSON
    James 394
    William 289,
466,478
WATT
    James 337,420
WATTS
    Ambrose 152
WAYNE
    Anthony 184
WEBB
    ---- 150
    W. . 647
    Zacheriah 131
WELBORN
    ---- 656
WELCH
    Myles 640
WELD
    Edward 291
WELLBORN
    James 385,394
WELLS
    William 291
WELSH
    ---- 184
WESKETT
    John 677
WEST
    Jesse 337,420,
491
    John 632
    John S. 89,399,
658
WESTCOT
    ---- 397
WESTON
    Isaiah 548
WHARTON
    Jesse 136
WHEATON
    Joseph 125
    Laban 578
WHEDBEE
    Benjamin 221
    James 214
    Lemuel 573
WHERLOW
    John 257

WHITAKER
    John 236
    M. C. 370,647
WHITE
    ---- 15,184,
268,673
    Ann 420,491
    Bun 654
    Isaac 574
    John D. 78
    Joshua 266
    Luke H. 265
    Priscilla 265
    Robert 266
    Saml. 136,578
    Samuel 268,700
    William 176
    Wm. 165
WHITEHEAD
    Swepson 217
WHITEHILL
    Robert 136,578
WHITESIDE
    Jenkin 578
WHITFIELD
    Bryan 415
    Needham 411,486
WHITING
    John 534
    Samuel 291
WHITLOCK
    Charles 280
WHITMAN
    Ezekiel 578
WHITMELL
    Drew S. 320
WHITTEMORE
    Amos 535
    William, Jr. 535
WHOKES
    William 666
WICKHAM
    ---- 117
WILBOUR
    Isaac 397
WILBOURN
    Isaac 136
WILDER
    ---- 315
    Francis 57
    John 57
    Michael 99
    Nathaniel 99
    Willis 62,99,
564
WILDS
    ---- 588
WILKINSON
    ---- 35,37,75,
105,109,110-114,
116,198,200,248
    George 99
    James 111,115,
121,184,199,245,
344
    James B. 35
WILLARD
    Nath'l. 131
    Nathaniel 564
    Prentice 239
WILLEY
    Hillary 311
WILLIAMS
    ---- 147,197,
248,328,353,411
    B. 354
    Benj. 153,355,
654
    Benjamin 148
    D. R. 136
    Ebenezer Heredall
673
    Edward 370,388,
654
    Elias 515
    Eliza 617
    Elizabeth 99,
669
    Enion 97
    Henry 640
    J. 654

WILLIAMS (Cont.)
    James 370
    Jas. 654
    John 378,491,617
    John Q. 574
    Jona. 344
    Jonas 654
    Jonathan 199,239
    Marmaduke 136
    Nancy 187
    Nathan 656
    Nathaniel 63,365
    R. 153,457,472
    Robert 388,654
    Stephen 370,388
    Thomas 466
    Thomas H. 248
    Thos. 370
    W. 153
    William 118,370,
603
WILLING
    Thomas 138
WILLS
    ---- 281,403,
412,413,466,478,
641,642
    Henry 18,55,77,
230,236
    James 1,73,
p. 103,229,405,467,
514,591,704
    Thomas 3
WILSON
    ---- 83,673
    Alexander 136,
445
    Elizabeth
    (SKINNER) 663
    George 666
    James 578
    Jas. 396,727
    John 83,157
    Peter 548
    Thomas 161,437
    William 663
    Wm. 85
WINN (See also
WYNN,WYNNS)
    Richard 578
WINSLOW
    John 458
WINSOR
    Peter 547
WINSTON
    Jos. 153
    Joseph 388
WINTON
    David 630
WIRT
    ---- 51
    William 698
WISE
    William 380
WITHERALL
    James 136
WITHERSPOON
    Robert 578
WOOD
    Eleazer D. 239
    John 491,572,573
    Reuben 153
    Richard 276
    Wm. 666
WOODBRIDGE
    Dudley 51
WOODS
    B. 153
    Benjamin 275,352
WOODSON
    Tarlton 438
WOOTEN
    John 176,378,654
WORD
    Thomas A. 457
WORKMAN
    ---- 248
WORSTER
    William 58
WORTH
    James 16

WORTHAM
    T. 654
    Thomas 388
WORTMAN
    Tunis 506
WRIGHT
    ---- 104
    David 654
    J. G. 472
    Joshua G. 147,
378,457,477
    Robert 646
WYNN (See also
WINN)
    Richard 136
    Thomas 458
    W. 449
WYNNS
    Benj. 90
    Thomas 164,225,
256,452,661
WYVILL
    ---- 152

—X—

None

—Y—

YANCEY
    ---- 161
    James 394
YANCY
    ---- 465
    Henry 647
YELLOWLEY
    Edward 551
YORK
    Abner 17
YOUNG
    ---- 504
    Joseph 333
    Wm. 491

—Z—

None

INCOMPLETE NAMES

    ---- Tom 135
    AWYER
    Enoch 487

164

www.ingramcontent.com/pod-product-compliance
Lightning Source LLC
Chambersburg PA
CBHW051319020426
42333CB00031B/3406

* 9 7 8 1 6 3 9 1 4 1 7 7 7 *